Ocean

ange

Mackenzie River

Ft Yukon
Beaver
Circle
Rampart
Chatanika
Eagle
Fairbanks
Fortymile
Nenana
Dawson
Big Delta
Klondike River

Broad Pass
Mt. McKinley
Paxson
Yukon
Ft Selkirk
River
Gulkana
Copper
Center
Chitina
Wrangell
Mts.
Lake Laberge
Chugach
Matanuska
Anchorage
Mountains
Valdez
Whitehorse
Carcross
Yukon
Cordova
L. Bennett
British Columbia
Mt St Elias
Chilkoot
Pass
Bennett
Malaspina
Glacier
Skagway
Yakutat
Bay
Glacier Bay
Nat'l Mon.
Juneau
Hoonah
Petersburg
Sitka
Wrangell

MAP OF
ALASKA
Legend
• • • • • • Boat • • • • • •
→ → → Auto or afoot → → →
↔ Airplane ↔
╫╫╫ Railroad ╫╫╫
— — Harry Jr. only — —
▨▨▨ Glaciers ▨▨▨

Ketchikan
Metlakatla
To Seattle

THE LURE OF ALASKA

BOOKS BY HARRY A. FRANCK

THE LURE OF ALASKA
SKY ROAMING ABOVE TWO CONTINENTS
ROAMING IN HAWAII
TRAILING CORTEZ THROUGH MEXICO
A VAGABOND IN SOVIETLAND
A VAGABOND JOURNEY AROUND THE WORLD
FOUR MONTHS AFOOT IN SPAIN
TRAMPING THROUGH MEXICO, GUATEMALA, AND
 HONDURAS
ZONE POLICEMAN 88
VAGABONDING DOWN THE ANDES
WORKING NORTH FROM PATAGONIA
VAGABONDING THROUGH CHANGING GERMANY
ROAMING THROUGH THE WEST INDIES
GLIMPSES OF JAPAN AND FORMOSA
WANDERING IN NORTHERN CHINA
ROVING THROUGH SOUTHERN CHINA
EAST OF SIAM (FRENCH INDO-CHINA)
THE FRINGE OF THE MOSLEM WORLD
I DISCOVER GREECE
A SCANDINAVIAN SUMMER
FOOT-LOOSE IN THE BRITISH ISLES

Juveniles:

MARCO POLO, JUNIOR
WORKING MY WAY AROUND THE WORLD
(*An Abridgment, by Lena M. Franck, of
 Mr. Franck's first book*)

Geographical Readers for Schools:

MEXICO AND CENTRAL AMERICA
THE JAPANESE EMPIRE
SOUTH AMERICA
CHINA

*F. A. Owen Publishing Co.,
Dansville, N. Y.*

An Eskimo mother and child

THE LURE OF ALASKA

By

HARRY A. FRANCK

Accompanied by

HARRY A. FRANCK, Jr.

With 100 reproductions of photographs, most of them taken
by the author

J. B. LIPPINCOTT COMPANY

PHILADELPHIA   NEW YORK

IN SINCERE SYMPATHY FOR
THE REST OF THE FAMILY, WHO SPENT
THEIR SUMMER IN THE WILDS OF
NEW HAMPSHIRE

CONTENTS

vii

CONTENTS

CONTENTS

ILLUSTRATIONS

xi

ILLUSTRATIONS

CHAPTER I

ESCAPE TO FAIRBANKS

*Family Split ... Rolling Bed ... Spare Driver
... Mt. Rainier ... The Inside Passage ...
Mere Hours to the Heart of Alaska*

RACHEL had been talked into deserting me for the summer, anyway, when someone suggested my going to Alaska. She was to go to her first girls' summer camp, councilor-like, with our two daughters, and only half a mile beyond there was just the camp for our two small boys. That left Harry, Jr., too, with a summer on his hands, so he came along with me. For though he had just received his up-holstered diploma from Harrisburg Academy, no one was waving self-respecting jobs in a boy's face, and he didn't quite feel like drilling in the hot sand of Camp Meade for a second summer. We had thought of Mexico, even Europe, but Alaska would at least be new to both of us.

Two of us of course meant driving to Seattle. We turned in the less aged of our faithful old Fords—the other was good enough for New Hampshire—and acquired a ... a car of another breed. Perhaps I had better not mention it by name, for the maker's modesty in advertising its most convenient feature suggests that he is purposely soft-pedaling it. Maybe he is afraid of antagonizing the hotel, tourists-accommodated, cabin-camp and trailer inter-ests. But the ... that particular make of car is just the answer to a constantly recurring question in my "pan" mail: "How can I sleep on my travels without having to pay for it?" or, "Now that my kids are too many, or too big, for all of us to sleep in a trailer, what do I do next?"

The answer is, get a . . . the only automobile on the market, as yet, that can be made up in a jiffy as a double bed, roomy and comfortable as a Pullman compartment. Normally one uses the front seat cushion as a part of the mattress, which of course leaves you stranded until morning. That seems to be as far as automobile manufacturers have thought, to date, along that line. But anyone with an ounce of ingenuity can better that arrangement—pick up an extra seat cushion somewhere, or, better still, fill in the hiatus with baggage which on shipboard would be tagged: NOT WANTED ON VOYAGE. Then one can sleep while the other drives.

For me there is only one thing better than being able to scorn city hotels, and that is to be able to thumb your nose at the cabin camps and tourist homes that make the scorning of hotels possible. Quite aside from any sordid matter of comparative expense, the convenience of always having with you your own bedroom, and one spare meal for emergencies, makes all the difference between delightful and worried traveling. Yet a trailer is just too much, at least on a hurried transcontinental trip and return.

Time certainly does step along! Here I was, practically falling asleep, while the baby we brought back from the West Indies in a basket only yesterday—well, at least only eighteen years ago—drove me westward at fifty, beyond Chicago at even more, miles an hour. Not that we ever speed; there is too much fun in life to be that foolish. Nor do we care for that all-night stuff on which some continental motorists pride themselves.

In my twenties I used to think it close to a miracle to lie abed on a train—it was usually on the floor of a boxcar in those days—and speed along at thirty, forty, once in a while at fifty miles an hour. The engineer thought he was doing a hard day's work—and he didn't even have to steer!

Beyond the Mississippi you can do sixty miles an hour,

Downtown Ketchikan overhangs the seashore

Ketchikan's fishing boats were tied up just then by labor union agitators

Industrial strife is now invading Alaska   A Ketchikan street

At Ketchikan, the new Federal Building bulks symbolically above mere Alaskan
buildings

often for a full hour without slowing down; out Montana
way you can drive a hundred and fifty miles without shift-
ing gears, and even then only because you choose to stop.
You can sleep or read or write notes, or just day-dream,
back there in the Pullman part of the car. Fields, hillsides, endless vistas of black-eyed susans . . . delightful
snatches of sound flit in upon you: the croak of a friendly
frog, the muffled shriek of a rooster, the operatic note of a
meadow-lark, thrown in at the open window as we dash
past, like a good-luck greeting, like a bouquet tossed in by a
roadside well-wisher. The upland air is delicious; for a
day or two we scarcely met ten cars an hour, some hours
none at all.

We put our car in cold storage in Seattle. Our lodgings
on the way had totaled $4. But that was because we were
extravagant, took a cabin now and then for more elbow-
room, stopped where we could get shower-baths and the
other luxuries of travel. It costs a hundred dollars or so
to take a car from Seattle to Alaska and there are only
1,500 miles of connected roads, 2,000 miles in all, none of
them what Outsiders would call a highway.

There really is a Mount Rainier near Seattle! It appears to be just over there, even from Olympia, where a
delightful classmate of my college days is now one of
Washington's nine old—I mean, middle-aged—men; he'll
be chief justice by the time you read this. As many times
as I had been in Seattle before, I always took that story
of a snow-clad mountain in the background with a grain
of salt. Whereas this time it stood out just across the
lake on which giant Boeings practising for their trans-
atlantic flights sit down. From the windows of the Fritz
Millers' I knew in high-school days it filled the horizon
with a majesty and a beauty that sometimes made Fujiyama, in retrospect, seem insistent and artificial.

The Inside Passage is not crowded with shipping even
in mid-July, when the Alaska Steamship Company sends

north the unprecedented number of six ships in five days.
Mount Rainier withdraws gracefully into the background;
by early afternoon Mount Baker monopolizes the snow-
clad honors. Those graceful flying garbage-cans, the seagulls, escorted us in swirling flocks. About four in the
afternoon we crossed a lane of ferries, some laden with
boxcars. It seemed to be the route between Victoria and
Vancouver. Even Vancouver Island has a peak snow-
patched and streaked in mid-July. It was comfortably
warm on the moving deck; and at 8:40 the biggest moon
I have ever seen came up out of the Canadian hills. Four
American destroyers gazed placidly at us somewhere along
the way.

Pine forests on rock hills; long silver waterfalls; snow
patches that seemed only a little bit above us, on almost
bald rock hilltops. Snow in profusion on the summits of all
high hills; more snow-capped mountains shouldering aside
the blue sky. Wooded islands of fantastic shapes, scattered recklessly. Time and again there seemed no possible
passageway ahead, yet miraculously we always found one.
Poets, and many less gifted, have sung the glories of the
Inside Passage. I shall not try.

Alaska is Seattle's most faithful and most important customer. In fact, Seattle did not become an important city
until Alaska's gold-rush days. Our holds were filled with all
the portable needs of our present northwest territory, the
lower decks with more of them. Weather-bitten men on
their way to the summer salmon grounds whiled away the
second day at cards and reminiscences. Old-timers hurrying back from what they felt were lost days Outside were
almost reluctant to retell their experiences of the year
when Alaska first became more than a name to most Americans, only forty years ago. Young ladies merely sight-
seeing bent, in place of the "Mames" and "Lous" whose
errand to Alaska had a more practical motive, shrieked

applause of Nature's gorgeous show, put on, they seemed to think, for their personal benefit.

Forty-eight hours after leaving Seattle we were tramping the streets of Ketchikan. They are wooden to their full width in places, and most of them lead up to stairways that climb a hill. Even the newer concrete pavements are flanked by good old resounding wooden sidewalks, recalling my youth. Main Street climbs a five-story stairway, then levels off again. Ketchikan is built on an island forty miles in diameter, and is pushed almost into the sea by steep, wooded mountains. Not only does the town itself stretch long and narrow at the foot of its mountains, but houses are scattered far out along heavily wooded shores in both directions. "Arterial Highway. STOP." A road runs a dozen miles out of Ketchikan toward Seattle, as if trying to escape—or does it resemble a welcoming committee? Another entices you as many miles in the other direction, close along the shore of the fjord. The business section is built on piles; the rest of the town on rock. Water pipes, perforce on the surface, are allowed to trickle if it is very cold. But Ketchikan is seldom colder than Seattle. That July day could not have been improved upon; even Ketchikan's "four hundred days of rain a year" had left it almost cloudless.

Modern business blocks . . . well, modern buildings, at least, give it the familiar American aspect. Without exception, as far as we saw, the homes are frame structures, some of which might look down their noses at many in our Middle Western towns. Flowers grew in profusion about them. The big new concrete post-office and Federal Building is beautified, if that is the word, by a huge brass plaque bearing the names of our current President, Postmaster General and lesser fry, in letters proportionate to their political importance. It was reassuring to realize that we were still at home.

A sarcastic, hand-painted sign: "This is not a public

woodpile." The inner harbor was full of motionless fishing boats. The forest of slim masts swayed ever so gently, as if eager to get back to work. But fishing had been tied up by strikes ever since the season opened, on July 5. "Soon's the fishing gets good they'll probably get together," said one of the burly loungers, with a trace of Scandinavian accent. More salmon, they say, is packed in Ketchikan than in any other city in the world. Another of its distinctions, we heard, is that it leads the world in saloons per capita. But somehow saloons are different in Alaska. Of the numerous Indians strolling the streets and hanging about the impatient fishing boats the one we accosted answered to the name of Peter McKay. Just then the *Baranof* gave its second warning whistle . . . after all this was only the tail-end of Alaska and we could judge it better on the way home.

Another labyrinth of heavily wooded islands. They say Alaska could produce a million tons of high-grade pulp paper a year. But who wants more pulps?

We were barely packed and dressed next morning when Louis Delebeque of the Pacific Alaska Airways stuck his head into our stateroom and said, "You're flying at ten o'clock." So all we saw of the Alaskan capital on the way up was the few blocks between the wharf and the hotel, with a side trip to the post-office. The rest of the time we spent in trying to reduce our 300 pounds of baggage to the 88 we were entitled to as plane passengers. It was convenient that the boy and I can wear the same clothes, except that I cannot fill his shoes—or hat.

It seemed at least ten miles out on the Glacier Highway to the airport. It's a wonder they can find enough level ground even that near Juneau. Once there, we had to wait for serum. An emergency case had been radioed in at the last moment—a real Alaskan touch. Finally we were off, at 10:45 of a Saturday morning, July 16, in a gleaming Lockheed Electra.

Snow-streaked peaks; great valleys full of frozen rivers, turned solid, like Lot's wife. Madly rushing torrents of dirty glacier water. Green lakes; lakes with surfaces like black polished marble. An endless sea of mountain peaks, all more or less snow-covered, some forever capped with ice. Here we sat, warm as toast, looking *down* on glaciers. Some of them were streaked from end to end with two parallel black lines, like the tracks of a wagon.

More sunshine, less vegetation inside the coastal ranges. A scrub-wooded plain opened out and we sat down, an hour and twenty-three minutes from Juneau, at White-horse, Yukon Territory, for a box lunch and hot coffee served, gratis of course, by a reticent Canadian lady. Then just a chat with His Majesty's customs officer. The town lay well below, uncrowded frame buildings among trees, a few more pretentious ones along the bank of the Yukon. The landing field had been gashed out of the forest on the top of a high bluff.

Up again half an hour later. Four women, three men, two youths as passengers; Pilot, Robby Robbins, one of Alaska's famous band of fliers; Walt Hall, co-pilot. The scenery was less spectacular after Whitehorse. Harry, Jr. felt that the trees needed a lawnmower and they looked as if one had once been run through them, as we crossed the international boundary, slashed like a firebreak diagonally across our route, stretching on over the horizon in both directions. For a long time there was no snow, even in Alaska proper. The land below was almost flat in comparison with the fantastic scenery we had seen on the way in. Muddy rivers; placidly clear lakes; rivers above and below them. Fog—no, a cloud ceiling—just over our heads. Harry, who had until then enjoyed his first flight, found the air a little bumpy near Fairbanks, where we sat down at 3:45. Fairbanks time, by the way, is an hour earlier than Juneau time, six hours behind New York, in the daylight-saving summer. We had flown about 725 miles in five and a half hours.

Co-pilot Hall had brought along a new wife, and a delegation led by genial Joe Crosson met us—or particularly, him—handcuffed and leg-ironed him and seated him on an open platform on wheels, an immense JUST MARRIED sign above him, and hauled him through town with a tractor. Just a mild sample of the lusty, Gargantuan, Paul Bunyan humor of the frontier, and Walt was not brought up to it. The last day I saw him on the way Out he was still mumbling, "And I thought those fellows were my friends." He didn't seem to realize that he got off easy; Fairbanks often includes the wife in such embarrassing antics.

CHAPTER II

OUT ALONG THE CREEKS

*Big Scale Placer Mining ... Thawing, Sluicing,
Dredging ... Miners' Pot Luck ... I Try "Stripping" ... A "Dragline" ... Air Prospecting*

THE morning after we got to Fairbanks I slipped into
heavy old clothes and our one pair of high boots, leaving
Harry to handle his own struggle with Morpheus, and
went out along the creeks with George Christensen of the
F. E. Co. It was Sunday, but mining goes on in Alaska
irrespective of days—though not of seasons. We went
as far as Chatanika, thirty miles out the Steese Highway,
where the biggest dredge in captivity, or maybe only in
Alaska, was working.

Seagulls here in the very heart of Alaska! Do they
come down, or up, the Yukon? The hills everywhere
were pink with fireweed, shoulder-high along the roadside.
Alaskans don't seem to appreciate it, perhaps because it *is*
a weed. But so are most wild flowers. People were out
picking blueberries; on the way back we found a slope
almost carpeted with them.

Tropical helmets in Alaska! Yes, indeed; a majority
perhaps of the workmen in the open wore at least some
cheap variety of one. The sun beats down here almost
like midday in the Andes.

We came to a dredge before we saw any thawing or
"stripping." But let's take things in their order. Along
about 1918 to 1920 Fairbanks seemed to be dying on its
feet. Then the F. E. Co. came in and now it is the most
nearly like a boom town of any in AAA—as you should

9

abbreviate Alaska.   The "F. E.," in case you don't know,
is the Fairbanks Exploration Company, a subsidiary of the
U. S. Smelting and Refining Company, whose quotations
you can find waving up and down on Wall Street any work-
day in the year.   The F. E. Co. is placer mining the creeks
about Fairbanks on the big modern scale.   The Sourdough passed it up, but it's pay-dirt again now, thanks to
dredges—and Roosevelt.   Curiously enough, his shenani-
gans with the gold standard did help some people, made
gold mining again worth while in the Fairbanks district,
for instance.   Most Alaskans think he devalued the dollar—"raised the price of gold" is the naive way they put
it—for the specific purpose of helping Alaska.   Whereas,
the . . . well, at least the boosting of gold from $20.67 to
$35 an ounce was a big help to its mining companies and
miners.   Incidentally, in case you have again managed to
lay aside a bit for a rainy day, Alaska wants and hopes
that the price of gold will be raised again.

They say the F. E. Co. spent $18,000,000 in this Fair-
banks area before taking out a nickel.   In other words,
mining in Alaska, like so many other enterprises, from
peanut-selling to exploring, has become a Big Business and
the little fellow without capital no longer has much chance.
Even the big mining companies have to be good gamblers,
keeping their cards close to their chests.   Gold is a great
game, in which a few men win and many lose—but what
isn't ?

The Fairbanks Exploration Company and others like it
throughout Alaska buy land, which they seem to own in
perpetuity, or lease a string of old-timers' claims, paying
them in cash or in royalties.   One glimpse of the land
convinces the layman that it is forever worthless after it
has been run through the company dredges.

But let's see if we can make modern mining in Alaska
clear to the complete ignoramus in that line, such as you
and me, without taking too much of our time.   When a

company buys land or leases old mining claims along a
"creek" the land is all frozen clear down to bedrock, no
matter how deep that may be. The first job is to thaw or
"unfreeze" it, as they sometimes say in Alaska. Pipes
¾-inch in diameter are driven down by hand in ten-foot
lengths in holes drilled until they strike ice, then driven on
down farther as the ice melts or the ground thaws. Seems
to me George said it is sixteen feet from point to point
(that is, upright pipe to upright pipe), the rows that distance apart, and staggered, the average distance down to
bedrock here fifteen feet. But I refuse to be a martyr to
mining science if I am all wrong.

Now look up and behold other pipes, four or more feet
in diameter, come plunging down steep hillsides, hurdling
the next ridge, huge pipes that gradually branch into
smaller ones and finally shrink to the same size and make
a sort of hose connection with the "points" in the ground.
The result is an entire forest of ¾-inch pipes, rising six,
eight, ten feet above the ground and bending over there
in a hose connection to horizontal water-pipes on the
ground, which feed water from as much as eighty miles
up in the hills into the "points" at some terrific pressure
to the square inch. On the bottom or in the ends of them,
down toward bedrock, these upright pipes have sieve-like
holes in them, through which the water spreads, circulating
from the bottoms of the "points" toward the top of the
ground. There is a complicated nomenclature of header
lines, feeder lines, nozzles with a man-killing pressure of
water . . . but let's keep things as simple as possible.

Now, strange as it may seem, while water from a sun-
warmed pond may be slightly more effective, ordinary cold
water brought from somewhere far away in header lines
to the slender vertical pipes called "points," driven down
as nearly to bedrock as possible, thaws out ground that
has been perpetually frozen probably for centuries, perhaps
for eons. I believe Alaska did its first cold-water thawing

in 1922 and that a bookkeeper at Nome first suggested it. Before that every one assumed that you had to use steam. It costs 4 to 6 cents a cubic yard to "unfreeze" with cold water; steam was several times that.

From time to time during the thawing they send down a scout, in the form of a rubber-covered thermometer, to see if everything is 32°; if so, the ground is considered thawed. They thaw from "break-up" to "freeze-up," four to five months a year, and not only will the ground stay thawed all winter but for as long as two years.

Behind the thawers come the "strippers." Across the valley of the creek are man-made chasms down in which, a man standing at the nozzle of each immense hose, arcs of water that often threw rainbows tore at the sides of the cliffs, or at times ripped at the ground nearer his feet, with a roar and a cloud of mud. The gold is all down near the bedrock and the earth on top of it must be washed away before the actual mining can begin. "Stripping," "hydraulicking," or "sluicing," they call this washing off the muck above the pay-gravel. Bit by bit the thawed ground is removed and the terrain made ready for the next process.

Dredges follow the "strippers." A mining dredge, in case you have never seen one, looks rather like a river steamer with a penthouse on top, or like some fantastic modernist building with two long protruding trunks. One trunk messes about beneath the little pond of dirty water on which the dredge floats and the other points at the horizon in the opposite direction. The groping feeler consists of an endless chain of immense manganese steel buckets, which dredge up the bottom. Incidentally, the buckets' lips are all battered and cold-sored from their amphibian circling; wear out with incredible promptitude for such apparently indestructible things.

Though we had official permission from the F. E. Co. boss himself, we had to wander nearly all the way around a dredge pond to get onto one dredge. The first one had simply lowered its portcullis, like the apron of a ferry, when George waved to the men on board. But in this case we had to climb up something that resembled the Eiffel Tower, crudely reproduced on a smaller scale in hand-chopped timbers . . . and there is nothing I love more than being made to think I am undergoing hardships in seeing the sights, or at least seeing the sites, which other less haphazard reporters call "gathering material" or "working." Finally we were rowed out to the dredge in a row-boat, boarded it much as a pirate did a captured ship in the good old days when pirates were a definitely recognizable caste.

Once there, it was a bit like being inside a huge power-plant. I remember, too, a long climb up the sloping canvas-roofed "cat-walk" beside the conveyor belt which carries away the big stones. All the coarse tailings, refused admission by the screen into the hopper with the perhaps gold-bearing gravel, travel up this belt and are piled behind the dredge as it inches its snout along the creek, like some rooting prehistoric monster.

I won't pretend to explain what goes on inside one of those huge dredges, with its three shifts of sixteen workmen each, except to say that somehow it separates the gold from the other stuff dug up. Old-timers will tell you that this new gold-mining equipment is so thorough that a workman who fell into the feeder came out of the stacker without a scratch on him—but minus his four gold teeth.

There is no mining without water and up to now water had been rather scarce this summer. Not only must there be water for "stripping" but the great dredges must have ponds of water in which to float. Usually the dredges operate from about May 10 to October 10, with a month or two of get-ready and clean-up work before and after those dates.

Operations begin at the bottom of a creek and work up

it, leaving the tailings in ridges, the valley a waste of stones in windrows, behind the dredge. Modern placer mining runs a whole river valley through its machinery, covering with riffles of rocks scenes once made romantic— at least from a distance—by the prospector with a pan. Ahead of the dredges, behind the "strippers," appears the mastodon-weed with pretty yellow flowers. As it grows only after the top soil has been stripped off, it is assumed that it must come from seeds thousands of years old.

On the way to a camp, when things began to smell like noon, we met a friend of George's who had been "skinning the cat." I used to be a "mule skinner" myself in my college vacation days, but I am afraid I have not been keeping up with the times even in language. "Skinning the cat," it seems, means nothing more cruel or acrobatic than driving a caterpillar tractor.

The camp was just sitting down to dinner. To say that the food was well-cooked and as great in quantity, almost in variety, as on a cruise ship is of course merely to say that even big companies like the F. E. Co. have to give some thought to the contentment of their hired help in these times. Veritable rowboats of beef, pork, lamb, potatoes, vegetables—which no doubt come by the ton from Outside—ketchup by the quart, gravies and sauces, arm-straining dishes of stewed fruit, pies, cakes big enough for a golden wedding, and sundry other appetite-quenchers which I have forgotten, passed, mostly in silence, from hand to hand up and down the long table. A man who looked as if he would rather have been swinging a shovel circled the table with a gallon pot of coffee. One or two men, with the air of college students masquerading as miners, helped themselves to less than heaping platefuls. Other men, their hands still damp from washing, dropped in and fell to; those who had gorged to capacity rose, with perhaps a "So long," and drifted away toward the bunkhouse or back to work. I was a bit flabbergasted at the ladylike attitude of the miners in the matter of conversation, compared with the cussing, blaspheming, foul-mouthed good old days when I used to work in mines and with railroad gangs. I hope to goodness they were not holding themselves in just because I was there, mistaking me perhaps for a stool-pigeon of the Big Boss.

The workers for the F. E. Co. are about fifty-fifty Alaskans and Outsiders. That is, something like half of them "stay in" all winter. They are furnished food and lodging and everything that goes with it, such as soap and matches. The company pays $4 a man for hospital insurance, including doctors, nurses and all the rest. Labor gets from $150 a month up, "pipers" and "strippers" 71 cents an hour. They work nine hours a day, seven days a week, but cannot at most expect more than six months' work a year.

I found "stripping" easy when I got a chance to try it later in the summer. It was out at Ester—more specifically Cripple Creek—barely ten miles from Fairbanks, where some thirty years ago Charles Strandberg and his brother Dave took out approximately a million dollars. I did my "stripping" with a "No. 2 Giant," counterweighted at the back end by a jockey-box full of stones. The immense hose, with an 85-pound pressure from the three-inch nozzle, but as well balanced as a Chinese wheelbarrow, handled as easily as a garden hose. We were shooting at an 80-foot bank and the mud cliff before me came down in cascades as the stream struck it with the force of an avalanche. The water, propelled by pumping stations from streams often far away or brought down by gravity, can be shut off in the immense feeder pipes by turning wheels like those still available to brakemen on the tops of freight trains, but it is simpler to waste some of it. What look like huge boulders are really frozen mud; that black stuff near the top of the cliff is protruding glare ice, probably thousands of years old.

"Pipers" leave their stream shooting straight at a cliff while they are gone to lunch, then raise clouds of mud and a noise like a swiftly burning building when they return. Firemen would love hydraulicking. They could knock holes right through the walls of any but a well-built stone house. Let one of those streams hit a man and it will break his back. Pity they didn't, or couldn't, use "stripping" nozzles in digging the Panama Canal.

"Pipers" work in three shifts, using flood-lights for night work. They change shifts every thirty days, so that each gets his turn at what sailors call the graveyard watch. Sometimes a man holds the nozzle for only six hours, then spends three hours on the "bull gang," laying pipes, setting up "giants," and the like. Standing at a nozzle all day has a tendency to make a man lazy, they say. Most of them insist that "piping" is not monotonous, but I'm afraid I'd pin a book out on the nozzle.

Men living in the company camp at Ester get an average of $200 a month, $45 more if they feed and lodge themselves. College men go up for the summer; here again there was evidence of education, even of bourgeois respectability, compared with the railroad gangs of my youth.

Out at Cripple Creek the mammoths of today, which are machines, make chasms vaguely resembling the natural abyss surrounding La Paz, Bolivia, except that there are none of La Paz's glorious colors in these huge blocks of earth, not stone. We were down in a great man-made chasm filled with what looked like huge tumbled boulders but were really mud, frozen for centuries, with volcanic ash in huge sizes in it—did this and the gases kill the prehistoric monsters whose remains "pipers" uncover in such numbers? Here in this man-made valley in the face of Alaska it is a hundred feet down to bedrock even after the 80- to 120-foot cliffs have been washed down. Flowers and fine beginning grass were already growing on the bottom.

They will take out at least most of this useless hundred feet of earth with a "dragline" like an immense steam shovel. High on the edge of the chasm stood a new one, the big Bucyrus-Monigan "walker," the daddy of all mining machines of its kind on the continent, I think they said, second largest in the world. It had just been brought here for excavating at Cripple Creek and rose, high on the bank above us, like a great modern man-made dinosaur surveying the landscape it was planning to devour. For days it had been practising walking, like a child learning its first steps—and what feet! Each of them was larger than a caterpillar tractor; the crane stretched its prehistoric neck surely not less than fifty feet into the air; the one dragline bucket picks up about a boxcar-load of earth at a time, handles from six to seven thousand cubic yards of material daily. This is about the same amount handled by the famous Ester dredge, which has a chain of buckets of six cubic feet capacity, whereas this dragline has a single bucket with a capacity of eight cubic yards.

Back in Fairbanks, having somehow convinced them that we have no gunman leanings, we were admitted to a back room of the one bank, and saw the gold in its final form, so far as Alaska is concerned; pans of gold dust melted down into huge gold bricks, big as a man can lift, to say nothing of running away with one. There were more than $250,000 in gold bars in that Fairbanks bank's safe, besides a big pan of beautiful gold "dust." Few bankers in the States come so closely in contact with real money any more. The miner, mere lone panner for the F. E. Co., brings his dust to the bank, which assays it and pays him nearly the full value then and there. The rest is paid when the final assay is sent in from Outside.

Nearly every professional man in Alaska, they tell me—doctors, dentists, railroaders, aviators—either has a stake in a large mining property or a "field partner" (a prospector whom he finances). You must have the gambling philosophy to be a miner—or a good Alaskan. You may prospect, personally or merely by the pocketbook method, for years without seeing a color. On the other hand, Long Creek, near Fairbanks, cleaned up $62,000 in nine days a couple of weeks before we left Fairbanks. Our taxi-driver there thought he had carried at least $200,000 in gold dust so far this year—just tossed it into the car; no gun, no guards, no bandits. In 1937 Alaskan mines produced $27,000,000, more than $20,000,000 of it gold. Copper had second place, by twelve times as much value as silver or platinum. Since 1880 the output of Alaskan mines has been $750,000,000. Nothing at all of course compared with a Federal deficit these days, but still quite a respectable handful of change. More at least than "Seward's Folly" cost us.

A lawyer (of all people!) says miners are lazy. Perhaps, intellectually. It's a lot more fun grubbing about in the ground than in a dictionary, a library, a ledger. But somehow I wish more people were contented to work with their hands instead of their heads. Just think how much better off the world would be with Hitler still hanging paper, the sacred Mikado pulling a rickshaw, Mussolini washing his own black shirts! But of course without intellectual activity we would also lack our marvelous inventions, too, such as the radio, which can blanket the entire continent with the inanities of a Jewish comedian, who formerly had to gather his victims under one vaudeville roof—and risk their overripe vegetables.

Alaska is prospecting from the air now. Experts find ore veins by merely studying a photograph. Everything, including men, is flown in to some mines, places that could not have been reached, much less worked, in the old-fashioned days. The Alaska musher or prospector has his pack dog as well as a pack on his own back, in summer.

Facing a mining dredge head-on

"Strippers" wash away the muck above bedrock

A mastodon tusk washed out by "strippers"

Just to give you an idea of the size of a dragline bucket

This thawing field happens to be at Nome, but the process is the same anywhere in Alaska

An Alaskan mining dredge floats on a pond and lays windrows of tailings behind it

(Between you and me, in case you don't know, a prospector is a miner who has never struck it rich—or hasn't got it now if he ever did.) But old-time prospectors are dying off and no young ones come up to take their places. "Young fellows nowadays can't take it. Any man who hasn't learned to work by the time he is eighteen never will" . . . you and I of course have seen examples to the contrary, but at least that is the Alaskan philosophy of life.

One drawback of mining in Alaska, they say, or at least against big mining companies getting a worthwhile foothold there, is that patented claims pay no taxes and often by the third generation there are so many heirs that it is impossible to run them all down and get a good title to claims you want to buy or lease. There are a lot of such patented claims and missing heirs, so that much of Alaska which might be producing gold is lying idle.

CHAPTER III

Visiting Denali

*Colonel Ohlson's Dodge . . . McKinley Park . . .
North America's Summit . . . Wild Game Lore
. . . Hunting and Trapping in Alaska*

WITH Colonel Ohlson himself at the controls we were off at 5 A.M. sharp, the sun already high, at thirty miles an hour, which is good speed on the Alaska Railroad. The colonel never lets a previous hard day's work or poker the night before interfere with an early start, and his reputation for speed has spread as far away as Washington, D. C. In fact, he spilled a Cabinet member out of this very car barely a week later.

The Alaska Railroad manager's private car was a Dodge with flanged rubber tires, a rigid axle, no steering gear and something resembling a station-wagon body. Besides the colonel and ourselves and two weather-beaten trainmen, taciturn at least in the colonel's presence, who seemed to have come along for the ride, there was John M. Holzworth, whom I had known in New York, and of course his inseparable bird dog, Jack. Jack has many thousands of miles, several lands and not a few birds to his credit, and lacks only the ability to read and write. Holzworth himself is a New York lawyer—except when there is something more interesting to do. He used to be quite a famous big game hunter but would rather shoot with a camera than a gun now. One of our stream-lined new magazines had commissioned him to bring back pictures of Japanese poachers in Bristol Bay . . . but they must have heard he was coming, for they had fled the week before, leaving Holzworth with a summer on his hands.

Colonel Otto F. Ohlson was born in southern Sweden, half a century ago now, built railroads in South America and India, spent seven years with the Pennsylvania Railroad, went to France with Atterbury, and was finally drafted from the Northern Pacific in 1924 to run Uncle Sam's new railroad in Alaska. They say he is a demon card player; at least he is good at driving a Dodge with railroad feet. Offhand he seems just the man for the job—except that he is politically Republican. Many a hungry Democrat's mouth has watered for that $14,000 a year, but so far the colonel has not been uprooted, so he must be good.

Even that early in the morning Harry got a great kick out of sitting up beside the colonel. Only two and a half hours to Healy—the regular bi-weekly passenger train doesn't get there until lunchtime. Healy is the entrance to the mountains, with a branch line to some coal mines owned by the railroad. Geologists say there is a great deal of coal—and probably great quantities of oil—in Alaska. But so far miners have been interested in more valuable deposits. The dull lignite coal from Healy, which lights with paper, costs $11 a ton in Fairbanks, but has to advertise to overcome the superior publicity of wood—and they say the railroad makes it hard for fuel oil to get this far north.

Tripod telegraph poles—I mean, instead of the usual single upright peeled pole, the two or three wires were held up by an endless series of smaller, unbarked poles, set together like the framework of a wigwam. Such poles are plentiful, labor expensive, I suppose; and perhaps high winds and heavy winters have something to do with it. I wonder if section gangs work as steadily when the colonel's car is not in sight? And why must the Alaska Railroad import its ties?

Speaking of telegraph poles, back in the days when Alaska was "Russian America" the Overland Telegraph Company set out to unite the United States with Europe by 1,600 miles of them. On July 8, 1865, the War between the States being over and the air full of ambitious young men ready for more adventure, twenty-four vessels left the Golden Gate with five hundred of them, tons of green-glass insulators and 1,200 miles of telegraph wire. Peter MacDonough Collins, whom President Pierce had sent to Siberia as commercial agent, was in charge. The founder and president of the Western Union, then several years old, had contributed $100,000 and Uncle Sam had chipped in $50,000. The Russians had already done three-quarters of their seven thousand miles—there was even talk in those days of a railroad from America to Europe, with a tunnel under Bering Strait!

Six holes were a good day's work, heroic hardships the mere commonplaces of existence. By New Year's Day, 1866, they reached the Yukon. But on July 27, 1866, Cyrus Field's last dollar spliced the first successful Atlantic cable—he had united the United States and England in 1858 for a few brief hours, before his cable parted, somewhere, and he became an international laughing-stock. So the Collins Overland Telegraph Company died, a few months after the first pole had been raised and $3,000,000 spent; obviously it couldn't compete with a transatlantic cable. But it took more than a year to call off all the workers.

For decades afterward Eskimos drank from green-glass insulators and Indians made suspension bridges with telegraph wire. Some poles lasted until very recently. Collins died in an obscure New York hotel in 1900, at eighty-seven; got one paragraph in the newspapers. Yet there are people who say life is not a poker game.

One of the CCC boys pottering around with shovels at McKinley Park station wore the only mosquito-net we saw in Alaska, except in the kit of a pair of tourists. Somehow I had pictured every one in headnet and gloves in summer, whenever and wherever they stepped outdoors. This lad, too, was a tourist, in a sense, for Alaska imports, against her will, even her CCC boys. Is it cause or effect that made these fellows look, in every line and manner, so nambypamby compared with the hardy young men who live in Alaska?

The president of the McKinley Park Association, who has since gone to his last reward, drove us in an aged car to Savage River Camp. Not so savage at that, except in price, with rows of floored tents, good food almost well served, ground squirrels sitting outside their holes scolding at you. There is horseback riding if you like, and can afford it, accommodations for a hundred people, ninety of whom were not there. McKinley Park netted 1,139 tourists last summer, the best tourist run in its history. It should have many times that number; the landscape vista alone is worth the trip, though perhaps not the rates. It might be wise to encourage visitors by making them more reasonable, instead of trying to make money on the venture (which is private) before tourists begin to come in serious numbers.

The Alaska Railroad was building a tourist hotel at the McKinley Park station, which by this time should be open. It is larger than was at first planned, because last August the Secretary of the Interior came along and said, "Here, you are not spending enough. Add another twenty rooms." The colonel, being a Republican, doesn't like debts, but orders are orders. The concessionaires in McKinley Park contend that it would have been better to have built at "66" or at Wonder Lake, or both. "The money is in transportation, not in hotel-keeping. [Tourists please note.] There is a much better view of Mt. McKinley at Wonder Lake; and as to mosquitoes, we could build high enough above the lake to be free from them."

"Montana Bill" drove seven of us, counting Jack, by bus to Wonder Lake, eighty-five miles in from the railroad. Ahead of us loomed Mt. McKinley against an azure sky, barely half hidden behind clouds, which is better luck than most visitors to Alaska's great national park have. I have seen worse roads—and many better ones. Quite a feat to have made even a passable one at all through these mountains, along the sheer edge of the McKinley River, without much modern machinery or any imported materials.

The winding road disclosed at every turn glorious panoramas of mountains, all lorded over by the highest peak on our continent, ice-covered from crown to foot. Patches of snow, some of them immense, lay below us. Yet yellow, blue, white, dark-red flowers grew in profusion along the way. Here and there white specks far up the slopes and crags turned out to be mountain sheep. There was something of a forest where the rangers, and now the CCC, have their headquarters, between the railroad station and Savage River Camp. Otherwise, except for a bit of evergreen scrub forest in the flat valley of the McKinley River, McKinley Park may be said to be above the tree-line; the tops of its mountains are not even grassed.

With the sun still well above the horizon, though it was hard to believe our watches, Denali (Home of the Sun), and I prefer the native name for the mountain we call McKinley, stepped forth from behind the great curtain of clouds which almost always hides it. They tell me that tourists, even old-timers themselves, have waited days, weeks, months, even years to catch Denali unclothed in all her beauty. By the time we had parked as near the lake as circumstances made possible not a wisp of cloud . . . or rather, one single wisp of cloud, like a puff from the pipe of an Indian chief enjoying his goodnight smoke, clung to it; and nowhere except in the Andes have I ever seen a more entrancing sight.

Dr. Cook reported it ninety feet higher, but Uncle Sam's

experts now credit Mt. McKinley with only 20,300 feet.
Yet in a way it is not only the highest peak in North
America but in the world. I marvel that any one could
ever have climbed it. For it rises 17,000 feet above the
timber-line in sheer snow and ice, higher above its base
than any other of the world's mountains. Mt. Everest's
perpetual snow and ice line begins at nearly 18,000 feet
elevation, so that there is only 11,000 to 12,000 feet of
snow and ice upon it. Mt. McKinley was first climbed by
a party of Sourdoughs who spent from December, 1909,
to April, 1910, at the task, coupled with some prospecting
in the vicinity. Only two of them, Anderson and Taylor,
got to the top, but the feat received so little publicity that
many people still think Archdeacon Stuck's party was the
first to climb it. In fact, even Alaska refused to believe
that the Sourdoughs reached the summit, until Stuck's party
found a 14-foot pole which the first climbers had carried
up the knife-edge ridge of ice and planted at the top.

All evening Denali stood forth in cloudless nudity, its
silver summit still sunlighted at 11 P.M. And next morning it had merely put on a gossamer scarf, which enhanced
its beauty with a hint of coquetry.

All seven of us slept on the wooden floor of the one tent
at Wonder Lake. Both "Montana Jack" and Holzworth
proved themselves prime cooks . . . and until you have
eaten a moose steak cooked on a camp stove in the wilds
of Alaska you ain't never et nothin'. But a stove in a
floored camp tent makes the mosquitoes outside mere an-
noyances by comparison.

Though most of us went fishing, both that evening and
next day, no one reported a bite. Lay that to us, however,
rather than to Wonder Lake. Three Alaskan youths in a
leaky rowboat had a catch to make Izaak Walton sit up
in his grave. There was a huge beaver house for the
boys to examine, moose flies whose bite made believable
the statement that they can make holes through moose

hides, not to mention swarms of mosquitoes that corroborated at last, and for the only time during the summer as far as we were concerned, the tales we had heard of Alaska as the land of mosquitoes.

On the way back a fox sat at the roadside as if he were waiting for the bus, and we saw a caribou or two, scores of mountain sheep high above us, but nary a moose, wolf or bear. Once the young and the active ones of us stealthily climbed a high crag in the hope of getting within photograph range of a cluster of sheep sunning themselves on a rock ledge. But we got there only in time to see two ewes leading a lamb each along an almost sheer shale hillside opposite.

So we fell back upon the bus and Holzworth's animal lore. Man and primates, it seems, are the only animals that do not have a fixed rutting season. A caribou bull maintains a harem, loses it as soon as a younger bull is able to take it away from him. There are what look like fights to the death between bulls, but caribou never carry their struggles to that extent—unless they lock horns, which means death for them both. Caribou calve in the late spring and twins are as rare as among human beings.

Alaska estimates its caribou all the way from 500,000 to 3,000,000. Migrations of 100,000 are nothing. In places the mountain slopes above us were streaked with scores of caribou paths. On the move they cross any river or lake; even steamers cannot turn them aside. They begin to migrate around the first of September, not necessarily toward the south, but to get out of the wind and to find new grazing. Caribou were so numerous only twelve miles from Fairbanks, out along the Steese Highway, about the time we left, in mid-September, that the surface of the hills seemed to be moving, so crowded that it was no sport to kill them. Licensed hunters may shoot three a season; Indians have no limit set, so that they feed their dogs on caribou meat. Nor is there a limit for the white man, if he can say that he was starving—if, for instance, the grocer failed to come that morning.

The mountain sheep also has a harem and fights to hold it, but rams' horns do not lock. Follow an old ram if you want a good pair of horns, a ring a year, because the fact that he is alone is a sign that some younger ram has taken his harem and chased him away. Mountain sheep have twins more often than the caribou; live to a ripe old age compared with the caribou's six or seven years. Males and females may graze only a few yards apart, but they mingle and graze together only in the rutting season. A ram stands sentinel for the rams; a ewe for the ewes.

They say in Alaska that mountain sheep seem to decrease when they are protected, as in McKinley Park. But this may be merely because the wolves that prey upon them are also protected. Alaskans complain that Uncle Sam, among his other unwise policies, maintains three thousand square miles of sanctuary for wolves in McKinley National Park, an ideal breeding place for them; that the government is competing with itself, so to speak, for there is a $20 bounty on wolves in Alaska. While rangers are authorized to shoot wolves, they are kept at paper work so steadily, Alaskans allege, that they have killed only four during the past several years. Let hunters shoot wolves even in the park, they propose. As it is, Uncle Sam protects them in the park and pays a bounty on them outside it; and the same goes for coyotes.

So men smuggle wolf and coyote skins, or rather the ulna-radius bones of the left front leg, with skin attached, which is all that is required, into Alaska from the Yukon Territory. Wolfskins are worth much more in Alaska than Outside, because Alaskans use them for clothing. So, including the bounty, wolf hunting is a profitable business. The game commission has no jurisdiction in our national parks and the park commission thinks all animals should be protected in McKinley Park. Meanwhile coyote and wolf depredations among caribou, mountain sheep and moose continue. Alaskans and big game hunters disagree with this policy and say that by the time the department concerned sees things from their point of view all other wild animals except wolves and coyotes will be gone.

Coyotes can breed and increase where wolves would starve. They are the most destructive of what Alaska calls the "predators," but they are not worth skinning, except for the bounty. The $80,000 appropriated for bounties during the last term of the Territorial Legislature was exhausted in one year and today there is a big deficit against the bounty fund. The law-makers, last I heard, were considering a bill to raise the wolf bounty from $20 to $30, but insisted that bounty bootlegging must be stopped. No longer will the mere front leg do. Skins must be dressed, taken to a postmaster or commissioner, shipped to the territorial treasurer and sold for the General Fund. That looks like another case of Uncle Sam going into business in competition with private industry. Turning in the pelts for the bounty may be all very well down in southeastern Alaska, where wolfskins usually bring only $6 to $8. But in the far north a gray wolf's skin may be worth $45.

Another Alaskan grievance is that there are only a baker's dozen of game wardens in all Alaska, and only recently have they been given planes in which to try to cover their immense domain. The Alaskans want to hunt wolves by airplane—one pair tried it this winter, found it easy, if all the ground was covered with snow. Alaskans claim that coyote and wolf crossbreed. Wolves follow a herd of caribou, two or more of them attack one, front and rear, and when the animal whirls around to get the wolf behind him the other one hamstrings him.

Muskox, on the other hand, form a circle, women and children inside, at the first sign of danger and jab their horns sidewise at anything or any one who approaches them. Even muskox calves instinctively and immediately form a circle, like a football-team huddle in reverse, horns out, when you approach them, and allow nothing to get inside the circle until they are no longer scared. But this protects them not at all against rifles. They say it is no sport to shoot muskox, because they are as tame as a cow—though even the young calves will attack retreating fur . . . such as the back of a woman in a fur coat.

Yet for some reason the muskox is much more nearly extinct in Alaska than the caribou. Once very common here, muskox were exterminated by 1865. You can find their bones on both sides of Bering Strait and all the way across Canada. So Alaska brought some of them from Greenland. The idea was to make an easy draft and meat animal for the natives. But the government put them all on an island, and there they have remained.

Alaska has black, brown, blue, glacier, polar, grizzly and Kodiak bears, the last reputedly the largest in the world. The bears on our calendars are all wrong, according to Holzworth. They do not stand up to charge, only to see better, being very shortsighted. The New Deal might look into the matter of fitting them with glasses. Bears do not strike at you with their claws but bite like a dog. They do not knock salmon out onto the bank but put their paws on them in the shallows, take them in their mouths and carry them ashore. There they clean them with their claws; do not eat the bones. They pick berries by stripping them from the bushes into their mouths.

The bear is monogamous, breeds every two years, but even then male and female stay together only two or three weeks, like couples with separate careers. The cubs, incredibly tiny, are usually born during the first week in February, while the mother is hibernating—a kind of twilight sleep, though she must of course be nearly enough conscious to suckle and cuddle the cubs. The average bear has two, sometimes three or four, cubs at a time. Only

mother and cubs travel together. The female will not let
the male into her cave; she comes out herself in June if she
has new cubs, otherwise in May, with the yearlings she
has taken in with her during their second winter.

Moose generally have twins at the first breeding—I am
still quoting Holzworth and take no personal responsi-
bility for the statement—but thereafter usually only one
calf. Eagles, with nests of sticks high up on inaccessible
crags, mate for life. There is a bounty on them, too, and
Alaskans say they also should be shot even in the park.

Wolverines are a godsend to the Alaskans, because, the
hairs being tubular instead of flat, wolverine fur will not
gather frost even at 40° below, hence is invaluable around
the hoods of parkas. But the wolverine is the bad boy
among Alaskan wild animals. Not only does it climb down
the chimney and wreck the place but it is so fond of wanton
destruction that it urinates on food it cannot eat or carry
away. The wolverine is a scavenger—eats the leavings of
bears and wolves. He is a formidable camp and cache and
trapline robber—yet strangely enough can lick his weight
in wildcats.

Those who have tried it say you soon tire of eating
mountain sheep, but that caribou and, above all, moose
meat can go on forever, as far as gourmands are concerned. There are Alaskans who eat caribou and moose
the year round, and many others who would like to be in a
position to tell the game warden, in the unlikely event of
having him drop in at an inopportune moment, that they
were in danger of starvation.

The season for mountain sheep opens on August 20;
for other game on September 1, and all run until New
Year's. Alaskans denounce, as who doesn't, the man who
goes hunting only because he wants another head to hang
in his trophy room, and leaves the meat to rot on the
ground. But Americans who go to Alaska to hunt have
what seems to be a justifiable grievance. A non-resident

hunting license costs $50—twice that for an alien. What's more, Alaskan game laws require any non-resident to hire a guide, for each hunter, even if he is only armed with a camera! The best guides in the United States must live in Alaska three—seems to me it is now five—years before they can qualify. Guides pay $10 a year license fee and are so hard to get that they exact a minimum fee of $15 a day. Natives pay only a dollar for a hunting license and may dispense with a guide.

The ostensible reason for this partiality against the non-resident is that the Outsider doesn't know the country and may lose his way or otherwise come to grief alone, whereas the Alaskan is assumed to know all about taking care of himself in the wilds. The argument becomes a little absurd, however, when you find that a mere boy from Brooklyn—or from Minnesota or Montana, let's say, since Brooklyn boys rarely venture that far west of the Hudson—who came "inside" a year ago and has been driving a taxicab in Fairbanks ever since, can get a resident license and go off hunting alone anywhere he chooses, while the man who has chased big game all over the world and knows his wilderness in any clime must be trailed by a licensed guide. Oh, well, big game hunters are generally wealthy, at least by reputation, and it is quite in keeping with the times to take it away from those who have.

Alaskans, on their side, complain that "aliens," by which they also mean non-resident Americans, who break the game laws of the Territory are treated too leniently. Just the other day a non-resident without a license and unable to prove that he was starving was fined $25 for shooting a caribou—and no doubt went out saying, "Well, that's cheaper than buying a hunting license!"

CHAPTER IV

DOWN TO MATANUSKA

*Caboose to Curry . . . Matanuskan Hospitality
. . . Colonists at Church . . . Pioneering de
Luxe . . . Reverend Fisherman Bingle*

THE colonel's Dodge would have room for only one of
us that afternoon and Harry was more eager than I to try
out Savage River Camp's riding horses, so I went on by
morning freight. There is no better way to travel, except
by airplane, than in the cupola of a caboose, stretched out at
full length on leather cushions made a perfect fit by generations of freight-train crews, feet braced against the win-
dow-sill ahead, all the train writhing along before you, the
engine so far away that, unless the wind is wrong, even the
smell of its black smoke is gone before you get there . . .
For seeing mountain scenery it can't be beat.

The thinly wooded country looks as if it barely knew
man by sight; ptarmigan and their chicks pick their way
suspiciously through the underbrush. A dissatisfied young
man from Outside served Gargantuan Alaskan meals at a
sort of railroad roadhouse; $1 to travelers; 55 cents to
trainmen. Broad Pass, the highest point on the Alaska
Railroad, is only 2,363 feet above sea-level, which is surprising in so mountainous a region. I assume there must
have been some practical jokers among those who named
its stations; Honolulu, for instance, one green building and
a water-tank on a siding, doesn't greatly resemble the
original.

But talk about your luxurious hotels in the wilderness!
Curry, Alaska, has a hotel where your feet sink inches deep

in rugs . . . and, I judge by his perpetual manner of dis-approval, the headwaiter is straight from Mrs. Vanastor's, which was a dreadful come-down from the days when he served royalty in Europe. The Curry Hotel is the only place in Alaska, at least as far as the public is concerned, where you can get the kind of meal your butler serves you at home. But the prices need halving . . . no, I believe the Alaska Railroad's halfway hotel runs a perpetual deficit, and the taxpayer is feeding too many joy-riders already.

I strolled across the Chulitna River by a swinging bridge behind the hotel and sweat for an hour up a trail head-high in grass, through masses of big ferns, to get another view of Mt. McKinley—but he had gone into hiding.

Harry and I shifted places at Curry. He spent the night there and came on by caboose in the morning; I crowded into the Dodge, graced with a chauffeur now, and went on with the colonel and his party. A moose or two crashed through the underbrush along the way; twice porcupines got out of the way just in the nick of time. Their quills, I understood the colonel to say, have been known to punc-ture a car tire.

It was dark, which means at least after ten, when Colonel Ohlson dropped me at Matanuska station on a Saturday night. An assistant manager of the colony, who had taken the trouble to meet me there, drove me to Palmer. There is an almost luxurious inn (they call it a dormitory) there, run by a lovely lady—except that, like so many government enterprises of that sort, it more or less runs itself. There was no finding either the lovely lady or anyone else . . . "probably they're all at the movies" . . . but the assistant manager just walked me upstairs and picked me out a room. It had all the comforts of home, in spite of being rather crowded with dormer windows.

In the morning, which turned out to be Sunday, there still being no one in evidence, I went for a stroll, hoping there might be some other place where one could get some-

Near the base of Mt. McKinley, loftiest peak in North America

The high slopes of the Alaska Range in McKinley Park

Palmer, center of the Matanuska Valley project

Typical home of a Matanuska colonist

thing that would serve as breakfast. There wasn't, but I dropped in at Palmer's principal garage, perhaps with the subconscious thought of having a drink of gasoline. The big garage man, from Duluth, said the winters are longer but less severe here than in northern Minnesota, not so cold as the blow-away farms from which a lot of Matanuskan colonists came. The Japan current helps, even this far inland. "Besides, zero here is like 28° above in the East. Chinook winds are warm and keep the snow down. But the winds are often terrific; every few years the wind raises hell, sweeps through from the Aleutians . . . usually it goes through the mountains to the south . . . and blows silt all over the valley.

"Rain? The first summer we were here they had the most ever. You've heard about us being mired when we stepped off the train. This year there has been too little rain.

"Oh, we're doin' pretty well, considering," he said. "Three years is not enough; we should have six—but we must start paying this fall. Still, ten years from now this will be a fine place."

I wandered back to the inn. Sunday breakfast was said to be at nine o'clock, "or maybe 9:15." Then it was reported at 9:30 . . . 9:45; was finally served at ten—which was 4 P.M. back home, and I had still not quite caught up on the time.

In spite of outward cordiality you are given the feeling in Matanuska that you are imposing upon them by coming; that it's none of your business, the public's, the taxpayer's business, what is going on here; that the great efficient government employee class will take care of everything without outsiders butting in.

This included even the pert waitress, the solid-footed cook, both with a government-official attitude—they all seemed rather to resent the existence of civilians; consider them at best a necessary evil, as authors are to publishers.

Fifty cents for a take-it-as-it-is-and-make-no-comments breakfast: tomato-juice, eggs as the cook prefers them (which happened not to be the way I prefer them), half a coffee-cake (too early to make toast or hotcakes), coffee (tea is too unusual), butter and jam . . . not bad, on the whole, but pretty slim, at least for a man who has been up hours already.

Across the table young men far from the hardy, wholesome Alaska-born type were discussing what clothes would be like this summer—smart-tongued, self-assured young softies, with white-collar jobs in town; quite different even from the government imported Alaskans who do the real work on the land, in garages, at the slaughterhouse in Matanuska. Funny how soon we divide society into its unfortunate ages-old divisions.

Then I went to church—three times, in fact. The three reddish peeled-log churches stood all in the same block— more government regimentation? The little Catholic church was already turning its dozen faithful loose; the Lutheran, I think it was, had even fewer. So I brought up in the largest church, with by far the largest congregation, either because there are more Presbyterians and those who can meet with them, in Matanuska, or because the Reverend Bingle is popular.

Born in Fremont, Ohio, thirty-some years ago, the Reverend Bingle is the sturdy, enterprising, two-fisted (what hams!), simple-minded type that makes just the fellow needed for such a job. I mean simple-minded in its best, its complimentary sense, the sense in which Uncle Sam is naïve compared with Europe, for instance—yet perhaps wiser, certainly happier, in the end. A homely, homespun Will Rogers quality; not all the everydayness sandpapered off by "culture"; obviously never a misgiving, a suspicion that perhaps mankind is not all worth the effort, the "saving"; obviously a hundred percent honest and sincere.

But it was quickly evident that there was good solid

homespun thinking under that burly red-faced Bingle exterior. The sermon, like the service, was down to hardpan, with no frills. But how man does run in the same mold, fall into the same sins, wherever you place him! It seems that even in Palmer there is a juvenile problem across the railroad tracks! "Beyond the tracks" is pre-Matanuska, non-colony Palmer, the unanointed versus the quality folks brought in by Uncle Sam. The preacher laid on with a heavy fist. But there was more emphasis on encouragement than on sin, constant hints that the fight was mainly against low morale. "It takes time and energy to swim up a stream in life; anyone can float down." Even his eyes, reddened from lack of sleep, told one that he had been at the salmon run all week. Some Matanuskans have the philosophy of despair; the Reverend Bingle, unquestioned leader in such community activities as laying up enough salmon for the winter, oozes optimism . . . whatever he may feel underneath.

You could see the whole story of Matanuska more or less. depicted here in church. Failures in the main; some stupid, some lazy, but the great majority too honest, too unsophisticated to compete in this cut-throat modern world. Some who have only the vaguest notion of what life is all about; some who never learned what real work is, and never will; a few who would have been all right in any society but just played in bad luck.

Most of them have a hint of resentment in their faces, some look a bit ashamed, as if being here were proof of failure, or as if they resented being shoved out of "America proper." Their once (some even still) pretty wives have droop-end mouths, as if they had long resented, brooded over, having married a failure. Different faces, an altogether different atmosphere than among Alaskans-by-choice. Some of the women still insist on up-to-date hats. There was even a hint or two of lipstick and rouge. But the youngsters (no lack of them!) born or nearly born here gave one a hint that they may prove to be the sturdy stock of the old pioneer days—unless they are weakened by too much grumbling and invidious comparisons with "God's country" by their disgruntled parents . . . or by a wet-nursing, initiative-sapping government.

Harry turned up early in the afternoon and Leo Jacobs, who has now been replaced as manager at Matanuska, generously gave us a lot of his Sunday holiday. He drove us about the colony, coming to a stop each time we crossed the Y-shaped branch of the Alaska Railroad serving some mines beyond Palmer—it would be embarrassing, he contended, to be killed by a weekly train—even took us to his log-cabin hideaway from perpetually importuning colonists on the high bank of the river, beautiful mountains in the background.

Brush only, down toward the Matanuska station on the main railroad; big timber and a hard job of clearing farther back, especially beyond Palmer. Hip-roofed barns and smaller commonplace wooden houses (yet as good at least as average farmhouses in Minnesota) stand out against an Alpine backdrop. They have the advantages of modern ideas on how to make a cheap house comfortable. Nor is there too much architectural sameness; a colonist could build his own style of house—within limits. Luckily, most of them built log houses and barns. They fit the landscape, the purpose of the colony. Some are neat white cabins with white and red-tipped log ends, against birch and evergreen. Frame houses, rust-painted barns, harnessed teams, washing on the line, children romping in yards that are spacious new clearings, playing on porches with their dolls. Girls, wives, get right out in pants and work.

Palmer, the principal, in fact only town of Matanuska valley, 241 feet above sea-level, has a slightly pretentious small-town atmosphere that is somehow definitely different from Alaskan towns that have just grown up like Topsy.

It sits within a bowl of mountains, its watertank on legs standing above all else, in a flat valley more than half surrounded, especially on the south, with rugged, jagged ranges streaked with snow, as if to keep you cool even in summer. The snow streaks barely wear off by the time snow flies again. Yes, Palmer has a beautiful close-up mountain background . . . if only you could live on scenery.

Matanuska colony has 170 families left out of the original 245. You know the story, of course, unless you haven't seen a newspaper, weekly or magazine for the past five years. No other pioneer project ever got so much publicity. In the winter of 1934 the Federal government rounded up nearly 250 families on relief from stranded lumbering and farming communities in Michigan, Wisconsin and Minnesota and carted them off to Alaska to make farmers of them. Critics at the time accused the government of sentencing innocent people to "Siberia," but now the complaint is rather of pampering, but also of hampering, them.

WPA field workers in those three States were told to nominate candidates for Alaska from the relief rolls, to choose only experienced farmers, preferably of Scandinavian ancestry. There are rumors that some agents got graft for putting a family on the list. But more of the colonists claim, "They told us about moose coming to the back door begging to be shot; other game and fish in proportion. Well, there are fish, an' no foolin'—in the season when we should be farming. But if it rained it must be good land, and nobody can deny that it rains. I've seen two farms blow away from me in the States and I wanted one that would stay put."

The pioneers, modern style, were fêted in San Francisco and sailed in May 1935, to the tune of massed bands, on the army transport *St. Mihiel.* It was a palace with every modern comfort compared with the *Mayflower,* but there was much grumbling even at that, and the colonists were much discouraged by mud and forest when they arrived. Maybe the first comers didn't know that Matanuska means "muddied waters," but they soon realized it when they were dumped from the trains. The chaos of the first months was beyond the power of words.

The government transported the colonists and their families and two thousand pounds of household goods from their home town to Palmer free of charge; but everything else, except community facilities, they were eventually supposed to pay for themselves. They got forty acres per family, of which the government cleared, or paid them to clear, fifteen. They drew their forties out of a hat; shifted, swapped and combined and settled down to work. They got farming equipment, materials and help in constructing their buildings, subsistence, food and clothing, and a grubstake to carry them along until cash crops could be raised. They drew livestock and equipment almost ad lib.; were expected to pay nothing back to the government until they became self-supporting.

They earned their grubstake by clearing that fifteen acres of land each, for which the government paid them $62.50 an acre! Genuine old pioneers could be heard turning over in their graves all the way from the Alleghanies to California. An energetic Swede could clear about two acres a month; a softy a few square feet. They cut down the trees and burned the brush. The government paid contractors to remove the stumps. Bulldozers were still tearing them out. They lay in high rows all through the valley. A man can burn up his trees or dispose of them as he sees fit . . . and ten years from now he will be hauling firewood. But even if he piled up his trees they would rot in ten years in this climate.

The kind of people the plan visualized no doubt deserve all the help Uncle Sam has given the Matanuskans. "But the trouble is, they turned out to be good, bad and indifferent, as in any community. For one thing there was no

medical examination, so that the first families included two
TBs, one diabetic, an angina pectoris *and* a wooden leg!
Lots of plasterers, steamfitters, streetcar motormen and
just plain loafers got mixed in by mistake. But some non-
farmers turned out best, as they don't know it all—ask the
Experimental Station instead of planting by the moon."

The turnover in families has been about fifty percent.
Twenty-seven left the first year; others have been replaced.
Originally there were 890 people in the valley; now there
are about 800—and a waiting list of 15,000. Of 173
houses built two burned down, one found no water. So
the government decided to keep it down to 170; hand-
picked the families needed for replacements, from the
thousands on the waiting list. Others were picked from a
number who came to Alaska on their own, hoping to "crash
the gate."

"But how great was the desertion in the early individu-
alistic colonization of the United States? And most of
those had to stay; they couldn't get back. How was our
great Middle West colonized? This is doing with public
money in a few years what it took three generations (and
not often the same family) to do in our pioneer days; men
who worked their heads off—and sharpers often got the
benefit of their hardships. At least there is no exploiting
[except of the taxpayer] in this case; a sort of socialism.

"Yes, it was a good experiment. But there were two
big mistakes—and a lot of little ones: no limit on the debts
they could run up, and the government's system of bulk
purchases made things worth three dollars which a Sears-
Roebuck catalogue offers for a dollar. [If only they could
keep out mail-order house catalogues—and newspapers
and other Outside publications—Matanuskans might be
more contented.] Some had no money sense; in some
cases that's why they were on relief. That kind ran up
big debts and then walked out. Some borrowed as much
as $16,000; the average was $5,000. Government money

flowed freely at first; then it got less and less easy, until now it has dried up entirely and a man must pay his own way and have his own money to get along. Extravagance, waste, graft, politics or whatever you want to call it"— not to mention giving reliefers better than many a taxpayer who pays for them has.

Thrifty people lived thriftily; prodigals wastefully, as usual. One colony woman is teaching in Palmer; one has started a beauty shop; one woman drives a taxi, and such as those are soon self-supporting, as in any group of people. Every forty was to cost $3,000, without interest for the first four years. Of the $5,000,000 Matanuska cost you and me, three-fifths was spent on roads and other improvements. Old settlers in the valley borrowed $26,000. The old-timers in the valley were mostly bachelors and "bachelors can't make a go of it, farming. They can in mining, but not in farming. Need a woman to help."

About $1,300,000 loaned the colonists is "secured" by mortgages on their farms and chattels. The government winked off the rest of it; heisted the debts of all to average up on the spendthrifts; hung a lot on the provident and required all who remain to sign (man and wife) three papers, promising to pay back an average of $5,000, at 3% interest, in thirty years. If the 170 families remaining all pay off in full the government will get back nearly $850,000!

But it was costing about $500 a year each to keep these families on relief . . . and they had little chance of getting off the relief rolls. The government officials justify the experiment with several other excuses: national defense job; military advantage! The Japs could cut off Alaska and starve them out if there were no local sources of food. (It will take a lot of Matanuskas to help much along that line, but the best of luck to them.) Yes, we have spent $5,000,000, they say, but a destroyer costs $5,000,000, and this is a better defense against the Japs. Maybe.

Then, too, say the sponsors of Matanuska, it demonstrates farming possibilities in Alaska which may cure scoffers among old-timers and possibly prove an outlet for more destitute populations in the States. To which Alaskans reply: "The New Deal rushed into Matanuska valley without proper foresight—as it does into most things. This project may do more harm than good in the end; failure may hurt future colonization, discourage hardier types from tackling farming in Alaska elsewhere. Besides, Alaska is perhaps not yet ready for such a colony; the territorial economy has run in other channels so long that it will take time to change it." As to the real old-timers, they are something between skeptical and sardonic; "and anyway," ends a Valdez editorial, "the colony is an existent fact, so what?"

Colonel Ohlson suggested Matanuska colony back in 1928; advertised in West Coast papers; got much "fan mail" but few results. Then he got the New Deal interested . . . and in a way it is his headache now. For the colonel is also president of the Alaska Rural Rehabilitation Corporation and to all intents and purposes Matanuska, transferred from the relief administration to the colonel's care, is a department of the Alaska Railroad, though the Division of Territories of the Department of the Interior technically has charge of it.

The biggest problem has been to get land enough cleared so that farmers can grow enough to make themselves self-supporting through the winter. They now earn, on the average, about $400 cash a year from their farms, but they need more. About a hundred of them work for the ARRC after they finish their work on their farms. I see by the papers that the government is to buy 110 cows to be distributed among Matanuskans, that dairying is to become one of the big industries of the colony.

They grow good hay, not bad wheat; produce rye, barley and oats abundantly. But the hay must be dried artificially,

in that large sheet-iron building you see on the road between Matanuska station and Palmer, before it will keep
for the winter. They say it is quite an elaborate process,
the hay passing over rollers or over vents somehow heated
—not being a farmer, drying hay is not the world's most
interesting problem to me. Matanuska grows huge vegetables—but some Alaskans say that although the vegetables
are huge they are tasteless. The valley is too cold for
corn, but more than 10,000 acres are now under cultivation.

I saw lots of white chickens; but why are there so surprisingly few chickens in Alaska? I always thought they,
like men, could be acclimated anywhere. Ah, I see, "It's
too cold for hens!" Not so much that, says an old-timer
who tried to raise them, but chickens walk themselves to
death in the long summer days. Evidently they need a
curfew law. But don't we create artificial daylight to keep
them awake and laying nowadays? Matanuska now sells
eggs at 45 to 50 cents a dozen; "ranch eggs," which seem
to be cold storage, cost 75 cents. But Matanuska had a
hard time convincing Alaskans that fresh eggs are better
than—well, at least just as good as—cold storage eggs.
Most of the old-timers still prefer the eggs on which they
grew up. "Matanuska eggs don't seem to taste right . . .
and there is generally two or three spoiled in a dozen."
Looks as if Matanuska should raid its nests more frequently.

But there is a growing demand for Matanuska dairy
and farm products in Alaskan mining and fishing communities. Cooperative marketing has helped to solve the
valley's problem. "Matanuska Maid" dairy products are
displayed in towns at least all up and down the railroad.
Colonel Ohlson dreams of a million-dollar market for
them along his railroad. "Well, how did towns on our
prairies grow up?" The cooperative paid a 3½% divi-
dend last year; it has driven or is driving out of Palmer

the Jews of boom days. Prices and the demand for fresh
stuff being what they are, the farmers of Matanuska should,
when they get squared away and settled down to contentment with their lot, make good money. Besides, they are
in a natural game country; can catch and pack their winter's supply of salmon in nearby streams in no time.

The trouble is that if a man makes a success at Matanuska he finds he is not entirely a free man. He cannot
sell his forty without government permission, even if it is
free and clear. That, they say, is to keep out speculators.
Four colonists were ordered out just the other day because
they refused to join the cooperative marketing association
in Palmer. One of them is considered the best farmer in
the valley; is said to have made $11,000 in two years; but
he had been marketing his stuff in Anchorage. He wants
to pay off Uncle Sam and withdraw from the colony,
financially, cancel his contract with the government and be
wholly independent, though willing to pay the cooperative
5% on what he markets. But the Corporation heads said
no, and the case has now gone to the District Court in
Anchorage.

One man with a wife and five children has been ordered
out for raising mink! The new manager says, "Colonists
who joined in good faith but fail to carry out the basic
idea and foundation of the community structure will not
be permitted to imperil the rights of the majority of the
colonists. The colony cannot be successful unless every
member belongs to the co-op. Supplies from farmers must
be guaranteed and they cannot be guaranteed without the
co-op movement." I never did understand big words and
philosophical verbiage, but to me all this smells faintly of
Russia.

Palmer has a good school and the publicity given the
colony project has attracted good teachers. Now it has
been turned over to the Territorial government. Buses

pick up all children in the valley, which is more than can be said of States on our eastern seaboard. There is another little school on two corners at Wasilla, a few miles from the center; and colonists sending their children there are kicking; they want to send them to Palmer, which has an accredited high school.

The valley now has quite a network of what were once bottomless mud roads, graveled and maintained by the Alaska Road Commission, on Federal money. Seems to me the government furnishes a snowplow but leaves it to the colonists to keep the roads open. They are even talking of a road from Palmer to Copper River, on the Richardson Highway from Fairbanks to Valdez, "much needed" —well, it would at least open up a new and much mineralized district. Alaska needs opening up, and roads help . . . "in spite of the colonel." To hear Alaskans talk you'd think he would forbid roads for all time, in the interests of his beloved railroad.

One last misgiving. No, it seems it isn't one. "The fever that made the tin pan mightier than the plowshare" in Alaska is not likely to attack the Matanuskans. They are not essentially gamblers; a farmer isn't, though he often feels as if he were. Perhaps it is partly this different philosophy of life that makes the hardy, self-starting Alaskans sneer at "pioneering de luxe"; why Sourdoughs "admire Matanuskan colonists' production in one respect— babies."

The Reverend Bingle called for us at 2:45 next morning and drove us until 4 A.M., which brought us to the remnant of an old pre-colony town on the muddy edge of a bay—or it may have been a river. Fish by the truckload were already being landed from the boats. We got coffee and hotcakes in one of the dilapidated houses. The man and wife were old-timers who liked to reminisce on their youthful days in some well-known eastern city, only a distant

memory to them now. Then we were off in a clumsy row-
boat, slimy as a slaughterhouse floor. Half an hour later
we pulled up and waded ashore in the slime. Up under the
edge of the high-washed bank, trees towering above us, the
Matanuskans assigned to fishing had rigged up a couple of
makeshift tents, a table with a lot of food, mainly from
tins, on it, to which they now and then waded, one at a
time, for a bite to eat or forty winks.

Somehow one got the impression that here were good
willing men, not mere lazy failures. One bewhiskered
fisherman had started life in Wisconsin, fought fate for a
living through Minnesota, North Dakota, Montana,
Washington, Oregon, California—"where I ended up
broke, with five kids. I tried to get in on this Matanuska
project when I first heard of it, but I didn't have the pull,
or luck. So I had to pay my own way up later, and this
time luck was with me, and now I'm in." His vocabulary
was almost professorial; and just to show what a fine,
ambitious fellow he is, for all his misfortunes, he claimed,
and gave pretty good evidence to prove it, to have read—
in libraries—everything I had ever written.

We helped a bit, slithering at every opportunity down
the long sloping bank of mud that was like heavy oil, to
pull in the long nets. The Reverend Bingle was one of
those bosses whose word is law without any hint of what
makes it so. Now and then he whacked a recalcitrant
salmon on the head with the same calm I'm-sorry-but-it-
must-be-done air with which he had whacked sin the morning before. He worked harder than any of his fishing congregation, jumped to the dirtiest jobs before they could
collect their slower wits, pulled loose badly "gilled" salmon,
and gradually there was a whole boatload of fish, huge fellows that little by little stopped flopping and lay still.

Finally, by the middle of the afternoon—oh, no, I see
it's only 9 A.M.! Getting up at 2:45 surely is a way to
make your days longer, to stop life from running away

like sand through your hands. The tide had gone out and
we slithered and slipped, waded and climbed back along
and now and then jumped across a small stream bordered
by high grass, or grass that would have been high if it had
not been so heavy with rain and tide-water that it could
not stand up, scrub trees and even some large ones vaguely
in evidence farther away on either side, fell finally into a
wide road. It was well laid out but knew nothing of modern surfacing. Somewhere along it, after a long sandy
climb, the Reverend Bingle's car appeared by some sort of
shaman magic and he drove us . . . that is, started to
drive us back to Palmer.

But one of Uncle Sam's fish wardens stood stranded
where some other lucky possessor of a car had dropped
him a few hours before, and Alaskan hospitality and good-
heartedness being what it is, even among as late comers as
Matanuskans, there was nothing else possible than that the
Reverend Bingle should turn around and drive the warden
and his burden of a week's provisions to the stream where
his duties began. There was a small bridge across it,
above a white slab of stone set in the stony bottom, over
which salmon are counted. Thus does Uncle Sam keep
tabs on whether enough of them are allowed to escape upstream to spawn, and die.

Once, on the way in, Mr. Bingle was so overcome with
two or three weeks of almost no sleep, while Matanuska
gathered its salmon for the winter, that we stopped under
a tree at a turn in the road. He dropped instantly sound
asleep, his hands still on the wheel . . . stayed asleep
twelve minutes by the clock, then drove us on in, wide-
awake and cheerful as ever, oozing optimism to gloomy
parishioners along the way.

Where we crossed a small river a father and son were
cleaning huge salmon on an improvised table within easy
dipping distance of clean water. Matanuska has its own

boilers in which the home-canned salmon are cooked, just as they are cooked on a larger and more automatic scale in Alaska's canneries. They cannot sell fish; no commercial fishing is allowed so far upstream as we had been. But they can charge 5 cents a fish for use of the net!

Children of the Matanuska colony, leaving its largest church

The Reverend Bingle superintends the salmon fishing of the Matanuska colonists

The Reverend Bingle as a fisherman

A CCC worker wore the only mosquito-net we saw in action in Alaska

Fishing at Russian River

A young Matanuskan

CHAPTER V

To Seward and Back

Anchorage and the Colonel . . . Off at Moose Pass . . . Russian River, If You Fish . . . Acrobatic Railroading . . . Seward—and the Alaskan Flag . . . Riding the "Brill"

WE thumbed a ride to Anchorage, trains from Palmer being infrequent, and bearded the colonel in his den. The Alaska Railroad, which so far has cost us $75,000,000, began operations in 1923 and has been annually more than a million in the red ever since, until last year. Its payroll alone is $1,600,000 a year—"and that is spent in Alaska, whereas steamer payrolls are spent Outside. This year there will be a net profit. I said when I sent in my annual report to the Secretary of the Interior, in October, 1928, that it would be self-supporting in ten years—and it is."

That may not seem to you cause for boasting. But if you know of any other government railroad in the world that is self-supporting, wire me collect. Matanuska helps, of course; so does $35-gold. But the government is finding that trying to run a railroad at a profit is a very different thing from merely taking in taxes the profits of one run by private enterprise.

Ohlson is of course hard-boiled. Any man who has to fend off politicians and deficits with one hand and yelping shippers and the Alaska climate with the other has to be hard-boiled to begin with; or would soon become so. Also Ohlson is a Swede and a railroad man, hence not always as gracious on the surface as a French dancing master. But that's the kind of man it takes for such a job. Ohlson's main task is to hold down the annual deficit; part of his method of accomplishing this is freight rates that send howls of protest all the way from Fairbanks to Washington. But he is only a Republican and knows no New Deal magic to offset the forces of nature in the field of economics.

"The Federal government," say those who pay those freight rates, "is doing all it can to keep people out of Alaska. Uncle Sam builds railroads in Alaska and expects fares and freight to pay for them—but highways are Christmas presents. Railroads in Alaska should be for opening up the country, not for an immediate return. The government should encourage men to develop the country and help them by not charging so much for transportation . . . and the cost of food of course depends upon the cost of transportation. It is the individual with a grubstake and the ability to stand hardships, not the big companies with dredges, that do the country good. For they bring in their labor and take out their gold—even ship in supplies to feed their men and their machines and give no profit to local dealers."

Passenger fares on the colonel's railroad are 6 cents a mile, plus an extra charge for the parlor-car. Freight, shippers complain, ranges from $80 to $120 a ton on the railroad, but is only $40 a ton by truck over the Richardson Highway. "Moreover the Alaska Railroad 'reclassifies' freight after it has been accepted in Seattle for shipment to Fairbanks, by the Alaska Steamship Company, which works hand in glove with the colonel, and charges us a lot more than was agreed upon, when it gets here. After the highway closes for the winter the railroad rates become fantastic. The colonel has tried to kill competition by getting the government to take graft on every pound of goods that comes in over the highway. But even with the toll, it pays to ship oranges up the highway to Fairbanks and back down the railroad to McKinley Park."

Colonel Ohlson's answer seems to have point: "Merchants kick at the railroad rates. But 16-cent veal in Seattle, paying 6 cents a pound freight from there to Fairbanks, sells there at 50 cents a pound—or more. Low railroad rates would merely mean that the Outside taxpayer would be subsidizing the merchants, miners and other people of Alaska."

But don't let's get our fingers mashed in a domestic quarrel. The most interesting observation the casual and disinterested—no, very much interested, but after all only in an academic way—visitor to Alaska is likely to have on this particular controversy is that high prices and high wages, if general, are of little advantage to any one— except to the government and perhaps to the man who lays aside some of his income. But there do not seem to be many devotees of that old-fashioned sport in Alaska. It has the frontier attitude that "there is plenty more where this came from."

Anchorage, which only recently gave up to Fairbanks third place among Alaskan cities, is a government-built railroad town of few architectural pretensions. As a port it is open about five months a year; it can never be a very good port, being subject to silt and icebergs—or at least to pieces of glacier. There is an occasional steamer from Seattle to Anchorage. But for the most part goods from Outside go to Fairbanks and its hinterland by the Alaska Steamship Company and the Alaska Railroad, connecting at Seward.

Tourists pull down the curtains against the cruel (!) Alaskan afternoon sun and read the *Satevepost,* through some magnificent mountain scenery. Two young Indian men just back from Bristol Bay—Yes, lots of fish. No, no Japs—gasp with astonishment when I turn around and talk to them. Passengers avoid the natives just as absurdly as white residents do. They had paid $68 each for a 2½-hour flight that saved them two or three weeks

on boats. They both wore Wrangell High School pins;
seemed average Americans in every way, except that plain
evidence of Indian ancestry. There is probably more
racial prejudice in the United States proper than in Alaska.
But Alaska does have social barrier trouble. Many an
establishment, even in Canada's Yukon Territory, is
adorned with the sign "No Natives Allowed," and in
places where they are allowed, it is the good old insulting
custom to smash a glass after a native has drunk out of it.

The day was almost hot. But the snow-capped mountains just across Turnagain Arm filled our windows . . .
yes, I suppose they do look like truckloads of vanilla icecream spilled all over the mountain-tops. The scenery
nearly always improves as you near the coast in Alaska.

At Moose Pass Holzworth and Jack were waiting to
assure us that it would be worth our while to visit Harry
Smith's hunting lodge at Russian River, a couple of hours
inland. Smith himself, once of New Mexico, was there
with a car as virgin as the scenery to add our names to his
guest book, if we could spare the time—and expense. Such
places are not cheap in Alaska, for several good reasons.
But they say this is the best sheep district, one of the best
moose districts in Alaska; lots of mountain goats, too.
And at Harry Smith's you can fish right out of the house,
so to speak; whereas from other accommodations for
hunters and fishermen in this region you must walk three
miles to fish, eat a cold lunch, maybe get wet and have to
stay so all afternoon. . . .

By this time the train had gone on without us and we
were headed for Russian River Rendezvous. Unfortunately, you can get nearly there by car now; twenty-five
miles along the new highway from Seward to Hope takes
you into the perpendicular mountain scenery of the Kenai
Peninsula, along big Kenai Lake, of greenish glacier water.
It was along the shores of Kenai Lake that were grown
the prize spuds (Alaska seldom says "potato") of all the

United States and its possessions, the distinction being
awarded them Outside. Where the lake becomes a river
you cross a good solid wooden bridge to Cooper's Landing,
named for an old-timer. Cooper's Landing has a citizen
noted for her beautiful flower garden, some feuds of long
standing and at least one delightfully unsophisticated old-
timer who "wouldn't live anywhere else for a pokeful of
gold dust."

Better still, a little farther on you have to abandon the
car and take to the trail—so nearly impossible a pleasure
for travelers nowadays. It was barely a three-mile walk,
when I at least would have liked five times that as an ap-
petizer, but there were glimpses of a real Alaskan forest
along the way.

Mrs. Smith and her two girls—no, her daughter and
a chum from Montana—were there to make us at home.
The Smiths had two daughters when they came to Alaska;
and of all places you'd think this region safe from the
hazards of life on street and highway which make Outside
so terrifying to the old-timer. But five years before, soon
after their arrival, the two girls went on a picnic, in charge
of a woman who not only was responsible by nature but
had lived most of her life in Alaska. So how could there
be any danger? But as the dozen or so children were
strolling gaily homeward along that road by which we had
come to Cooper's Landing, a chunk of the mountainside
fell off and . . .

The Smiths can handle ten guests in their two-story log
house, six more in cabins. Well built by the fox farmer
from whom they had bought what was once a Russian
penal colony, it is just the place for a comfortable hideaway, and incredibly well furnished for so isolated a spot.
It was hard to believe that all the furnishings had been
back-packed in. There are legends and even rusted im-
plements testifying to Stalin-like cruelties back in the days
when this was a place of exile. In the back yard is Russian

River, outlet of a beautiful lake only three or four hundrew yards away, above which is a higher lake, backed by a gleaming glacier.

Where the river takes a picturesque tumble just beyond the house, Harry and I went with the hired man to hook salmon, their eggs being needed for bait. You use a pikepole with a sharp hook at the end of it, pick out your salmon from the schools of them bent on fighting their way up the falls. Unfortunately, males are no good for bait purposes, and it is harder to distinguish between the sexes in a whirlpool than in a modern swimming-pool. We hooked four males to two females, and it was too far from salt water for the fish themselves to be edible. But one female salmon furnishes a lot of eggs.

Even I caught a dolly varden, 'steen inches long, at the first cast, a rainbow trout even longer, a larger one still while trolling in the lake. They have rainbow trout here up to—well, Harry's measured thirty-six inches. Lake or river, it makes little difference. There was a bloated dead moose floating along the shore of the lake; it seems moose sometimes break through the ice in the spring.

The Smiths, like so many isolated Alaskans, have their own radio station; fixed hours in which to talk to the outside world. In Alaska broadcasters often give not merely the hour but the day of the week and of the month. Some one might sleep the clock round in winter, or stay awake too long in summer, I suppose, and lose track of the calendar.

The Smiths teach the Moose Pass School, when school keeps. Eight pupils, two teachers, and their daughter's proficiency even on the typewriter was evidence that there are advantages in small numbers, that isolation need not necessarily mean a scanty education.

We took the trail back to the highway, the car back to the train, forty-eight hours later. Another trainload of tourists. A moose . . . right over there, lumbering away through the underbrush. Don't mistake 'em for a mule; and the plural is not "meece," as some tourists seem to think. Glaciers, tunnels, bridges high over gorges, with rivers of sickly-looking glacier water foaming far below, a loop on which the train would tie itself in a double bow-knot if it were long enough. This part of the line was already built when Uncle Sam took over the job.

The train stops long enough for passengers to photograph the largest glaciers and to see Nellie's place at Lawling, a log cabin full of imposing trophies. Nellie was a friend of Buffalo Bill and lives partly on collections from three-minute lectures to train passengers—mere pin-money, I suppose, which is all money is in many parts of Alaska. As to the more serious problems of life, Nellie keeps a line out in Kenai Lake just behind her house and when a fish is caught it rings a bell and is dragged through the kitchen (a pause here for cooking, of course) into the dining-room.

Nellie says she shot most of the big game on the walls herself; that the job is not to kill but how to take care of a big animal after the killing. Personally I'd rather see those huge handsome moose heads out there in the under-brush, proudly and suspiciously raised, rather than adorning a log-cabin wall, no matter how brave, hardy and hunting-wise is the woman who killed them and now gloats over them. But . . . I suppose they'd all be dead by now anyway, even if man, or woman, never came to disturb them.

Seward lives to meet its incoming steamers. The town itself lies low on a little peninsula jutting out into a bay surrounded by mountains, rising in one place to 7,000 feet. The bay is open to ocean traffic all the year round, so that Seward calls itself the Gateway to Alaska. There is a common belief in the States that steamers ply to Alaska only in the summer, whereas this is true only of Nome. Seward has its weekly steamer even in winter. Some of its houses are sumptuous for such surroundings, nearly all of them replete with inner comforts.

In the outskirts is the Jessie Lee Home with 312 acres, founded by Northern Methodists in 1890 at Unalaska, moved here in 1905. There were a hundred children there at the moment; twenty more live there when school is in session. Only pupils with some native blood are admitted. But though probably a majority of them were full-blood Indians, they are so mixed with the Scandinavian that there were several blonds. Some Jessie Lee graduates become valedictorians in the Seward High School.

Besides mission schools like the Jessie Lee and the Sheldon Jackson School at Sitka, and two native vocational boarding-schools, at Wrangell and at Eklutna, just north of Matanuska on the Alaska Railroad, there are two distinct kinds of public schools in Alaska. Territorial schools, supported by the Territory and the incorporated towns and school districts in which they are situated, serve nearly all the white children. Natives may attend them, but most of them go to the public schools for natives, maintained by the Federal government. These are under the Bureau of Indian Affairs of the Department of the Interior, which has been responsible for the education and medication of the natives since 1931.

At last account there were 237 teachers in the Indian service—and twenty-two communities in Alaska with a school population of twenty-five or more were without schools. Uncle Sam is gradually remedying this situation but he wants a minimum number of pupils *assured* before opening a new school. The Territory spends almost half its income from taxes on education and in addition, the Territorial schools outside incorporated cities get one-fourth of the so-called Alaska fund, consisting principally of federal taxes collected in Alaska. Much of this comes from the fish tax, so every time you buy a can of Alaskan salmon you are helping to support Alaskan schools.

The Territory pays its teachers well; $200 a month is almost a minimum; but the mortality among schoolma'ams in Alaska is terrific. Go northwest, young woman, go northwest. Alaska is a great place to pick up a husband, even if you are past your prime. Many of them are still real he-men, too (though not exactly the sort of fellows Alaskan novels picture), and while you must expect rougher living in some places than Outside, my guess is that Alaska's miners and pioneers make less troublesome husbands than the average city plodder.

Whenever possible Uncle Sam appoints both man and wife to teach in his native schools, especially in isolated places. But do not expect a sinecure. A teacher in the far north finds, sometimes to his surprise, that he must also be the postmaster, village doctor, secretary of the village council, manager of the co-op store, superintendent of a PWA project, responsible for several thousand reindeer, and has other jobs to keep him out of mischief. For instance, in one native school we visited, the showerbaths in the basement are open to adults at certain hours: ladies, 3-5 P.M. on Thursdays; men, 1-5 P.M. on Fridays—no doubt leaving the teachers the Saturday night rights.

Until 1884 there were only missionary schools in Alaska, and for some time after that the government subsidized these, so that teachers were also missionaries. There are places where those in the Indian service are still expected to change their calling on Sundays. The boys of Alaska show a decided preference for men teachers, and if one may find fault for a moment, the native schools seem to cling too closely to the curriculums in vogue on the mainland. Uncle Sam always seems to feel that every one under the Stars and Stripes must have the same education, that an Indian who must earn his living by fishing and trapping should have the same schooling as the boy who is going into business in New York. In fact, but for their faces it would be hard to distinguish between native and white children in Alaskan schools—though many young Eskimos and Indians use the English they learn in school only when they do not want the old folks at home to know what they are saying.

It was a native schoolboy at Seward who designed the Alaskan flag. In the autumn of 1926 a contest for such a flag was opened to all seventh and eighth grade pupils in Alaskan schools. Every State and every other "possession" of the United States had a flag, so why not Alaska? Of the 142 designs submitted, that of Benny Benson, then thirteen, won the engraved gold watch offered as a prize and in 1927 his design was officially adopted by the Territorial Legislature. The Alaskan flag has eight gold stars on a blue field, showing the Dipper and the North Star—"which will in time be the 49th star in the American flag" . . . maybe.

The scenery is magnificent from Seward to Anchorage, then less so for some time. Turnagain Arm, so named by the Captain Cook who died at the hands of the natives of Hawaii, because he found it a closed passage, looks very different when the tide is in. Cook Inlet, you know, has the second highest tide in the world, sixty feet above low tide, and the incoming waters rise to a bore eight or ten feet in height.

They are talking now of spending $10,000,000 of our hard-earned money to shorten the Alaska Railroad. The new branch, if this comes to pass, will leave the present right of way at Mile 63 and run twelve or fourteen miles to Portage Bay, bringing Anchorage within two hours of the coast—and no doubt killing Seward, named for the man who bought Alaska! But first of all they must do some drilling to see whether the mountains between Anchorage and Portage Bay are of a material that will stand tunneling. The proposed new branch would require one 13,000-foot tunnel, another of 4,600 feet, and the glacier above may be too deep down to make them pos-

sible. Opponents of the plan say a railroad from Portage
Bay will not develop any new country but that one from
about Mile 84 to Homer, a beautiful place with a marvelous harbor, would open up the Kenai Peninsula, though
they admit that would require a costly fill across Turnagain
Arm.

Seward, of course, and many other Alaskans are opposed to the colonel's new plan. But he insists that it is
nonsense to talk of the job costing $10,000,000; that half
that amount will do it, in two years. Portage Bay is shel-
tered and free from ice at all times. Such a branch would
shorten the line from tidewater by 53 miles, make possible trains in one day to Fairbanks, reduce the steamer
running time from Seattle considerably (denied by the op-
position), make it possible for the Alaska Steamship Company and the Alaska Railroad to compete with steamers
that have been bringing goods up Cook Inlet to Anchorage
and cutting the rates from Seattle, make possible a lower
freight rate on the railroad, so that it can compete with
its bitter rival, the Richardson Highway, in summer, perhaps even reduce passenger fares. But the main argument
seems to be that such a shortcut will do away with the most
costly portion of the railroad to maintain—and with some
of its best scenery and most interesting acrobatics. Slides,
mountain ranges and other natural obstacles make the
Seward end of the present railroad a constant expense;
the roadbed has already been raised and replaced three
times.

The colonel assures Seward that it will survive the
change; there is a road from there to Hope, he reminds
them. But his mention of "opportunities for the people
of Seward to move to the new terminus" sounds ominous.
And if tourists can reach the McKinley Park Hotel, or
even Fairbanks, in one day, what will happen to the
sumptuous Curry Hotel and its lofty headwaiter? We

might be able to move it, but hardly him, to some backward town in the United States proper.

There are no sleeping-cars, at least for the mere public, on the Alaska Railroad. But there is the "Brill," made of course in Philadelphia. Twice a week two light electric cars, furnishing their own power, carry the hardier type of Alaskan travelers through the night. There is a rocking-chair, ocean-voyage quality about Brill travel over such a track which adds to the pleasure (shall I call it?) of a ride through the luminous Alaskan summer night, the sky at most like a semi-opaque glass dome overhead even at the end of July.

Curry for a midnight lunch, with no headwaiter in sight. Then a nap perhaps as the Brill sways onward, though that seems foolish when one can have but one such ride in a lifetime. In the morning, if there is such a thing during the Alaskan summer, rain, badly needed up here, was falling. There is much more sunshine in the interior of Alaska than down on the coast, and Fairbanks gardens had been protesting. Garden truck, flowers, every seasonal growth, were farther along than farther south. But a rainy day makes this part of Alaska as flat and mountainless as our prairies.

We caught a murky glimpse of what fellow-Brill-riders said was a big forest fire down the Tanana below Nenana, which had been burning for weeks. Nenana, by the way, takes its accent in the middle, Tanana on the first syllable, and Alaskans warn you that mispronounced Alaskan place names with a native derivation have a way of making you say something very different than what you intend to say, to the raucous delight of listening natives.

That bridge across the Tanana at Nenana cost $2,000,-000 and boasts a gold spike driven by Harding, the only President, Alaskans rather bitingly remind you, who ever came to Alaska. A section gang was working busily on in the rain—though whether that is hardihood or uncertainty as to when and where the omnipresent colonel may appear, I can't say. But Alaska is still too near the pioneer stage to be much given to malingering, or for that matter to speeding up just because the Big Boss comes along.

And so at the end of our first month away from home we came back to Fairbanks on the fair banks of the Chena. Somehow, though we had certainly enjoyed every hour of it, we seemed to have been away more nearly three hundred than a mere thirty days.

CHAPTER VI

SKAGWAY FROM THE REAR

*Back to Whitehorse . . . It's in Canada, You
Know . . . That International Highway . . .
Route of the '98ers . . . Windswept Skagway
. . . Old-timers, Living and Very Dead*

JOE CROSSON himself flew us from Fairbanks back to
Juneau that last Sunday in July—except that Harry and I
left the plane at Whitehorse. The Electra's full load that
day included the small son of Ben Eilson, on his way Out
with Ben's brother, to go to school in Michigan. Alaskan
aviation has a few bitter memories, among them the death
of Eilson, the pioneer who taught Joe Crosson. Eilson
was up around Bering Strait somewhere with Dorblandt,
the bad boy of Alaskan aviation, in that he was always in
trouble, often by his own fault, his own impulsiveness, getting furs out of a stranded ship. The weather was bad.
But Dorblandt said, "If we hang around for good weather
we'll never get this damned stuff out."

"Too bad for flying," said Eilson, "but if you go I will."
(Never take a dare is no longer standard policy among
Alaskan aviators.) Dorblandt took off, found the weather
even worse than Eilson had thought, made a circle and
sat down again, no doubt thinking that Eilson, who took
off just behind him, was following him back to a landing.
But the weather was so thick that Eilson only saw him
start, took off just behind him, went on and was killed in
the Arctic wastes, where Joe Crosson and Harold Gillam
found him days later.

We landed, unexpectedly, at Tanana Crossing. A head

65

wind, Joe said, and just as well to be sure of gasoline. An Indian who looked as if he had never come within nearer than hearsay contact with civilization came running out to the airfield, which resembled a pioneer's clearing before the first plowing, with a mailsack or two. Mails rarely miss a chance to catch a plane in Alaska. Even in Fairbanks barnstorming aviators call up the postmaster and tell him they are flying to so-and-so and is there any mail. The government authorizes him to pay 25 cents a pound from Fairbanks to any other town in Alaska, except to Nome, which pays 50 cents, then 25 cents more from there to Barrow. I am speaking of course of ordinary mail, not airmail, which pays double postage from anywhere in the United States or Canada to anywhere in Alaska.

Above the White River we were up 10,550 feet, flew directly across Lake Labarge, and landed in time for that box-lunch on the plateau high above the town of White-horse. There were of course no formalities, just a brief friendly chat with His Majesty's customs officer.

Whitehorse sits on the flat bank of the Yukon, backed by a high bluff. It used to be across the river; before '98 it did not exist at all. Today it is a great airplane center. You can fly from there to Edmonton and on to Toronto, Montreal, Quebec, and of course to anywhere by chartered plane. Eighty-seven people were flown into or out of Whitehorse in one day.

Americans were the first to land here in a plane . . . and was that a Whitehorse holiday! But the Canadians are doing their share now. They can repair a "ship," even build an entire plane at Whitehorse; a mechanic gets credit for factory experience there. People go in forty minutes to places it took from two to four weeks to reach by any other form of transportation. The Church of England bishop in this region covers in ten days what four months won't do otherwise—and easy days, compared with the early bishops, who went down the Yukon on a raft, with

Mrs. Pullen of Skagway   Chilkoot Pass in gold-rush days

Quiet Skagway may be just the place for those jangled nerves

Our steamer on the Yukon from Dawson to Nenana

Dawson on the Yukon, and the mouth of the Klondyke

Indians . . . one of them, a Bishop Bompas, I believe it was, even ate his own boots!

It is half an hour's walk from Whitehorse to the famous rapids of the same name. They seem tame indeed compared with rapids I have shot, on the Essequibo River in British Guiana, for instance; the stream hardly looked deep enough to drown any one, and there is no jungle alongside. Yet the cemetery that grew up beside the rapids was well patronized—probably there were many canoeing greenhorns among those who rode on boats and rafts made of whip-sawed green timber. As soon as they had themselves organized the Canadians refused to let women and children shoot the rapids, soon required a licensed pilot for every one. To hear them talk nowadays, old-timers didn't find robbers or the Whitehorse rapids nearly as bad as they sound now from the tales of Klondyke days; yet men were robbed and drowned.

Now there is a mosquito-netted building beside the rapids, to save the poor sightseers from Alaska's chief hardship today—though we simply must keep in mind that this is not Alaska, but Canada's Yukon Territory. Somehow the Klondyke always seems American. Here visitors can sit in rocking-chairs and imagine with tears in their eyes the old '98ers rushing past, perhaps to destruction . . . there is even a book provided in which they may pen their poetic thoughts on the subject and hand their names down to posterity.

Whitehorse says there is good fishing at Whitehorse rapids. Miles Canyon, a little farther on, is like a spaded ditch of clear blue rushing water, now with a bridge over it, though it leads to nowhere in particular. There are remnants of the alternative to shooting the rapids, a 4½-mile pole tramway around the canyon and the rapids that had sprung up by the Klondyke's second winter.

Whitehorse Inn is a nice enough place, rather too luxurious for so out-of-the-way a spot, though $4.50 seems a bit high for a box-like hotel room with twin beds, no bath and half-inch partitions—and even in Canada there are inconsiderate travelers who carry their own radios. The Inn has a strong English accent but the meals next door are rather American. The waitresses are English enough to show astonishment, however, that any one should want a glass of water at breakfast. That Sunday's dinner ($1.35) included lake trout, moose steak, mountain sheep, but also "Maryland" chicken. It is open season the year round in the Yukon Territory and game can be sold, which the law forbids in Alaska. There is the same spread, however, between a resident and non-resident hunting license, and here we were not merely non-residents but aliens—and $100 is a lot of money.

The Hudson's Bay Company opened a new store in Whitehorse that Monday morning and but for a candybar sold to a Siwash youngster we would have had the honor of being its first customer. If you think Alaska prices are high, wait until you get to the Yukon Territory! A sack of potatoes, for instance, only $1.50 in Skagway, costs $9.50 in Whitehorse. Freight pays 5 cents a pound for that 110-mile trip and there is a handsome profit to the retailer; 5 cents more a pound from Whitehorse to Dawson, where there are retailers also.

"You just get so you refuse to think of price," said the young Church of England minister in Whitehorse; "put it out of your mind, like the other inevitable things of life."

Yukon Territory has the second highest mountain in North America (Mt. Logan, just under 20,000 feet) and an area of 207,076 square miles, far more than any State except Texas . . . and about 5,000 inhabitants. In the gold-rush days Dawson alone had 50,000, the Territory probably 80,000. Today's white population is estimated at 2,200, Indians about the same, the rest Eskimos. Few Americans settle in the Yukon Territory, but there are many Englishmen, Scots, and samples from most countries in continental Europe. Until this year, said the young minister, there was a job for every one. A few down-and-outers drifted in, but they were absorbed. "Any young man who drifts up from Saskatchewan or Manitoba can get a job here. This summer I offered 75 cents an hour, six to eight weeks' work guaranteed, for easy common labor . . . and could get no one.

"A Church of England missionary has to be a man-of-all-work in a place like Whitehorse. I give about 10 per-cent of my time to my religious duties. The school takes a lot of it, and there are a host of other things, some of them far indeed from the cloth. Our Indians nomad so fast that it does little good to build good school buildings for them. The Eskimos are more intelligent, industrious, trustworthy, better in almost every way, than the Indians. But there is a vast difference between Indian tribes, even living near each other. The Teslin Indian chief sent back the government-given fishnets, with some strong words about his people being mistaken for mendicants, while the Indians of Whitehorse prefer the dole to any personal exertion. There are a few pagan natives left in the Yukon Territory; and Christian Indians are a better lot in every way than those who have remained pagans"—which is con-trary to the experience of most layman travelers in many countries.

"Fifty below zero is more pleasant here in Whitehorse than ten below in Skagway. Here the atmosphere is so dry that you can freeze an ear off without knowing it. Yes, we have Indian, even Eskimo, priests. The book-reading record of Whitehorse is higher per capita than that of any other city I know—and they read very little trash at that. They get the best and the latest books at once [no doubt in so far as publicity makes them "best"] and even a year later you can get them only if you are in the library when they come back. Every one has a radio, is familiar with the best music; there is plenty of social life and genuine culture. Radio reception is marvelous, especially in winter, when we need it most. London comes in as clearly as if the speaker were in the same room—you know London points its antennæ toward the different parts of the British Empire at different hours."

They call the United States "America" even here, though Canadians this far west seem more like Americans than like the English. Yet there is a hint of dislike, or envy perhaps—not inferiority complex, surely—toward Americans. No wonder, with some of the tourists we send them. One of the minister's tasks is to give lectures, sometimes several times a day, with slides he has been at great pains to collect . . . and an audience of a score or more left 40 cents (besides our contribution, which is a secret) on the plate at the door. Being British, the minister was too modest to ask openly for a contribution. But the register they all signed showed that almost all of them were Americans from the East. That is, they were paying hundreds of dollars for the trip, $10 or so each for overnighting in Whitehorse—and few of them left the poor church a dime.

Robert Service worked in that ugly frame Canadian National Bank building in Whitehorse and was warden of Christ Church, the "Old Log Church" where we met the minister. He wrote most of his early poems in the vestry of this church, kept the minutes of its meetings. They tell this story of him, both in Whitehorse and Dawson; and I sincerely hope it is true:

He asked the bank where he worked to lend him $500 to get his first volume of poems published—must have run into one of those play-it-safe publishers. Of course the bank refused any such absurd risk. Finally Service talked one of the bank officials into making him a personal loan. He offered him half his royalties, but the man of course preferred his note.

Six months or so later Service came to the official and

repeated his offer of half royalties. The man still vociferously preferred his personal note.

"Very well, sir," said Service. "Then will you take your $500 out of this" . . . and he pushed across the desk his first royalty check—for $8,000! However, don't jump to the very erroneous conclusion that the mere author often gets the laugh on the banker; rarely is it even the ghost of a smile.

Some day Whitehorse will be as familiar to you as Cheyenne. For you know of course that they are talking of a highway from Seattle to Fairbanks—and beyond— which would of course pass through Whitehorse. The Seattle-to-Fairbanks portion of the International Pacific Highway—they already have it named—would be 2,256 miles long (from Vancouver 2,204), of which 1,073 are already completed (with reservations). Of the 1,183 incompleted a thousand miles are in Canada, the rest between the Alaska boundary and Fairbanks. The estimated cost of that thousand miles is $12,000,000; of the 183 miles, $2,000,000.

Our President has already appointed an International Highway Commission and a voluminous report has been printed at government expense. Already Alaskan newspapers frequently run such optimistic headlines as REALIZATION OF GREAT HIGHWAY SEEMS NEAR. They are already talking of pushing it on from Fairbanks to Nome. In fact, Donald McDonald, its leading sponsor, dreams of an International Highway from Buenos Aires to Siberia— the talk of tunneling Bering Strait is old, you know—thus linking by automobile every continent except Australia!

It would be Good Neighbor policy, say Canadian Premier Mackenzie King and Premier Pattullo of British Columbia, to let the Americans run a road from Seattle to Alaska. In fact, British Columbia has appropriated $25,000 for a preliminary survey. The hitch seems to be that Canada will have to pay the lion's share of the cost and get the lamb's share of use out of the highway—unless and until British Columbia and the Yukon Territory become populous. Well, then let me pay for most of the Canadian part, says Uncle Sam. At which of course Canadians make the grimaces and sounds of protest of an Englishman offered charity by a stranger of lower social rank. Then let me lend you the money, without interest, cries Uncle Sam—good old Uncle . . . if only he didn't take it out of your pocket and mine. One Congressman suggests that Canada sell us—or give us, as an instalment on the war debts—a corridor . . . not realizing, evidently, that Canada is a proud country. The Outs, the opposition in Canada, say, "The Alaska-Yukon Highway is unreasonable, unnecessary and extravagant." [Well, aren't most things?] "And if we appropriate the money ourselves a lot of it would go into our politicians' pockets," adds the outspoken far-western Canadian. I'd no idea they were so American as all that.

Meanwhile optimists talk about the work starting "soon." The sponsors are singing that familiar old patter: "It will cost only $15,000,000, maybe $20,000,000, the price of one cruiser, and it will be worth it even if only for the road's military value." Can't you see us rushing five hundred thousand men overland to Nome, to repel the Japs? Maybe not; but I can see a procession of overladen flivvers coming up to see whether there is any chance for a man to earn an honest living in what our grandfathers called "Walrussia." Or will they be only tin-can tourists?

A hundred million dollars' worth of gold passed through Whitehorse during the first few years of the rush. The mines back beyond it are still producing well. But here, too, the sluiceboxes and hand work of the first prospectors have now for the most part given way to hydraulicking and dredge work and mining has settled down into the steady stride of Big Business.

The station of the Yukon and White Pass Railway at Whitehorse, colorless on Sunday afternoon, was enlivened on Monday morning by several bright-red coats and Canal Zone Police hats . . . why, it was like reading Laurie Erskine! The RCMP—"Canadian Mounties" to you— keep close tabs, unostentatiously, on every alien entering the Yukon Territory. Men have been greeted out on the Yukon, hundreds of miles from anywhere, by red-coats who knew every checking station they had passed without complying with the law to report. Mounties sign on for five years; reenlist for two, three or four, if they choose. Every one of them we met seems to have what it takes to police an enormous wilderness with a scattered handful of population.

You may smoke anywhere in Alaskan or Yukon Territory trains. I wondered why almost all the "natives" sat on the right-hand side of the car, as if we were in the tropics—until the sun came out from behind the curtain of clouds. For nearly two hours we rolled across a high wooded plain, wooded, that is, along the banks of river and lakes, because the water thaws the earth there. Elsewhere never more than a few inches of the surface is thawed and such land can produce only low scrub.

The story has been too often and too well told to need repeating, how that rip-roaring Irishman, Michael J. Heney, performed this railroading feat of building 110 miles of narrow-gauge line over the White Pass and on to Whitehorse in little more than a year. British capital, but American energy and ingenuity, and brawn of many nations. No wonder fares are still 10 cents a mile—and the observation platform alone is well worth the extra dollar it costs to ride in the parlor-car.

But I wonder why it seems to hurt the feelings of railroad men to answer the traveler's simplest questions. Their manner is so different from that of airplane employees . . . ah, no, I see it is just that they are Norwegians. Many

Norges, some Swedes, work on this railroad; hence that reserved air you may at first mistake for a perpetual grouch. That lack-luster, dead-codfish eye, that reticence and lack of animation are not stupidity or surliness but merely racial. Like old sea captains they do not easily meet people socially. But they are used to such a climate, find no hardship in it, and apparently find nothing unusual in such lofty scenery.

Or is it overwork? The Norwegian conductor, when he had thawed out, said he hadn't lost a day going over this line in twenty-six years. I hope he didn't mean it literally. The CIO might hear of it. Anyway, in winter trains run only twice a week—though sometimes it takes two and a half days from Skagway to Whitehorse.

The view of Miles Canyon and its lonely bridge is about all the first hour or so has to offer the sightseer. But there is a wealth of scenery and remarkable railroading before the journey is over. Beautiful lakes, some of them a glacier green, crawl past on the way to Carcross, formerly Caribou Crossing. The Caribou Hotel—no, for people. Carcross, they say, is the third driest place on the continent, six inches of rain and snow a year. It has lectures for tourists, too, by a member of the party that discovered the Klondyke; something Alaska lacks. If there is time, Carcross is the place to take a steamer to Ben-my-Cree, due south, up West Taku Arm of Lake Tagish. They say it resembles the Scotch Lakes, and the lone man and wife who live there in complete isolation but astonishing comfort nine months a year welcome all comers with open arms and unrequited hospitality in summer. A delightful old house, furnished as Dickens would have liked it, in unbroken wilderness at the foot of snow-peaked rocky mountains.

The train stops for dinner at Bennett, merely a railroad station and a ruined church on a hill. It was a big tent town and (amateur) shipyard in '98, before there was any Whitehorse, but soon reverted to what it is now. There is time, and it is worth while, to climb to the abandoned log church, built with such hopefulness in 1899, when the place was crowded with gold-rush boat-builders. You may be able to picture the furore of throwing all sorts of craft together at Bennett in the spring of '98, the clear blue lake covered a little later on with makeshift boats and sails as numerous as the craft Cortez saw gleaming in the sun on the waters about Tenochtitlán. But it is 650 miles from Bennett to Dawson, and other hazards besides the Whitehorse rapids lay between.

We pass a forest of big tumbled rocks, sinister even on August 1, with a heavy blanket of clouds just over our heads. A rocky wilderness indeed! Higher up come endless snow fences, openwork structures of narrow horizontal boards at first, then long snow-sheds. The Stars and Stripes and the Union Jack grow ragged in the wind side by side at the summit. The White Pass boundary is only twenty miles above Skagway. The English wanted Skagway, too, you know, but they didn't get it—quite.

How the '98ers would have laughed to hear us call this cold; yet how we suffered during that five minutes outside the train! But there were clusters of beautiful pink flowers; white, yellow, red—adventurers of the vegetable kingdom. "Mushers must report here," says a sign on the office of the RCMP—as if there were mushers over the White Pass in these effete times! Or are there?

The summit of the once dreaded White Pass is 2,888 feet above sea-level and water falling on the northern side of the slope flows 2,150 miles to the Bering Sea. Three miles below, at Inspiration Point, stands a monument to the 3,000 pack-animals that left their bones in Dead Horse Gulch below. The Trail of '98 lies grass-grown and untraveled down near the bottom of the steep gully, placarded here and there for the vicarious suffering of tourists. You can still walk up the Trail of '98, but it is merely a stunt now. Joe Brooks, who had 350 pack-animals on the Trail between August of '97 and May of '98, came back in 1934 and climbed the pass, camped and slept on the spot where he once had a cabin at Old White Pass City —and died in the night.

The train feels its way cautiously along the east side of the gorge, crosses an appalling side gorge by a steel canti-lever bridge incredibly high above it, makes an immense loop around another gorge, crosses smaller ones . . . seems lost in a labyrinth of sheer rock mountains. There is the inevitable Bridal Veil Falls; and a cross on a 100-ton rock that fell on two workmen. I am not sure but what this is the most amazing railroad construction I have ever seen, especially taking into account the climate.

Streams like rivers of milk pour down from snowfields in plain sight, joining larger streams boiling headlong down to the sea. We catch sight of the ocean and Skagway, seven miles away, then lose it again. The train once more seems bewildered, finds the exit at last . . . only to be blocked by a slide when all its troubles appeared to be over. Half an hour and a quarter-mile farther on we are wel-comed by customs officers. Then the train puffs jauntily right down the main street of Skagway. They call it Broadway, and Skagway objected when Heney proposed to lay his tracks there, so that he had to build that section in the middle of the night. If the tale is true, opinion seems to have changed: hands wave in welcome from win-dows and sidewalks as we screech down the main thorough-fare of what once dreamed of becoming an important city.

A scattered old town of largely unpainted frame houses, some mere shacks, many of them falling in upon them-selves. Whole blocks grown up to tall grass and weeds. Raspberry bushes clutch at your knees as you thump cau-tiously along wooden sidewalks with many a slat missing. Strawberries, white clover, grow in what were once resi-dential blocks. In one of these now vacant, weed-grown squares sits the statue of Molly Walsh, who ran a grub tent, forerunner of Alaskan roadhouses, high up the Klondyke trail, during the winter of 1897-98. It seems she had two suitors, but quarreled with the first and apparently favored one, Jack Newman, and married the other fellow. She might have done better, for he murdered her in Seattle, in 1902. Newman went back to Seattle and married, but evidently could not forget. In 1929 he put up a monument on the White Pass trail, where he had been a head packer—where, too, probably, his early romance had blossomed and died—and the following year erected this one to Molly in Skagway. When he died a year later he asked to be buried on the trail. But his wife disallowed it; didn't want him linked even in death, evidently, with his former sweetheart.

"Deserted, wind-swept Skagway" was originally Skagua, which meant Home of the North Wind. But we seemed to be getting a south wind, cold, too, from up the Lynn Canal—no, not dug by man. The thermometer insisted it was 67°, but the high wind and hurrying low black clouds made one shiver as if it were below freezing. November weather was rather a relief, however, after almost too much heat at Whitehorse. The drifting tide was strewn with seaweed; heckling gulls glided, banked and sideslipped down along the rickety abandoned pier. Out along the other pier an occasional car rumbled to a big white steamer tied up before a cliff on which at least a generation of amateur artists and letterers have tried their skill.

Canadian steamers bring most travelers to Skagway, though most of them are Americans. They dodge our coastwise shipping laws by having them change steamers at Vancouver. That law against foreign ships (and airplanes are legally ships, you know) plying between two American ports sometimes makes queer complications, has even been known to provoke profanity. For instance, it is a nuisance that you can't travel from Juneau to Skagway by Canadian boats, larger and more frequent than the weekly American steamer between those ports. Why not a reciprocal arrangement?

I see by an old photograph that Skagway had a SHOE-MAKER, with a very conspicuous sign, in '98. But those enterprising days are gone; now if you want to get half-soles you must send your shoes to Haines, a hundred miles or so down Lynn Canal . . . "and they fall off the first time it rains." Such signs as "Tea Room, Home Baking, Cup Reading, 50c" give some hint of the struggle it is to make a living in Skagway today.

So its loyal citizens are playing it up as a health resort: good water, no mosquitoes, a climate said to make for longevity—and certainly no heart-taxing rush! I can't think offhand of a more restful place, if you don't mind the wind. Nearly every one works either for tourists or for the railroad, or both. Stores? Of course; some of them incongruously up-to-date . . . though the little wooden bank refused to risk cash against a letter of credit. A drugstore merchant, on the thirty-second anniversary of his arrival in Skagway, sits near the stove and yarns, looking up, vaguely curious, faintly hopeful, each time some one passes the window.

Winter, no doubt, has its compensations, but the chief summer sport of Skagway is growing flowers. A Mr. Blanchard (or rather, his women folk) has delphiniums seven, eight feet tall; blossoms of many species that make our own seem tiny, more kinds of flowers than you, or I at least, can name. The Blanchards have taken flower prizes even in California. But they tell me Charlie Walker, a well-to-do bachelor, has the edge on them when it comes to flower gardens.

Skagway's old-timers include Martin Itzen—pronounced Itchin', so that facetious or envious fellow-townsmen call him, surreptitiously, "Itchy Scratchy." Martin owns the only streetcar in Alaska—and that isn't a streetcar. He drove the only hack in Skagway, had just imported its first gasoline buggy, when the idea came to him. Around a Ford motor he built what looks at a hasty glance like a stream-lined streetcar. On the back platform, big as life, stands Soapy Smith, labeled, I suppose for respectability's sake, "Marshall." Soapy *was* a Fourth of July marshal, you may recall, only four days before he was shot.

The only gold rush in Skagway now is of tourists, and Martin gets nearly all of them. He gives a witty lecture on Skagway and its past and present and runs his "streetcar" at one and the same time. Martin is on the verge of being a town joke, but he probably makes a bigger haul, at least when the salmon—I mean the tourists—are running than any other of the 490 people left of the fifteen to twenty thousand who came to Skagway almost overnight in '98. On the side he is the local Ford agent, the Skagway undertaker—not a bad combination, come to think of it—but gets the doctor to save his deaths for the wintertime, he says, when there are no live tourists for the streetcar. "Skagway is a very healthy place, anyway," he patters, "and plenty big enough. As long as the population is under five hundred an undertaker doesn't need a license. . . ."

Martin is a bachelor, among his other distinctions. But they say he is so good a housekeeper that women rave over his orderly diningroom-bedroom and well-provided kitchen. A few winters ago he took his streetcar down to Hollywood, invited none other than Mae West to come up and see him some time. But so far she has not kept her promise. Martin wears a nugget watch-chain, all gold and waistcoat wide, a handlebar mustache dating back to '98, a streetcar conductor's cap. His fellow-townsmen rather resent his exploiting of Soapy Smith, because Martin was up-country when Soapy was shot . . . and no one can claim membership in the First Families of Skagway who was not on the spot when Soapy collected his just reward.

Mrs. Harriet Pullen, now nearing eighty, is probably Skagway's other most picturesque living citizen. She came up from the State of Washington in '97, a widow then or soon afterward, with three children and nothing to feed them on. First she got $3 a day cooking for stampeders; later she bought seven horses "and made $25 a day clear that winter." Then she ran a Home Bakery, built a home up against the mountain wall that keeps Skagway in its narrow place. Now the Pullen House is probably the most delightful hotel in Alaska, the only one, by the way, that serves meals—except of course the Curry Hotel and all roadhouses, by force of necessity.

Mrs. Pullen is almost eighty now, yet she tosses a huge piece of beam on the fire with the ease of a basketball player making a goal. Skagway burns beams, boards, rafters from its old abandoned buildings . . . and a fire was welcome, too, those first two evenings of August. The Pullen House itself is a museum, especially the big glass-walled living-room, quite aside from the room it will cost you two-bits to enter, Mrs. Pullen herself as guide and lecturer. Nothing much that has to do with the history of Skagway is missing in that collection: Soapy Smith's gambling gear, Indian relics of the long ago, everything that might but for her have gone into the limbo of out-of-date things. When she is dressed for museum visitors Mrs. Pullen's left side gleams with more medals than a general who has always managed to stay snugly back of the front lines can display. Her son Dan, notable in football at Washington University in Seattle and later at West Point, to which he was appointed by Theodore Roosevelt, ended the war as Lieutenant-colonel Daniel D. Pullen, Chevalier of the Légion d'Honneur, Officier de l'Ordre de la Couronne of Belgium, Distinguished Service Cross, won for bravery under fire in the Bois de Cuisy on September 26, 1918. "He directed a tank attack and rallied the infantry in the face of withering machine-gun fire." Pershing is said to have remarked, "I wish I had a regiment of Pullens."

But Dan is dead now, and so is Mrs. Pullen's daughter, and the other son is far away. So she has little more than her memories and those medals left, and she wears them with a naïve satisfaction.

Skagway's chief glory, however, is not her living nor her dead war hero but the ghost of Soapy Smith. Soapy might have made a good modern gangster, for he was a great leader of men—the wrong kind of men. But no, on second thought he probably was too naïve and honest and soft-hearted to have held his own among the politically protected rats of today. Just what Skagway would do without his memory, however, is something hard to contemplate.

Jefferson Smith won his pseudonym of Soapy back in Colorado, where he once sold soap—in his own way. He cut up hunks of blue lye-saturated soap into bars, wrapped a dollar bill, now and then a five, ten, even a twenty-dollar bill, around some of them, and sold them at two-bits each . . . his stool-pigeons of course retrieving those so attractively wrapped. The stampede to the Klondyke was just the place for such a man to go into business on a larger scale. Incoming '98ers naïvely carried their money in a safety-belt; or a man coming back down the trail with a full poke was more inclined to boast of his luck than to hide it, and Soapy's pals were quick to recognize pay-dirt. He sent his stooges out made up as prospectors, feather pillows in their packs, to act as come-on men. Soapy or his men ran a shell game every here and there along the trail. The rubber pea was always between the player's fingers, not under any of the three walnut shells, but simple as the fraud was there were many suckers. They craved attention, kind words, recreation, excitement, sudden for-

tune; and what better combines all those than gambling?
Now and then, just often enough to keep the suckers biting, one of Soapy's fake prospectors dropped in to pick up
a winning shell or the right cards and ostensibly went on
up the trail . . . to sneak back and play the same game again
as soon as possible.

One of Soapy's harmless little tricks had to do with the
longing of '98ers for news from home. On a Skagway
building Soapy put up a Telegraph Office sign and charged
only $5 for a telegram to Seattle, plus the rate, which he
ostentatiously looked up in a Western Union rate book,
from Seattle to whatever other point in the United States,
or Europe, the sender named. Oh, yes, Soapy was very
meticulous in his financial dealings. His telegraph and
cable line was perfect, too; the sender invariably got an
answer (always collect, of course) within two or three
hours.

Mrs. Pullen says she was standing "as close as that" to
Soapy when he was killed (some of her fellow-townsmen
allege the distance was definitely greater, but envy is an
ugly trait) and that "he was a fine-looking man, with snap-
ping eyes, good manners; looked and acted like a minister." Witty, too; at least they attribute to Jeff Smith the
line: "The way of a transgressor is hard—to quit." He
offered to raise a regiment for the Spanish-American war,
but his ardent patriotism was flouted in Washington.

One day in the summer of 1898 a young miner named
Steward came down the trail. He had a well-filled poke
and made no bones of admitting it. Besides, it was the
fashion of the time that when a man came down from
"inside" he ordered drinks for the crowd and nonchalantly
handed his poke over to the bartender. That worthy
weighed out the amount of gold dust that covered the
transaction and handed . . . or, in Soapy's place, sometimes
neglected to hand back anything. Things were so easy-
going in Alaska and the Yukon Territory in those glorious

The current-operated fishwheel is the most persistent work of man along the Yukon

The devil, you say! No, it's merely a greeting to visitors at Purgatory on the Yukon

An old-timer of Dawson, born in Belgium and now forever done with prospecting

Frank Yasuda of Beaver and his athletic daughter Hana

Indians of the Upper Yukon

days that thousands of dollars' worth of pokes were often left lying behind the bar until the owners sobered up. Except for Soapy's outfit, really known for what it was only to the chosen few, there was very little open theft. "Let's see your poke" was not usually notice of a hold-up, but if the inquirer found it empty he and perhaps his pals poured some of their dust into it.

Steward, whose poke the bartender claimed never to have seen, was not the kind of fellow to let himself be robbed without a squawk. Skagway was getting tired of Soapy and his gang, anyway. It resented the reputation they were giving the town, so that miners were beginning to make their way into and out of the Klondyke by some other route. Some fifty citizens gathered out on Silvester Wharf next morning to discuss the situation. Among those told off to keep Soapy from joining the posse was Frank Reid, one of Skagway's most reputable citizens. Soapy and his gang, it seems, had broken up a similar meeting in the town the day before. Skagway's old-timers who were there are more or less agreed that they had no intention of killing Soapy but were planning to appeal to his civic pride, that at least the posse would have been contented with driving him and his gang out of town.

But Soapy was not the sort of man who likes to be left out of important discussions. He fortified himself with a few drinks and came down to see what it was all about; insisted on shoving his way in; said he had a feeling that something was afoot against him and his partners, and that it was a public wharf. Reid said, "Jeff, you can't come in here." "Who's going to stop me?" "I am" . . . and so on, through the usual dialogue of the pulps. Jeff raised his rifle—no, it was a sawed-off shotgun, insist some of the bystanders. Reid pushed down the barrel and let Soapy have three or four slugs from a six-shooter. They say Reid would be living yet if his first cartridge had not been a dud. Soapy died at once; his body lay there until two o'clock next morning, when some nice women carried it away. He evidently had a way with women, even in death. But Reid had been shot in the groin and died some ten days later.

It's an old story, of course; Soapy was killed on July 8, 1898, aged thirty-eight. But Skagway would not consider a report on Alaska complete unless it included the saga of Soapy Smith. They still talk of Soapy; Soapy's death is the big bone of contention in Skagway to this day—though New Deal neglect now runs him a close second. (The PWA is building them a public school, but they want a new wharf, paved streets, what not.)

One version is that it was not Reid but his fellow-outpost, standing some distance away, who shot Soapy through the heart. His gang fled, but were rounded up and fifteen of them sentenced. That broke up what Alaska proudly boasts was the only organized gang in the history of Alaska. Steward's poke and most of its contents was recovered, upstairs in Soapy's trunk—they'll still show you the building if you are interested. Smith's beautiful wife and ten-year-old son arrived in Skagway a month after his death to settle his estate—which consisted of a total of $500 in debts, like that of so many other famous and "successful" men. But no one in Skagway's history has so nearly achieved immortality.

There is a big granite monument to Reid, with suitable inscription by a grateful community, in Skagway's mighty rocky cemetery, well out of town. Most of its gravestones are moldy wooden boards bearing the names of children who died around 1898. One tall marker is legible only to those who read Chinese characters. Soapy's small stone is protected by wire netting . . . people used to carry off bits of it as souvenirs.

Soapy's saloon, now a tourist sight, is just a big dry-goods box in comparison with the "Board of Trade" on State Street, said to have been the biggest saloon and gambling house in the north. Those must have been gala days.

Tales of '98 are still plentiful in Alaska, but it is not so easy as you might think to get Skagwayans, or whatever they call themselves, to anecdoting—except on the subject of Soapy Smith. Most '98ers were from inland; many had never seen the sea until they sailed from Seattle. They didn't know about tides and all that sort of thing. They tied their horses, left their stuff and went uptown for twelve hours or so to the dance-halls, saloons, and worse. They came back to find the water at the same level, nothing to show that it had ever been at any other level . . . and went and complained to the sheriff that some son-of-an-outcast mother had carried off their belongings, well, ruined them, anyway, in some cases killed their horses! They tried to bake beans in a skillet greased with pieces of bacon. They tried to make coffee with sea-water; they cooked rice and it flew all over the place—but that's old stuff; I've done that myself.

Charles Carter, who combines burying others in and around Juneau with presiding over its Chamber of Commerce, and is still in the prime of life for a pioneer, says he was working as a freighter for Joe Brooks in '98, over the White Pass trail. Brooks got the Canadian Police contract to bring in 50,000 tons—seems to me Carter said at a dollar a pound! Some fabulous amount, at any rate. The average cost of transportation was 10 cents a pound. Horses fell off the trail, into the snow, unhurt, but you had to roll them and their loads down to the return trail and go clear back to the end of the line and begin all over again. "One trip I lost three horses, worth a thousand dollars. I went back to Skagway expecting to be bawled out, fired and probably lose what Brooks already owed me. But Brooks merely asked me if I got the freight through; and when I told him I had he said, 'Well, go down to the stables and take up another load.'

"Women? You mean decent women? Oh, yes, now

and then we had a woman, at least helping, or sometimes taking the place of her husband for a day or two until he sobered up or got doctored up . . . walking along at the left front side of the horse, the boss's place. Oh, you mean that kind of women? Yeah, there were a lot of them even in the first rush. Tough women were already installed and open for business in Dawson by the time most '98ers arrived. I didn't meet a man who claimed to have got there ahead of all of them."

, During the Spanish war Skagway boys sold papers at 50 cents or a dollar each. Big gamblers told the boys to bring them the first copy and gave them a cartwheel; then glanced through it and tossed it aside, and the boys picked it up and sold it over again for two-bits, sometimes four-bits.

It is a pleasant five-mile walk across Skagway's heavy-timbered bridge and up over the heavily wooded rocky hill to the site of Dyea (the original Indian name was Taiya or Tai-yeh), from where the first prospectors followed an Indian trail over the Chilkoot Pass. Skagway still sells photographs showing the endless line of mushers who climbed Chilkoot Pass every day for three months in the spring of '98. Some of them froze to death, not because they had too few clothes but because they wore too many—sweat in fur coats, sat down when they got tired . . . and "went downriver" a few days later from pneumonia. Early in '98 there was an epidemic of spinal meningitis; men died in snowslides and from other catastrophes on the trail. Skagway still talks of the big snowslide at Sheep Camp, on Sunday, April 3, 1898, as if it were yesterday. The men wanted to stay in camp, especially as it was Sunday. The Indians, too, had given warning that there was likely to be a snowslide of unusual size. But a woman started . . . and the men were not willing to admit that a woman could outdo them. The woman and a few men got through alive, but some seventy men (the guesses run from 61 to 83) perished. Not until the snow melted were some of the bodies recovered.

Dyea was completely abandoned almost overnight when the White Pass was discovered. It was lower and the grade easier; horses were virtually useless on Chilkoot Pass. But demand soon brings supply. In '98 George A. Brackett of Minneapolis built a toll road, from Skagway to White Pass City, nine miles from the summit—it was twenty miles in all to the top of the pass, forty from there to Lake Bennett—then sold it to the railroad, which put an end to hardships that are a saga of the Klondyke.

CHAPTER VII

STERNWHEELING DOWN THE YUKON

*Wood Piles . . . Fish Wheels . . . Dawson Then
and Now . . . The Klondyke Today . . . Service's
Cabin . . . Back to Alaska . . . Fort Yukon . . .
Frank Yasuda . . . Purgatory . . . Up the Tanana*

WE went back "inside" over the route the stampeders
of 1897-98 took to get to the Klondyke. With them it
meant weeks of hardships; we did it in seven hours of
railroad and thirty-six hours by boat.

At Whitehorse we not only saw Sam McGee's cabin but
Sam himself. He waved good-by to us from the bank.
The man made famous by Service looks like any other old-
timer. He was "inside" from 1898 to 1907 and again
for a few months about 1919; since then he had been
mining and road building in Montana. Now he had just
flown in, planning to prospect for gold up the Liard River.

The sternwheeler *Casca,* our steamer from Whitehorse
to Dawson, looked rather like a floating three-story tene-
ment house. On the Yukon they burn wood and now and
then we saw an Indian hut or a white man's camp with a
heap of 6-foot wood piled up on the river-bank, conspicuous as a billboard. There were more of them than
we could patronize, but two or three times a day or night
we wiped the bank clean.

For about thirty miles the Yukon runs across Lake
LeBarge, the channel lined with gasoline-tin buoys. If I
understood the captain, they now lay lampblack and oil
across it in the spring and this helps the sun to cut a
passage for steamers a little earlier in the season. In

gold-rush days the Indian chief who claimed Lake LeBarge charged a party of stampeders who broke through the ice 50 cents each for bathing in it!

At 8:30 P.M. the sun came out from under clouds and lighted up the tops of high brown hills, one long one topped with new snow. An Indian had a big fire burning at the edge of the woods where the brief night set in; rowed out to us and loaded two baskets of fish; got one empty basket and faded away again into his native wilderness.

It was as cold as November on August 3, but the 4th was partly sunny and almost too warm, even squirming down the Yukon. The Yukon winds and twists; is narrower (and bluer) than I expected. We cut sharp corners so recklessly that you wouldn't think the captain or the pilot could ever drive a car safely. We glided along with the smoothness of a magic carpet. The colors can't be described: the green seems double in intensity, the light-greens of birches gleaming against darker evergreens. No big trees, but big woodpiles. The bank, perpetually undermined by the stream, looks as if it has been spaded down. Ahead, high mountains always seem to have the exit blocked, but always it opens out, the river constantly coming up to meet us. Toward sunset, a gap in the hills ahead is brilliantly lighted, like a welcoming city.

We stopped at eight next morning to "wood up" at a clearing, the only Texas hat on board—a Jew from the Bronx—helping like a good little boy. I imagine he will long remember and dote on his days as a hardy and hardworking pioneer. The place had an Indian family, but three or four young white men, comfortable in a long sod-roofed log cabin, seemed to be the woodcutters.

Fish wheels—Ferris wheels for the fish, an old lady tourist calls them—work all night as well as all day long; why, here's perpetual motion. Anchored to the shore and turned by the current, they lift a broad scoop high twice each revolution and run their fish, if any, off to the bank. Automatic, lazy man's fishing, instead of hard work with line and tackle. Women do the work, cooking, or drying, the fish. A tent on shore and barking dogs almost always means a fish camp, the Indian's summer outing.

A lone, unshaven man was shoveling the river-bank into a horizontal revolving cylinder, evidently run by water. More woodpiles; a houseboat, white smoke oozing from its stack, a white woman hanging out clothes, a thick-shouldered young man in "overhauls," a tow-headed boy of twelve or so. . . .

Every now and then we drift up to shore, turning around to face the current, stick out a gangplank (a real plank, with cleats) and a steamer man in uniform goes ashore with a book to sign and leaves to a menial the job of carrying ashore an express package twice the size of a shoebox. That's keeping in touch with civilization, maintaining contact with the outside world, living up to British social rules. Or perhaps we land a box of oranges on the wharf, barricaded with a bag fortress of what seems to be soft coal.

Some of us had heard of Five Finger Rapids. Only one of the fingers is practical for navigation. Sure's fate we're going to hit that center rock! No, miraculously we miss it and are speeding onward. Going back up the river the steamer picks up a cable and pulls itself along it. At Link Rapids a crew was cleaning up a wreck; there was another very much smashed boat farther on.

At Fort Selkirk an old man came leisurely trundling down to the shore a wheelbarrow filled, if that is the word, with one small sack of mail. Evidently he knew the steamer must wait for him. A minor transportation company won the mail contract this summer from the Yukon S. S. Co., which seriously cuts down its profits. But such are the hazards of competition. Scores of people, some of them Indians, men flourishing rifles, gaze at us from the bank with a hint of bored suspicion. Actually to come down and see us tie up and push off would, I suppose, be to admit that they envy us. The gaping tourists probably strike them as a sort of slumming party.

Yukon Crossing; there is a winter "road" from White-horse to Dawson, a hundred miles shorter than this 460-mile river road, which is open only about four months a year. It crosses the Yukon here on the ice.

The steamer's hull whangs on the river bottom every little while, showing that the Yukon is not nearly so deep as it is wide. Sheer cliffs; castle-like headlands; queer strata, suggesting volcanoes erupting eons ago; great pitching cliffs, diagonally strata-faced with what look like myriad intricate stone carvings. Light-green vegetation trying to color the cliffs, like a hurried painter. Calico Bluff, some one has named one prominent headland. Cliffs in striking colors, especially a very rusty red; a cliff like an old-fashioned theater curtain, chaotically stone-faced, with streaks of forest in its fissures. Vistas like fjords ahead; row upon row of high hills, apparently cutting off our escape. . . .

One seagull followed us all the way from Whitehorse to Dawson, encircling, hovering over us, going on ahead or bringing up the rear, like a protective spirit, or a plain-clothes man.

Dawson is so conscious that her glorious past is gone that she has carnivals in which the rousing scenes of '98 are reproduced. This mid-August she was to celebrate her fortieth anniversary, but we were a fortnight too early. Fairbanks would come over, even by plane, to help her Canadian forerunner make it a gala occasion. Once there were 30,000 people in Dawson—60,000, including the surrounding creeks. Now there are perhaps two thousand Klondykers, as residents of Dawson are still called, with a trend toward increasing again. But the high cost of transportation, hence of living, tends to keep out new blood and

there is much the same difference in the industrial atmosphere of Dawson and Fairbanks, for instance, as between
the United States and Canada.

Here are some winter of 1897-8 prices in Dawson,
direct from her newspapers and handbills of the time:

Flour, $75 a sack; brooms, $14 each; padlocks, $25;
nails, $3.50 to $8 a pound, once $28! Six small window-
panes cost $35 to $50. In the rush they forgot to bring
glass, so most of them used canvas, or made windows of
bottles that first winter. An ax, $17, or one ounce of gold
dust; a pick the same; but shovels were only half as much.
I suppose their leaning qualities were not appreciated in
those days. A 5-cent sack of salt cost $5; a package of
Bull Durham, $1.25. If you were studiously or corre-
spondencely inclined, candles were $1 each, kerosene $40
a gallon, writing paper 40 or 50 cents a sheet, envelopes
two-bits each—and no ink in the stores. It cost $1 to send
out a letter. Rope cost $1 a foot, so that the unlucky
could not even afford to hang themselves. Horses were
less restricted; for hay was $300 a ton and men found it
cheaper to shoot a horse in the fall and import a new one
in the spring.

Today its scanty four-page newspaper costs 25 cents and
Dawson still does not feed you at Broadway Automat
prices, but . . . well, here's an early Dawson Bill of Fare
(December, 1897):

Soup $1.00	Doughnuts, pie or sand-
Mush and milk.........$1.00	wich, with coffee or tea $1.25
Canned corn...........$1.25	Beans, coffee and bread..$2.00
Canned tomatoes.........$2.00	Plain steak............$2.00
Stewed fruit...........$1.25	Porterhouse (and they say
Slice of pie...........$ .75	a razor wouldn't cut
	it) $5.00

There were times when an egg for breakfast cost $2,
especially after "Swift-water Bill" bought them all up to

keep his estranged dance-hall flame from getting any. The man who got the first copy of a Seattle newspaper telling of the destruction of Cervera's fleet hired a hall and charged several hundred dollars' admission to the five hundred men who crowded in to hear him read it. The line at the post-office stretched for blocks and lasted for days; impatient men paid $20 for a place near the window. Miners threw nuggets at female performers in dance-hall and "Opery House"—though every one except the sex-hungry prospectors must have recognized that overripe vegetables would have been more to the point. But of course in Dawson nuggets were cheaper. Dawson's socially elect sat, well-screened, behind the curtains of boxes. Dance-halls, saloons and gambling places ran wide open twenty-four hours a day; streets, or what passed for them, were packed day and night. Miners from the creeks threw their wealth at any one who took their fancy (and almost anything in skirts did) until their pokes were empty —then back to the mines. Five thousand dollars' worth of gold was recently washed out under a former dancehall.

Dawson, like Skagway, calls its main street Broadway. It is built on a glacier, two feet, some say only sixteen inches, under the surface. Excavations sink in summer and rise in winter, with the effect of an earthquake; so brick, stone or plaster are impossible. But here, too, there is pride in flower growing, in flourishing vegetable gardens. Frame houses and log cabins, punctuated by the sharp steeple of an occasional frail wooden church, are sprinkled up the rising slope, lost in weeds higher up.

Dawson's population, like that of Alaska, seems to be largely Scandinavian—though the old-timer who ran out to ask me to take his picture when he saw me photographing his frost-bitten flowers and half-acre of potatoes turned out to be Flemish. Twenty years or more since he had sent a picture back to Belgium; they'd appreciate it. Wouldn't we come inside? It was a spacious house for a

man who had lived alone for twenty years. He had lost
his wife on the *Sophia,* in 1918, near Juneau, with three
hundred others, every one on board. He was astonished
we had not heard of it, obviously the big event of his life.

Now his spuds were frozen, though his magnificent bor-
ders of flowers had almost survived. The thermometer
stood at 58° that August 5th afternoon, as if trying to
hide the fact that potato tops and water-pipes had frozen
the night before. Would we have a bottle of beer? He
lifted a trapdoor in his living-room and brought up a home
brew that tasted and looked a bit like beer. These lonely
old-timers are eager to talk. Nearly all of them show
physical wear and tear beyond the average for their years,
mannerisms due to a lifetime in a slow-witted environment
. . . or were those who came to places like this originally
slow-thinking people, content to shovel gravel in a creek?

We climbed the 1,500-foot Dome behind the town.
Down the face of it lies the mark of a great slide which,
they say, took a heavy toll in Indians. All the town and
miles of the Yukon and the Klondyke, its tributary, lay
below, far western Canada piling away into the distance.
We drove out along the Klondyke—it's a river, you know
—crossing it by a big modern steel bridge carrying a passable highway. The Klondyke is not very wide, considering
its fame. The valley of the river itself and its creek tribu-
taries are riffled with dredging for mile after mile. Miniature mountains of tailings lie on both sides of the Klondyke,
like the mess left by burglars, or children, looking for
treasure. Wrecks of old machinery, from wheelbarrows
to huge stationary engines, red with rust, peer from rampant vegetation.

The individual miner is passé along the Klondyke. Yet
he can still make good if he is lucky enough to pick good
ground—and has plenty of water. But it is better now to
rent or sell your claim to one of the big companies. An
old miner in that log cabin with grass and flowers on the

sod roof has a claim on Bonanza Creek and gets 10 percent of whatever the dredge takes out; got $12,000 on half the creek, one side only, so far, worked out. On the other hand, I understood the guide to say, an individual can work on big-company property, paying 15 percent.

Bob Henderson's grandson Chester was working excompany ground alone. "Dad owned this claim, but a company had worked some of it." He was a mixture of bashfulness and the want-to-talk of isolation. Pick and shoveling, hand sluicing—but water is scarce this summer. He had taken out two ounces and two pennyweight the first half of the week; cleans his riffles every week or two, then pans it—but for that matter even dredged stuff is finally panned by hand. If you liked mud pies as a child you would like this hand placer mining, but I think I'd rather get mine out of a bank. Though, come to think of it, so does Chester Henderson. Born in Dawson, he lives in a fine house in town, with his parents and sisters; goes out every day on a bicycle—nothing like the old days.

Gold was reported on the Yukon (and on Seward Peninsula) by the post-hole diggers of the Collins Overland Telegraph Company, and some was taken out ten years before the Klondyke (the native name was Tron Deg) discovery was made in the summer of 1896. Bob Henderson, a real prospector, had been looking for gold for eleven years when he made the original Klondyke strike in July, 1896, at Gold Bottom. On August 17 George Carmack, a happy-go-lucky squaw-man, and his two Indians, "Skookum Jim" and "Tagish Charlie," discovered gold by accident, up Bonanza Creek. Or rather his squaw discovered it, while washing meat for supper. They got twelve dollars' worth of gold in the first pan. Carmack beat Henderson to Forty Mile (there was no Dawson then) to register his claim. But Dawson gives Henderson the credit; after all, Carmack was only a squaw-man. The government gave Henderson, who lived most of the time in Dawson, a $150-a-month pension, until he died three or four years ago.

Carmack did right well by himself, too; died not long ago. He had married a white woman later but his half-breed daughter fought in the courts to get her share of what he left. The Klondyke produced more than $40,-000,000 the first year. Millions were taken out of 85 cubic feet of ground. Dawson grew up overnight.

Only British subjects were allowed to stake claims in British Columbia, but Yukon Territory (and Alaska) made no distinction. In 1902-4 there was a rush from Dawson to Fairbanks, and they say men were tired of living alone and determined to start housekeeping in a town that was to be built on a permanent scale.

"But why didn't Henderson and Carmack keep their discoveries to themselves?" a tourist wanted to know. The guide, panning for tourist benefit and finding only a few faint colors, looked up, amused:

"Discoverers couldn't have worked it themselves even if they had been able to keep it a secret . . . and the average prospector is too much of a boaster and spender not to tell the world about it . . . and, anyhow, they had to register it in Ottawa."

There were big fields thawing farther up the Klondyke. Here, too, pipes are driven down as it thaws, to bedrock, no matter how far down, where the gold lies. We had seen a man-made cliff of yellowish soil, where half a great hill or ridge had been hydraulicked away to get down to pay-dirt—and sometimes there is none there. Out at the big company headquarters I handled $28-an-ounce bricks worth $9,000 or more each, bricks so nearly pure gold that they are worth $444 a pound—the price, you know, went up in Canada just as it did in the United States when our savings were reduced. They bring the gold dust in from the dredges on mats that look ludicrously like the one you wipe your feet on at the door; wash them by hand.

Men locked inside an unimposing little building then melt the stuff down into bricks you could hardly pocket.

Up on Eighth Avenue, close against the half-wooded, thickly weeded hills, some low woodland below it, is the cabin where Robert Service lived after he moved to Dawson. Flowers and flowering vines half smother the one-room-and-a-porch cabin, with a lawn in front, rustically fenced. The rough-papered walls of the room are covered with homemade mottoes: "Don't Worry—Work," "Difficulties Are Only 'Strength Tests'—Down Them," "Rebuffs Are Only the Rungs on the Ladder of Success." Pretty platitudinous . . . but maybe a man not only trying to lift himself by his own mental bootstraps but living alone and intellectually isolated has to surround himself with such urgings.

The original bed, not uncomfortable, though certainly not luxurious; furniture made of packing-boxes; an old-style washboard; and, as I live, a small icecream freezer! The kitchen at the back has been torn down; there wasn't enough of it to be worth saving. A tin stove seems hardly adequate. The only real decoration is an enlarged photograph of "A Moose Fight in the Klondyke," by J. Doody, 6/17/1910.

Service wrote on long rolls of a kind of towel paper. Locals were bored by his poems; but today Dawson takes vicarious pride in him. Born in England, but educated in Scotland, he came to the Yukon at twenty, worked in banks in Skagway and Whitehorse. He had a strong English accent—no, not Oxford. His parents, Dawson whispers, were little more than peasants. His father died soon after he came to Canada; his mother only last year. He left behind the impression of being almost painfully quiet and reserved; a sarcastic fellow, however. Though he couldn't dance he belonged to a dance club. He lived in Dawson, the last years as a private bookkeeper, from 1908 to 1913, when he went to Europe to study. Caught by the war he

Yukon Indians resent unrequited photography and people passing behind them

This is the life, most Alaskans contend—but it is no summer sport

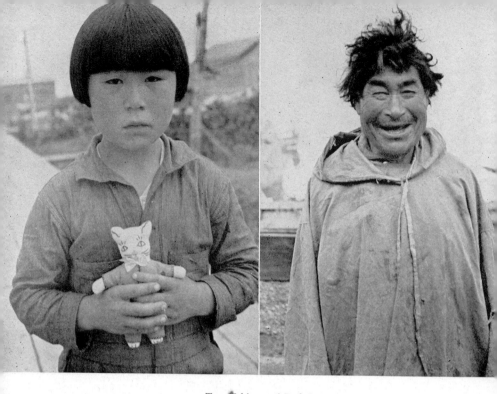

Two Eskimos of Bethel

Bethel at the mouth of the Kuskokwim

drove an ambulance all through it; picked up his own brother. He has two daughters and lives now outside Paris . . . must be about sixty-five. They say he is writing a book on Mexico . . . goes to some place near Tia Juana each summer. . . .

The informant, Hostess in charge of the cabin and its tourist register, was definitely a Service fan. Dawsonite? "Yes, indeed—though I came here, thirty-seven years ago, from Brooklyn."

Sometimes, by a combination of luck and energy, the trip in or out of Dawson was incredibly fast for those early days in the Klondyke. The father of Fairbanks' present mayor tells me he got from Dawson to Seattle in twelve days in 1899!

There is a cable-hung ferry across the Yukon at Daw, son, which seems to run on impulse rather than schedule. Just around the bend below lies Moosehide, a large Indian village, much older than Dawson. Farther on are more or less isolated Indian houses and three-story racks of fish, red as salmon, hung up to dry under canvas roofs. Tiers of dogs, river-bank grandstands of dogs, howl unto high heaven at the slightest provocation. Those inevitable racks of split salmon drying, mainly for dog feed, face every Indian village; always a three-story, canvas-roofed fish-drying place down on the shore; but usually there was just a red touch of fish in one corner, as if the Indians were lazy, or unlucky . . . only the latter, I suppose, since no one can hurry an automatic fish wheel. Besides, a lazy man just lays his split salmon out on the rocks to dry. But half-starved dogs, tantalized by the sight of fish they cannot quite reach, until winter, thirsty dogs, chained up all summer, each has worn down his little leveled space on the bank, by perpetual running back and forth the length of the chain, incessantly barking at the least disturbance. Yukon dogs howl at the boat whistle as if they were trying —and come very near succeeding—in imitating it; attain the same very sad note.   Friendly-looking huskies, some of them; it seems a shame to keep them always chained.   But Alaskan dog-fights, it seems, are no tame bloodless bouts.

The Yukon is 2,300 miles long, ten miles wide at its mouth and discharges more water than any other river except the Amazon.   Unlike most of the world's big rivers, it flows mainly north and west, up the map, which is easier on the ground than it looks on paper.   That is why in the Yukon Territory they speak of "down north" and "up south."   In the early mining days men came in by way of Manitoba and Saskatchewan, down the Mackenzie River, up one of its branches, over to a branch of the Yukon and up that.   Some came by the "millionaire route," up the Yukon from St. Michael.   But the Yukon is so long that at first they did not realize it was the same river and that ships could come up it.   The first steamboat ascended the Yukon in 1866.

But so seldom is Nature marred by the hand of man, so impressive the solitude, that you can stand at the bow of one of these Yukon steamers and imagine yourself the original explorer, the first man ever to have passed this way.   Never a sign of animal life, either, except occasional birds.   The gull that followed us to Dawson picked up a mate there; or at least from there on two gulls escorted us. But we didn't see a moose, a bear, a wolf, a caribou or a mountain sheep, not even a fox, except in captivity, in all Yukon Territory, though we ate several of them, at White-horse and on board the two sternwheelers.   We . . . but there goes the dinner gong to tell us to dress for dinner. The only way we could dress would be to put on another shirt—or our pajamas.   For we had come by air, and in a hurry, to Whitehorse.

It was dark, even in August, by the time we blew our next greeting and set the dogs to howling.   Forty Mile, doorway to much of Alaska in the gold-rush days and the junction for Chicken, well up Chicken Creek, is the last sign of life in Canada. Forty Mile was discovered—one can hardly say founded—in 1886, by a man named Lambert, ten years before Dawson first saw the light of day.

Uncle Sam, obliging for once, had a customs officer at Dawson to ask whether any one had found anything worth buying in Canada, thus sparing those who do not care for that sort of thing (not to mention the customs officer at Eagle) from being routed out at 2 A.M. We stayed up, but there is no need to do so. Eagle has an old barracks, built for U. S. soldiers in 1899; otherwise it is just another town on the Yukon.

Where we stopped to wood up next morning a path diagonally up the steep bank led to the home of a man from Missouri. The big two-story log house had cost him $6,000, besides his own work, from chopping trees into logs down to the last trimmings. Tourists rambled through his obviously bachelor bedroom; admired the bearskin covers. His spuds were in full blossom, though this is farther north in Alaska than frost-bitten Dawson is in Canada . . . close call, however; the mercury had dropped to 32.5° and eight miles farther up Coal Creek, where the dredge is at work, they had a real frost.

The scenery is pure Alaskan from Eagle to Circle, where we found it quite a job to unload a truck for Frank Palma. Noel Ross, too, and others from Fairbanks were there to greet us, though they had not come precisely for that purpose. Circle (formerly it was Circle City, but now it is of age), where the mountains end, was founded in 1893, when gold was discovered on Mastodon Creek. For a short time it was the largest log-cabin town in the world. Now it has a radio tower and a highway to Fairbanks. These towns on the Yukon are not very exciting; mainly one-story and mostly log houses on the flat land ten or twenty feet up the river-bank, down the face of which hang howling dogs and drying fish.

It had been cold up the Yukon, farther south; down here

in the Yukon Flats, where the river spreads out in many
puzzling channels, it was pleasant to sit on deck, watching
Alaska slip lazily and noiselessly past us, and read of a
heat wave all over the United States—though it wasn't
cold even here.   River after river . . . there is a sort of
all-one-big-family atmosphere in Alaska which extends even
to tourists on the Yukon—except couples bored with each
other, with travel, with anything and every one.

8:30 P.M., August 6: Mountains again! Hardly a mole-
hill since Circle.   9 P.M.: Brilliant sun flooding all the
landscape, a dead-flat landscape, only water and scrub
forest as far as the eye can see.   It must be hard to pick
the right channel between the many mud and gravel bars,
especially with the sun in the pilot's eyes.   He must do it
by instinct; at least he could not for the life of him tell
us why he chose this channel instead of that.   Cry of
loons; wild ducks and geese fly away before us.   The river
is constantly undermining the banks and big bushes and
trees are forever falling into the swift, muddy, glacier-
colored stream.   It looks like wonderfully rich soil; and
this region certainly has a beauty of its own.   Not a sign
of man for thousands of square miles; only a rare tent and
the piles of the woodchopper.   The delicacy of the sunset
. . . streaks of pastel-colored clouds miles long, indescrib-
able shades of pink and blue, reflected in the flat swirls of
the river's surface . . . a flat landscape carpeted with
slender sharp evergreens as far as you can see.

The sun was still above the horizon when we crossed
the Arctic Circle—marked, so help me, by a round sign-
board stuck up on the bank!   What people won't do for
tourists!   Dusk is endless, quite the opposite of the tropics.
In fact, even that August night brought little darkness,
though we were a month too late to see the midnight sun
this far south.

At Fort Yukon, the N. C. Co. store was still open at
midnight!   Indians, children and all, but especially women,

sat in a long row along its porch, backs to the wall, and stolidly appraised the tourists. There is nothing an Alaskan Indian dislikes more than having some one walk behind him. Probably an instinct of the wilderness, where wolves and perhaps human enemies and vague unknown dangers once lurked, for that matter are still lurking. The Yukon Indians resent being photographed—unless you pay them for the privilege; and when natives reach that stage they are hardly worth photographing. We landed flour, beans, sugar, to a symphony of howling dogs, until a great heap of burlap bags was piled on the shore. Fort Yukon, barely inside the Arctic Zone, ranges in temperature from 78° below to 110° above, and must lay in its supplies in summer. The trading center for a huge district, the largest village on the Yukon, with a population of 600 Indians and some 300 white men, it is one of the few places where the Indian birth-rate exceeds the death-rate. Yet they say the Indians hereabouts are one hundred percent tubercular.

Fort Yukon has several buildings more imposing than the average one-story Alaskan log residence. One two-story frame house in particular might have been brought intact from one of the wealthier New Jersey coast resorts. The town occupies the site of a Hudson's Bay Company fort, built in 1847. For a long time it was thought to be on the Colville River, which flows into the Arctic Ocean, and it was many years before it was discovered to be on the Yukon, emptying into the Pacific. The Hudson's Bay Company claimed the post here—though it is suspected that they really knew they were in Russian territory—until two years after we purchased Alaska. Then an American army captain settled the controversy, not with bloodshed but by astronomical observation, and the Britishers retired up the Porcupine River. It must have been a bit galling to them, for what is now Fort Yukon was the oldest English-speaking settlement on the river, and the farthest of their posts from headquarters.

In the old burial-ground are headboards with dates in the 1850s and a monument "to the memory of all the Hudson's Bay Company servants, pioneers, explorers and discoverers." Here, too, is the granite-shafted grave of Archdeacon Stuck, roomily surrounded by an iron-posted chain. How time flies! It seems only yesterday that Stuck was in the news, as leader of the second party to climb Mt. McKinley—which gave him more fame than a lifetime of really important work. And now Dr. Grafton Ross Burke, who came from Texas to join Stuck of the U. S. Episcopal mission in the summer of 1908, and succeeded him, was too ill to be disturbed, at least at midnight, in his forty-bed log hospital with its spacious solarium. I had looked forward to seeing Dr. Burke. Not many days later he was flown to Fairbanks, on to Juneau, sent by steamer to Seattle . . . from where his ashes were flown back to be buried beside Stuck.

I strolled on into the log-house outskirts, dogs still howling, mosquitoes biting, with a preference for the back of the neck. The church out there has a beaded buckskin altar cloth and a pulpit cloth worth seeing. In the other direction I ran across the smaller and less important trading-post, rival of the N. C. Co., to be found in almost every Alaskan town of any size. This man had a liquor license, hence a bar; ran the local movie house on his premises, importing his films in summer for all the year.

The half-dozen men left around the big but just then hardly necessary stove at one o'clock in the morning had that same surprising vocabulary, serious-mindedness, self-thinking and world-wide information one never ceases to marvel at in Alaska. Our widely traveled tourists were child-minded ignoramuses by comparison.

"No, trapping is our only income up here. But at least we are not working for a boss. [Prices of furs are not

low even here, at least not in the N. C. Co. store, whatever
the trappers may get for them.] Statehood? Good Lord,
no. We didn't even want to be a territory. District was
better, for then the Federal government paid for everything. Now we are cursed with politicians . . . and we'd
have a lot more of them and of taxes if Alaska became
a state. Now our two dollars a year trapping license is
our only direct tax, because we are not incorporated . . .
and don't want to be."

But just when the discussion was warming up the *Yukon*
blew her semi-final whistle. Pity one must always be moving on when he has found a reason, or at least a fairly
good excuse, to stay. It is really the truth and not mere
company propaganda that, if you can spare the time, it is
better to go up the Yukon rather than down it, especially
as the steamers make longer stops on the way up. Yet
the company rarely fills its passenger space on the upriver
steamers, while people going downriver are often crowded
off for lack of accommodations.

The Yukon is about twenty miles wide at this point and
continues so for a long time thereafter, laced with many
channels. In gold-rush days they had to station men along
here to pick out the navigable route between myriads of
small islands.

Frank Yasuda's log store at Beaver is the supply depot
for miners in the Chandlar River district behind it and the
point where the overland winter trail leaves the Yukon for
the Koyukuk region. But to a mere wanderer Frank himself was of more interest. So I was delighted to find, soon
after we were under way again, that he had jumped into
modern clothes and come along with us, having decided on
the spur of the moment that he needed a vacation.

Evidently sixty-seven now, though he hardly looks fifty,
Frank Yasuda, born in Sendai, left Japan as a whaler in
1888, when he was fourteen, came to Alaska on the revenue cutter *Bear* in 1890. He lived for fifteen years at

Barrow, married an Eskimo; has been at Beaver since 1910. He brought a lot of Eskimos down from Barrow with him, a two-year trek, led by a Japanese Moses. Now there are about twenty-five of them in Beaver, "getting along with the Indians fine." But he doesn't think much of the younger generation: "They can't live on the country." His daughter Bernice is married to a half-Irish, quarter-Russian, quarter-Indian, which makes his grandchildren—well, figure it out for yourself. The grandson I saw was a handsome little boy and seemed to have lots of get-up-and-go. Hana, the younger daughter, now married to Noel Ross, was the best athlete and by no means the worst student among University of Alaska girls.

The Santa Claus of Beaver, known (and liked) all over Alaska, has made several stakes but "you can't let people starve." One winter he had $83,000, laid most of it out in supplies, gave most of them away. Yasuda is the kind of man who slips in ahead of you and buys your ticket to the movies, if you know what I mean. Once he went to Fairbanks for a coffin, but couldn't get it into the plane, so he went home and made one. "He was my friend."

Frank has done a lot of mining; rides a dog-team or a plane with equal equanimity; says a plane seems slow compared with a dog-team. Rogers and Post flew right over his house in Beaver . . . and the next thing he knew his radio told of their death. He has been Outside several times but never back to Japan. "A lot of us were exiled from Tokyo in 1888 for trying to get a constitution. Now they want me to come back"—his uncle, they say, is a big man there. "I planned to go back last year, but the war in China put a stop to that. I'll go over for a visit, in 1940, if . . ."

Alaska's most famous Japanese Sourdough is a regular subscriber to the *Reader's Digest, Nation, Current History,* New York *Times,* Seattle's Japanese daily, two Tokyo magazines; reads the latest good books. He has an accent, of course, but is Sourdough rather than Jap, even in his gestures, his philosophy of life, so American in his thinking processes that sometimes he is not even particularly Japanese-looking. His is no expressionless Japanese face—evidently theirs are frozen only by custom. Now and then you get a foreigner completely translated—and find they are not so different from us after all.

Yasuda raises mink. The furry little creatures had nosed our fingers curiously through the chicken-wire of their cages. They live on a chopped mixture of several kinds of food, including dried salmon. But mink-raising is also a gamble. One mother mink had killed ten of her thirteen "puppies," and "furs are cheap now, even ermine"—which, as you know, is a species of weasel. Frank's wife speaks only Eskimo, the children only English! She makes parkas; insists on good work; has more orders than she can fill. She learned bead work from the Indians—"must work all the time. I have to tell her it is time to go to bed."

Forty miles below Beaver the Purgatory Brothers— pardon, I mean the Yanert brothers at Purgatory—have their little clearing. They live here alone by choice—yet are so anxious for company that they invite all the passing tourists to stop. They have a "patron saint" in the form of the devil and his pitchfork, who waves his arms and wags his head in welcome whenever a steamer approaches, and a bust of the devil jumps out of a jack-in-the-box just in time to make timid tourist ladies almost fall off the gangplank on the way ashore. Their cozy log house and general layout is the last word in pioneering.

William Yanert was a sergeant who came up here in 1898 on an exploring expedition with a Colonel Glenn of the U. S. Army. In 1901 he settled down here on the Yukon and named his place Purgatory, "because it is a hell of a place to live." Herman came to join him in 1910, and they have lived here ever since, despite the prayers of their many friends. William with the white goatee is still pretty sturdy but is worried now about the health of his "kid" brother. Our tourists, scanty on self-entertainment, could not understand how two lone brothers could live here contentedly on their own mental fat. Yet isolation has its advantages. But, gee, I'd hate to be marooned in Purgatory myself with nothing but my pen—even if I used one.

Isolation has affected the Yanert brothers so badly that they write, or at least one of them writes, poetry, sometimes rather biting poetry:

> When the river freezes over and the Yukon breezes blow,
> And you see the ice floes jamming and down the river go,
> You know that Old Man Winter is haunting you again.
> He stays until the breakup, from the fall into the spring,
> And around your cabin for a long time, his northwind solos sing.

That Sunday along the Arctic Circle would have been too sunny and warm ashore. Fort Hamlin, established by the Alaska Commercial Company in 1897, was the place where steamers from St. Michael and the mouth of the Yukon usually laid up for the winter, to be reloaded and sent on to Dawson in the spring. No wonder Dawson developed a dislike for fresh eggs! Beyond what remains of Fort Hamlin come gentle, heavily low-wooded hills, then vistas like fjords ahead again. The Yukon narrows between high rocky banks once more, which are welcome after meandering through a wandering river forever undermining trees.

A day of winding brings you to Rampart, where Rex Beach built himself a cabin in '98 and divided his time between writing books and chopping wood. Once a prosperous mining "camp," Rampart is due for a revival, they say, thanks to modern mining methods and the higher price of gold. It is almost all log houses, and in its store are hats that were in style a generation ago.

The Yukon gorge ends at the mouth of the Tanana, largest Yukon tributary . . . in which we were promptly stuck for two hours on a sandbar when we turned into it during the night. Yukon steamers use walking beams, like huge crutches, to push themselves off sandbars. Even when we were not stuck, five miles an hour upstream against a head wind was the best we could do—another argument for taking the up-Yukon trip.

The Tanana, like the Yukon, is perpetually washing away its banks, forests and all. It looks like splendid truck-garden soil under those falling trees; not a stone in sight. But they say it is "sour" land and must be sweetened up before it will produce in abundance. Ice may block the water, too, and flood what looks like a good place for an agricultural colony. And though you may get a good crop, frost usually comes along before you can harvest it. But they grow good cabbages, beets, celery along the Tanana, and sugar-beets should do well.

Fish wheels, Indian camps, woodcutters, a fox farm, almost endless forest, a new slough of a road to a mining operation farther inland, crawl past along the hot and almost windless Tanana. Once there were thirty steamers plying up and down the Tanana and the upper Yukon; now there is one every two weeks, and they can have their pick of captains and pilots.

Nenana, where Yukon steamers make contact with the Alaska Railroad, two hours by train from Fairbanks, is famous for its Ice Pool. They say the spring breakup is a sight which even the oldest Sourdoughs come a-runnin' to see. Immense cakes of ice shoot up into the air, fall back and dive beneath the water, turn over and over, end over end, ceaselessly grinding with a roar that can be heard for miles. Gambling on the Ice Pool is one of Alaska's great pastimes. Tickets must be sent by express, because our pious post-office, which carries the daily quotations of Wall Street without a murmur, will have nothing to do with them. But they are prominently sold everywhere in the Territory. School-children are well paid for a week or so to make up lists of ticketholders and the like, but the only other overhead is a $15-a-day secretary. An electric clock records the exact minute of the breakup, so the game cannot but be "straight." Last spring the prize was $80,000. But any number of people may choose the same minute and that prize was split among dozens of individuals—which is hard on Uncle Sam, who is right there to collect his share.

It is a long journey from Nenana down the lower Yukon, worthwhile, they say, only if you have ample time and patience. The Nulato storekeeper, whose hospitality you must ask if you stop over there, does not like women; told one of them, "There's the kitchen. Help yourself." Skins are the principal medium of exchange, but the Indians do much of their buying with dried fish, which the storekeeper sells as dog food. Lower Yukon village names include Dog Fish Village, Whiskey Creek . . . but down at Holy Cross nuns and priests are giving the native boys and girls a training that fits them for the life they must lead. When the Russians came the delta of the Yukon was densely populated; but there are very few people there now.

CHAPTER VIII

Our Alaskan Headquarters

*Fairbanks on the Chena . . . Log cabins de
Luxe . . . Bed and Board . . . Dreaming Sour-
doughs . . . Alaska's University . . . Geologist's
Paradise . . . Prehistoric Remains . . . Canoe
Explorers . . . Winter and Some Dog Lore*

FAIRBANKS, named for a forgotten Vice-President,
nestles in a reverse curve of the river Chena. It was
founded here because a boat lost its way, built a trading
post on the spot and sold out its supplies. But it really
owes its origin to Felix Pedro, weary and footsore Italian
coal miner, who in July, 1902, made a "gold strike" sixteen miles from the Fairbanks of today. Recently it passed
Anchorage and became Alaska's third city. Almost
exactly in the center of what we might call Alaska proper,
it is the focal point of all central Alaska. Once it was
like a seaport. But the Chena has been filling up with
mining soil for years, so that now it is shallow and there
is little shipping, except with wings. Green ridges rise
high in the distance, the ice-capped Alaska Range is partly
visible on very clear days.

When we first landed there we did not realize that Fairbanks would be our headquarters and rallying point all
summer long, until it became more familiar to us than
home. But nearly all Alaskan roads lead to Fairbanks
and we came to it six times, spent a total of fourteen nights
and nearly that many days there. It is distinctly a frontier
town—though my Texas hat, a present from Leo Welling
that had been lying around unused for years, turned out

to be as much out of place there as in Detroit. It is just as distinctly a real American town, even in its rosy dreams of the future; a mixture of the pioneer days in our West and the casual acceptance of the latest in modern contributions to comfortable living. It is also definitely a white man's town; there are scores of towns in the United States where you would be more likely to see an Indian, and Fairbanks hardly knows an Eskimo by sight.

Probably there are more log than frame houses: one-story log dwellings, often with tin roofs; lots of log mansions, low and cozy and homelike and obviously snug and warm in winter. Nearly every little log house has a huge front window; all have electric lights (meters or transformers decorating the front porch), most of them have radios, many have telephones. Inside, overstuffed chairs, capacious modern sofas . . . you can easily imagine yourself in a New York apartment. True, there is a suspicious number of public baths in town, but of course it has a great many visitors.

Flowers and bright weeds enliven earth-covered roofs of old log cabins. In Alaska, by the way, a log house is a "cabin," a frame dwelling, a house. Of the several small churches I liked best the tiny log one with a toy belfry, near the public library. The library, also built of logs, sits square-shouldered on a choice corner, its veranda rail a mass of pansy blossoms. It has more window area and probably more books, at least books worth reading, than the public library of any town of that size in the States. The local ladies are proud of it, to the point of strictness, Harry discovered,—keep your feet off the chairs!

The place is well supplied with trees for such a latitude; cars of recent vintage are numerous; at least one chain store has the latest in ornate delivery trucks. In short, signs of prosperity are general in Fairbanks. Not that it is rough and splurgy for a mining town. There is an occasional drunken brawl, now and then a hilarious party rather too near your own hotel room, a red-light district with wares of all colors, but on the whole it is a very respectable and above all a self-respecting place.

To be sure, Fairbanks needs pavements and sidewalks. Few of its streets are what you would call paved, concrete has not replaced many of those resounding wooden sidewalks so general in Alaska, and Fairbanks has its share of broken slats, missing sections and weed-grown stretches. In places it is wise to walk in the street itself, as in Europe, and when it rains the unpaved streets are apt to be pretty gooey with fertile black mud. But PWA money was flowing freely when we left: $45,000 worth of sidewalks, sewers, pavements and a school. Fairbanks voters approved a bond issue of $2,000,000 at the last election; voted $175,000 for a community center, $78,000 of it to come from Uncle Sam, who also offers to buy Fairbanks' $740,000 PWA 4% bonds, to be finally paid in 1963. Thus do even Sourdoughs mortgage the future and the most self-reliant of hardy individuals accept easy money, at least as a group, for what they consider pressing necessities. But the city on the Chena is determined not merely to hold but to make more prominent its place on the map.

A score or more of new houses were going up in Fairbanks and repairing and renovating were legion, thanks partly, as I recall it, to the Federal housing program. Captain Lathrop's new 'steen-story concrete building on the main street was nearing completion, his Fairbanks *News-Miner*, one of the best newspapers in the territory and only ten cents a copy now, already installed on the ground floor. He's said to be the richest man in town, and the breathless way in which his name is pronounced is an added proof that Fairbanks is thoroughly American.

The big new Federal Building, four stories high and one of the very few places in Alaska where you can ride up and down, houses most of Uncle Sam's officials and a very modern post office, not to mention an energetic and enterprising postmaster. True, the post office was closed from Saturday before we arrived until 11 A.M. on Monday, which was rather hard on people so lacking in foresight as to have their letters sent General Delivery. But Postmaster Sheldon had an explanation for it which did not seem to involve government-employee loafing.

There are two real hotels, a few minor places of lodging, a boarding-house or two, but very few houses with rooms to rent, at least in summer. As to renting a house, they tell me that four rooms and a cache cost $50 a month, including heat and light; but that it is hard to get a house with more than one bedroom and that houses for rent are always furnished. If it comes to the point of owning a house, the City Council has again fixed the Fairbanks tax rate at 12½ mills per dollar valuation, and they say that although it has had its ups and downs, especially during the World War, when men went Outside to get $15 a day in shipyards, no one has ever lost money on real estate in Fairbanks.

"Outside," by the way, I may have forgotten to mention, is the only term Alaska uses for anywhere else on earth. I can't remember ever hearing an Alaskan say "in the States." "When do you get Out?" "How long are you in for?" are familiar questions, though they do not imply that its residents think of Alaska as a jail. To them everywhere else is the Outside world, as contrasted to "God's country."

Sourdoughs are perhaps a little more inclined to gather and yarn and gamble—oh, yes, and to drink now and then —over at the Pioneer Hotel on the banks of the Chena. But the newer Nordale on the short main street also has its meed of old-timers. As is the Alaskan custom, the hotels do not serve meals. Every one eats, if not at home, at one of Fairbanks' four "Cafés."

When you first walk into one of them you will conclude that Alaskan meals are expensive. The standard price

Howard Hughes landed at Fairbanks not many days before us, on his round-the-world flight

Fairbanks, a metropolis of central Alaska, nestles in a reverse curve of the river Chena

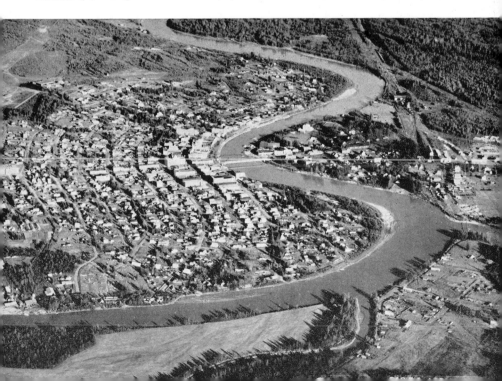

I found "stripping" a much easier but no less monotonous job than it looks

A Fairbanks home, and by no means an uncomfortable one

is a dollar, though underbidding has begun to show its
ugly or welcome (depending on which side of the counter
you are facing) head and the place with the most voluminous cook even has a few choices at half a dollar. There
is a hint, however, in the way in which they take so small a
coin, that this is a charitable concession to fellows down on
their luck. But by the time you have tried to make away
with "three squares" a day you will realize that you get a
lot for your money. Alaskan meals are of the ravenous
farmhand variety, more plentiful than dainty; and every
one, irrespective of size or sex, eats like a miner just off
location, or whatever it is miners go on. Even the meal
hours suggest hungry miners. Come as late as 5:30 in
the evening and you will find lines drawn through all the
"cheap" choices on the menu. Of course I am speaking of
meals for sale; I know next to nothing about the meals
served in Alaskan homes.

Nor will you save anything by going à la carte, trying to
pick your own menu, to make it a snack instead of a
gorging. A lettuce and tomato salad, for instance, or lamb
chops on toast, costs a dollar and the only item under half
a dollar is "Hamburger Sandwich on Bun . . . 25 cents."
Just the ordinary dish-slamming restaurant, mind you;
there is nothing swank about Fairbanks public eating places.

Your meal includes tea or coffee, but not milk. There
are now a couple of flourishing dairy farms outside Fairbanks, but fresh milk is unknown in most of Alaska; in
Fairbanks it costs 25 cents a quart, in restaurants 15 cents
a distressingly small glass. That seldom troubles an Alaskan, however. Almost to a man or woman, if not child,
they prefer canned milk to the real variety. They use
so much canned milk that some one has invented a patent
gadget which pokes two holes in a can of milk at one slam
of a waitress' fist. Your can of milk sits as omnipresently
before you on any restaurant table or trough—I mean,

lunch counter—as the sugar, salt and pepper and ketchup bottle.

I saw no evidence that tipping is much of an Alaskan habit, though our first Fairbanks waitress said she got generous tips from residents, in addition to her wages of 50 cents an hour, and small ones from tourists. But I suspect she was hinting. Meal tickets lie in unguarded rows on the cash register counter, and every now and then a man telephones or sends a note to let So-and-So "eat on my meal ticket."

In the stores; well, a loaf of bread is 25 cents, three bananas the same; canned goods, including Alaska salmon, cost more than twice what they do Outside. In short, though there are exceptions, prices, like wages, average about two and a half times as much as they do in our eastern States. They lay it all to the freight rates on the Alaska Railroad. But one gets the impression that Alaska's high prices are something of a habit, a hangover from gold-rush days, a sort of civic pride, rather than a necessity.

Yes, its prices are high, but there is nothing picayune about Fairbanks. There is no charge for local telephone calls in hotels, for instance. No one uses telephone numbers in Fairbanks; they just call by name, though the telephone book had been out two months when we got there. People used to leave a call with the telephone central and the girl on duty would call a man by name at the time he specified, and two or three times more to make sure he had not fallen asleep again. But those bucolic days are over; the frontier character of Fairbanks is changing, and the time is coming when people even will have to look up telephone numbers.

When traveling take your poke with you—but in Alaska make it travelers' checks. Alaskan banks are unfamiliar with letters of credit, looked mine over as a curiosity, said they had never seen one before, in one case refused to honor it, though they have been cashing travelers' checks of the same company for years.

Alaskans, like the Pacific Coast, abhor paper dollars; I suppose it makes them feel big and strong to lug a pocketful of silver. Time was, not so long ago, when two-bits was the smallest coin in circulation in Fairbanks. The bank paid $5 for a $5.12 check but $5.25 for a check for $5.13. But a few years ago the Piggly Wiggly brought in dimes, nickels and even pennies—and were its fellow merchants sore! Women of Fairbanks tell me that for a long time they were ashamed to accept dimes and nickels in change.

Saloons, or at least beer parlors, are numerous; Fairbanks, with perhaps three thousand population, issued twenty-six beer and liquor licenses for the current year. I don't know where it gets its water supply, but if it is as bad as it smells, especially when it is hot, no wonder people drink beer. Seems to me some one told us its strong aroma is merely a mineral water smell and that Fairbanks water is very good for your health.

But bottled water goes like beer at a policeman's picnic in the Hotel Nordale. Every half-hour or so the German handyman up-ends a bottle of imported water in the lobby water-tank and old-timers use up paper cups by the gross, as if they were making up for lost opportunities. Ice-water, I suppose, was rare in summer in their mining days. Sourdoughs, limping old-timers, retired prospectors, occupy most of the red-leather streamlined chairs in the Nordale's more public lobby—there is a "blue room" on the other side of the entrance, but that seems by common consent to be reserved for ladies and paying guests. The Fairbanks', or Sourdoughs', conception of hospitality is still so frontierlike that although the Nordale leaves a place of relief open for them, it has to lock its public bathrooms, lest mere lobby sitters take advantage of them. If it is so popular in the summer, think what that Nordale lobby must be in the winter!

Do the old fellows who sit there dreaming over the past and disapproving the present still look forward to making a fortune? At any rate I picked up under one of the red leather chairs in which old-timers loll away their declining years in the Hotel Nordale a sheet of paper with the following penciled upon it:

$$
\begin{array}{r}
800,000 \\
22 \\
\hline
176,000,000
\end{array}
\qquad
\begin{array}{r}
176,000,000 \\
600 \\
\hline
105,600,000,000
\end{array}
$$

No, I am sure it wasn't the musing of a New Deal government official.

Sourdoughs and Cheechakoes ("cheechalker" is the way Alaska really pronounces its word for tenderfoot) mingle freely in the streets of Fairbanks, especially in the summer, when workers as well as tourists from Outside are numerous. Among the old-timers themselves a man is a real Sourdough only if he has been in Alaska (or the Yukon Territory) continuously (brief trips Outside allowed on sufferance) since 1898. Or there is the more facetious definition:

Tourist: "Say, what's a Sourdough, Mister?"

"Well, son, to be a Sourdough a man must have done three things: Shot the Whitehorse Rapids, killed a moose and lived with a squaw."

"Are you a Sourdough, Mister?"

"Naw, I never did shoot me a moose."

Far from being the profane roughnecks one pictures old-timers to be, many of them talk more like college professors; even those with a Scandinavian accent have surprisingly large vocabularies. They have a gentle way about them, too, an easy-going manner rare in the States, or at least in the East. There is much less striving to be tough, to show the hard-boiled attitude, than among the flabby clerks and scornful ticket-sellers along Broadway.

The Sourdough does not easily fall into reminiscences, either, at least before strangers.   But in places like Fairbanks one gets the impression that cabin bachelors come to town, or town cabin dwellers drift into the two hotels where outsiders congregate, to have a good talk with any one who will listen.

Some of them are funny old derelicts left behind when gold mining became Big Business.   There are many old-timers stranded all over the Territory now, broken in health and, in probably more cases, financially broke. Money meant nothing to many of them in the good old days.   They say the average prospector was like a beachcomber, or a sailor just landed; drank up fortune after fortune.   "Well, at least I've tasted money in my time," they say now.

Your real prospector in his declining years scorns mere work; refuses to shovel snow even at a dollar an hour; buy each other drinks if there is anything to buy them with.   Hard-bitten old birds, quite indifferent to personal appearance—or rather, wearing what looks mannish and outdoors to them, scorning to follow the fashion.   Firm-jawed, cheerful in adversity, ready gamblers, good losers, haters of confined spaces; men who say, "Oh, Switzerland is okeh but it is too much cleaned up," or "that place is too crowded now [it has nine houses].   I'm pulling out for the North."   This sense of needing unlimited elbow-room may in some cases be put on, in some mere habit.   But most of them seem really unhappy where people congregate.   Alaska laughs at Admiral Byrd's lone vigil in the Antarctic; there are thousands of men in Alaska who live like that, and worse—and like it.

Old chaps hanging about the Nordale Hotel say casually, "I have six grandchildren I've never seen; a son and two daughters I haven't seen in thirty years."   Last summer one old-timer met the Reverend So-and-So, his son, age 37, for the first time.   It's rather hard on those old

Sourdoughs who went without any domestic affection from the time they left home in '98 or even earlier, until they married a schoolma'am, too late to have children, in their late forties . . . to see her die a few years later, as a mine manager I flew with in a plane one day had just seen his wife die, sitting in a rockingchair in the hotel after being discharged from the hospital as cured. And here he was flying back to . . . well, a pretty lonely place at best.

On one of my days in Fairbanks I called on Elam Harnish, who was Jack London's partner over the Chilkoot Pass and on to Dawson in '97. It was a nice warm, quiet early-September afternoon and Harnish was stretched out on his Alaskan divan on the front porch of his log cabin in one of the back streets—308 Wendel Avenue, to be exact—shoes off, half asleep, with something in his face that suggested he was always in more or less pain awake . . . I hated to disturb him. Born near Lancaster of Pennsylvania Dutch stock, he "golded" and lumbered and worked at many other jobs all over Alaska, until "Old Man Rheumatism put an end to all that."

"Who, London? Oh, Jack was hard to get up in the morning, but he was okeh after that, and good company. He got scurvy and lost his teeth and went out in the fall of '98. Made quite a name for himself, I guess. Yes, I went out once myself, in 1917; but I soon came back. Now I've been laid up with this rheumatism eight, nine years."

London made Elam Harnish the hero of his "Burning Daylight," or at least gave the hero his name—the rheumatic old fellow on the log cabin porch didn't show much evidence of ever having been the gold-tossing hell-raiser London pictures. But then, personally I did not meet a man in Alaska who even remotely resembled the Jack London type of Alaskan hero. Perhaps I was only unlucky. Nor was Elam's nickname "Burning Daylight." Note the great novelist's imagination in action! Jack got the phrase from Elam all right, but it came from his final

effort to get him up in the morning. When it was time to
hit the trail Elam would say, "Come on, Jack, you're burning daylight." Subsequent publicity did not go to Elam's
head; he takes his honors casually. Sourdoughs are like
that.

Sivert Bredie, born in Denmark, who "came in" in the
early days, is now the Fairbanks shoemaker, the only one,
in fact, in many thousand square miles, quite contented now
apparently to get Fairbanks' prices for his half soles and
rubber heels.

"Once I made a stake of $86,000. In '98 I got a stake
of $36,000, but I got typhoid and went back to Denmark.
When I got back to Skagway I had just forty dollars. I
asked a fellow I'd known there in '98 to lend me a hundred
dollars.

"'Can't do it, Sive,' he said. 'Smallest I've got is a
thousand dollar bill.'

"So I took that . . . he wouldn't listen to anything else
. . . and when I got to Dawson I had just exactly the
original forty dollars left."

Yes, the Alaskan woods are full of old-timers, every one
of them with a tale of luck and hardship, always with varia-
tions, to tell. But you can't look them all up and pump
them all dry in one summer.

When the summer sun shines in Fairbanks, as it often
does, long and ardently, you will find a coat almost as
burdensome as at home in July and August. The weather
was almost uncomfortably warm the first time we were
there, though we were nearly 65° North. The air and the
telephone wires were full of swallows. There had been
but one rain recently and both miners and the few farmers
around Fairbanks were suffering for lack of water. But it
rained cats and dogs all July 30, when we came back from
Seward. Don't bring your umbrella to Alaska, however.
I did, and it made me very conspicuous. There were some
raincoats but all the rest of male Fairbanks at least scorned

to carry an umbrella. Newsboys, busy youths, Sourdoughs in hats and without hats were all getting wet; evidently it is a proof of hardihood. Or rather, only one man besides your correspondent dared carry an umbrella; Fairbanks' dapper postmaster and president of its Chamber of Commerce, Bob Sheldon, is the kind of man who makes his own customs. I wonder if that is why he is one of the few '98ers who shows no signs of wear and tear. Now that Bob has become president of the McKinley Park Association and plans to retire as postmaster as soon as a successor with anything like his qualifications can be found . . . well, Fairbanks, I fear, will never be the same again, at least on a rainy day.

By August 9, when we got back again, dust was thick and Fairbanks was sprinkling its streets, privately. When we first came the nights were nothing more than one of those very long twilights of the north; now there were nearly three hours of actual darkness. A few brief months more and the sun would barely glance at the city on the Chena, around noonday.

They should have picked the site of Fairbanks with more care, as in the case of so many cities. The Chena overflowed its banks once while we were in Alaska, though we were not then in Fairbanks. It had made ready to entertain a flood; had a flood once which filled its cellars; wants to dam its river. Now I see the War Department is going to start work high up the Tanana and spend $576,000 for flood control, so that Fairbanks may live in peace, at least in that one particular.

Some one has said that Fairbanks in summer is merely a Middle Western mining town; that one must see it in winter to know the real Fairbanks. No doubt; but we found it a place worth seeing even when the fireweed is in bloom. Old Sourdoughs go stomping through the streets, down the corridors of the hotels; Noel Ross in a tropical helmet scurrying about in quest of news; cheery Dave

Adler, bubbling over with enthusiasm and still marveling
that a man born on New York's East Side should have
come to have the only exclusively bookstore in Alaska and
the most erudite wife in Fairbanks; the immaculate Mrs.
Ford tearing down another of her buildings . . . no,
there is no lack in Fairbanks of what a Frenchman calls
"types."

By the middle of August Alaska's often head-high fireweed begins to go to white puffy seed. But raspberries
were just ripening. "I picked a gallon of raspberries yesterday." There are blueberries, salmon berries, mammoth
strawberries in Alaska; the only trouble is that they cost
35 cents per small box, hardly a pint, in Fairbanks. And
by the way, "Alaskan strawberries," in the Sourdough
vernacular, are what the AEF doughboys called "whistle-
berries," in other words beans, out of a can.

Until a few years ago Fairbanks could be reached only
by way of the Yukon in summer or by dog-team up the
Richardson Trail in winter. Today it is probably Alaska's
greatest transportation center. The Steese Highway runs
163 miles northeastward to Circle City on the Yukon; the
Richardson Highway plods 372 miles southward to Valdez,
with several branches; the Elliott (seems to me he was
another general) Highway climbs 84 miles up the map to
Livengood . . . "and we badly need a highway to Forty
Mile, among other places." The Alaska Railroad ends
at Fairbanks; Yukon steamers, though they dock at Nenana and send their passengers up by rail, virtually make
it their terminus, and it is the greatest commercial airbase
in the Territory.

We never got to Livengood, though Don Adler did
offer us his car. When we had time, because planes were
held up by weather, the road was too slippery to be safe,
especially in heavy fog and a borrowed car. But we lost
interest, anyway, when we found that Livengood has a
long "i" and is not a sarcastic slap at early living condi-

tions. It is named for a miner who is still living, an old-timer who first discovered gold there in 1914—yes, for that matter, who is still prospecting, now at Forty Mile.

Livengood has the distinction of having a woman prospector. During recent winters its population has averaged about eighty, in summer nearly twice that. Now it is enjoying a boom, a big company having settled down on it, with all the modern aids to mining. Though there is not a farm in the district, many of its miners have good gardens. By the first of November, when caribou began moseying through the "camp" asking to be shot, there was fresh meat in almost every cache. Farther north still are towns with such expressive names as Coldfoot; Wiseman, Alaska's most northern mining "camp," where living is incredibly expensive and the population is still incensed at a man who wrote them up so thoroughly in a book.

Five miles from Fairbanks by car, though only three by train or afoot, is the University of Alaska, the most northern university in the world. Outwardly it does not greatly resemble our oldest institutions of higher learning. But the cluster of new frame or at most stuccoed buildings on a knoll are constantly increasing and inside them is one of the most important mining schools in the United States, with $65,000 worth of laboratory equipment. One third of the students lived in town last winter, but more dormitories are under construction.

Two out of five of the 200 students enrolled at last account were girls, and 68 of the 200 were enrolled in mining, or more than in any other department. Not a very large student body, even President Bunnell admits. But what it lacks in numbers it makes up in variety; twenty-two States, Canada and another foreign country were represented at last report, and another score or so of students were expected to turn up when mining froze down and people arrived from distant places.

There is a very interesting university museum, its ex-

hibits including the first, and last, automobile ever manu-
factured in Alaska. Fairbanks Postmaster Robert E.
Sheldon made it, from a description of a gasoline buggy
which he read! It is rather a queer-looking vehicle; to
almost any motorist of today it would be considered just
an amusing toy; but it got there just the same.

The university museum is noteworthy mainly for its
remains of prehistoric animals. Alaska is a geologist's
paradise. There could be no better vacation job for a
college student specializing in paleontology than to go up
to Alaska and become a "stripper" in its placer mines.
Alaskan miners, at least by the modern hydraulicking and
dredging method, are quite familiar with the extinct animals of the pleistocene era. They dig up in the muck huge
tusks, bones, fossils, now and then a whole head, of bison,
horse, mastodon, mammoth, camel, lion and sabre-tooth
tiger. But their idea is to wash them out with their hose
nozzles with the least labor, and geologists weep at the
damage done. The remains of lions found in Alaska scientists explain by guessing that not only was it once warmer
but that in those days the lion wore his hair as long as a
bison, and only the mane has survived.

When a "cat" driver turns up a 28-pound mastodon tusk
in the tailings, as one did just a day or so before we
reached Fairbanks, it belongs to him, to sell or to contrib-
ute to the scientists, as he sees fit. Some of the tusks
are very good ivory, but most of them flake off until only
the inner core is of any value. A skull and tusks found
near Chatanika stand almost as high as the average
man is tall. Huge skulls with horns similar to but larger
than those of the water buffalo are found only five to
twelve feet below the surface. Sets of perfect mastodon
teeth, about the size of a tractor plowshare, are so common
that Alaskans themselves hardly notice them. The geologists' guess is that they were buried anything from ten to
thirty thousand years ago, and that mastodons were car-

nivorous and mammoths vegetarians; and the great difference in their dental equipment makes it easy for the
layman to follow their arguments.

Out at the University of Alaska there are prehistoric
femurs weighing forty to fifty pounds, bigger than a locomotive drive-beam, if that makes their immense size clearer
to you. One of the latest finds in the university museum—
no, it was still in the clean-up room, along with truckloads
of other remains—was the whole hide, tail, and hind legs,
hooves, hair and all still intact, of a prehistoric creature
much like the water buffalo. Its hind legs were cramped in
a way to suggest that it had suddenly been overwhelmed by
an avalanche or similar disaster.

In Fairbanks and again at Valdez we met, on their way
Outside, Professor Wesley Bliss of the Department of
Anthropology of the University of New Mexico, and half
a dozen anthro—well, at least wanderlust-minded youths
who were paying their own transportation and food expenses for the fun they got out of a trip I should have
liked to make. They had started down the Sikanni River
in northern British Columbia as soon as the ice went out,
late in April, in three canoes and with more than a ton
of grub—you know what early-twenties appetites are even
in ordinary climates and under normal summer exertions.
None of the party had ever piloted a canoe on rivers before, so it shows good management or luck or something
that as far as we could see they had come through without
any serious mishaps.

From the Sikanni they went north into the Nelson, then
into the Liard. Men have been drowned where the Nelson
meets the Liard, but this party made it safely. The Liard,
swift and treacherous, has some fifteen miles of rapids a
short distance above its junction with the Mackenzie.
On the Mackenzie winds blowing against the currents
sometimes make waves so high that even "big river boats"
have to tie up. By using an outboard motor, lashing two

canoes together and towing the third, they managed, with
the usual virile adventures, to reach Aklavik. Some of
them, in one of the large canoes, went out on the Arctic
Ocean and along the coast as far as Shingle Point.

The Mackenzie carries more water to the sea than the
Mississippi. It has such a labyrinth of mouths that even
trappers who live in the delta sometimes get lost. In July
it was so hot at the mouth of the Mackenzie that they
worked stripped to the waist—and did the mosquitoes love
that! But no, the professor corrected my surmise: "We
only stripped out on the river when the breeze, often a
strong wind from the north, kept the mosquitoes away.
We used our shirts and head-nets as soon as we landed.
Sometimes we worked twenty hours or more at a stretch
without realizing it, thanks to the continual daylight and
the exhilaration of northern latitudes."

From the mouth of the delta they found themselves
heading into the mountains on a swifter and swifter stream
that was not on the map. Eventually they reached the
main Peel channel, went forty miles from Aklavik up the
Peel, then into the Rat River and up that to the rapids at
Destruction City. This is an abandoned camp where, during the Klondyke gold-rush, men coming down the Mackenzie headed for the Yukon had to break up their outfits in
order to track up the swift current of the Rat. Bliss and
his party had two weeks of tracking, the water cold and
the current like a waterfall, pushing upstream the two
canoes they had remaining.

They made three short portages between the Rat and
the Little Bell, between lakes at the top of the pass, and
got their canoes into water flowing into the Pacific; went
from the Little Bell into the Big Bell, then into the Porcupine. From the day they left the Peel River until they
got to Old Crow on the Porcupine, a period of three weeks,
they never saw another human being. At Old Crow they
thumbed a boatride with a trader on the way to Fort

Yukon, where they sold their canoes, got another boat-ride to Circle with two Indian wood-cutters, chartered a truck from there to Fairbanks and later to Valdez.

They had obviously had a grand summer and looked none the worse—in fact, considerably better—for wear, though they were not dressed in tuxedos. What's more (and here is the point to all this digression) they had found a few things of scientific interest, such as obsidian artifacts and abalone shell pendants indicating, by their similarity to those widely scattered farther south and east, early trade movements from Wyoming or our west coast. They found shells and coral on the coast of Alaska which show that evidently it was once much warmer than it is today, though not exactly tropical. Artifacts have been found which indicate that all central Alaska escaped heavy glacial movements, as moving glaciers would have ground them to bits.

Bliss and his boys had done some ethnological work among the Slave Indians of the Sikanni, Nelson and Liard Rivers, who live by hunting, fishing and trapping. They found them still using stone tools for some of their work, such as hide scraping. They use sinew from the back muscles of the moose and the deer for sewing. They tan hides for making moccasins and clothing, cut strips of babiche to use on snowshoes, toboggans and for coarse sewing. Some of the old tribes are completely extinct, mainly from tuberculosis. Overheated cabins in winter and sudden changes from this heat to intense cold outside, and trying to live in the white man's way, are at least partly responsible for their decline. Some people think they are a weak stock and therefore are dying out. But they are closely akin to the Navajo and Apache of New Mexico, Arizona and Mexico; in fact, they speak almost the same language, and the Navajos and Apaches are a very hardy people.

Bliss found evidence of early man in a test trench they

dug in a caved-in limestone escarpment near Blue Fish
Lake, north of the Nahanni Butte on the Liard. Other
caves in this area showed smoke-darkened walls. Along
the Little Bell there was evidence that an ice-free corridor
probably existed throughout the pleistocene era from
Bering Strait to the Mackenzie delta. But they had no
time to dig down through the blue clay overlaid with ash
to see whether there was any evidence below it of occupation by human beings—which would definitely prove
that man existed in North America prior to the major
advance of ice in that region, in the pleistocene age, which
was probably only about 50,000 years ago in this area.

Fairbanks has a central heating plant which heats several
business blocks and some residences. Its pipes run beside
the water-pipes and keep them from freezing in winter.
During the winter cars are left running while people are
in the movies, at dances (Fairbanks' "Sourdough dances"
are famous), flirting or spooning, because crankcase oil
freezes at 20° below. But they tell me Fairbanks is never
more gay and lively than in the winter, especially during its
Ice Carnival in March, when it builds a fantastic castle of
ice, has a Dog Derby to which even Dawson sends entries,
selects a queen from among the beauties dressed in parkas
and furs. Almost all Alaskans say winter is their best
season—and apparently they are not whistling in the dark.
I must fly up some time and see Fairbanks when even its
own citizens admit that it is "different."

Men fly south like geese and return in the spring, is
another version. "Everybody but officials, professional
men and drones go Outside in winter," the wet blankets go
on. "The rest hole up in the back rooms of saloons and
play endless card games until spring." But that seems to
be only a minority report, and every one agrees that the
spring stampede is catching. Old prospectors, after hot-
stoving it all winter, set out again, hopeful as ever.

There are public kennels for husky dogs in the outskirts

of Fairbanks and across the Chena. Out at the Pacific Alaska Airways airport you will find Fred Milligan, a famous dog-team driver from 1911 to 1932, now the airport manager. A great come-down, perhaps, but life cannot always be high adventure. For twelve years Milligan ran the mails from St. Michael to Tanana; eight years from Nenana to Flat; one year from Ruby to Ophir. In the summers from 1926 to 1932 he lived on the floating Yukon hospital, the "Medicine Boat" *Martha Angeline,* which started on its 1,400-mile mercy journey soon after the ice broke up and plied the Yukon and the Tanana until freeze-up.

Fred used dogs only six months a year, from November to April inclusive. A good dog cost $50 ($25 in summer; $100 in mid-winter) and lasted only two years. Each harness cost $7, a good sled $150. During the working season it cost him an average of 40 cents a day to feed a dog, on a mixture of tallow and dried fish. He paid his Indians $300 a month and all expenses. In the summer he boarded his dogs out in a fish camp at $3 a month each. No wonder dog travel was never cheap, nothing like as cheap as airplane travel is today in Alaska.

People knew the mails had to go through, so after a storm they knocked at Milligan's door and let him break trail, sometimes day and night for three or four weeks, while they followed more easily in his wake. While he had a government mail contract he kept sixty to sixty-five dogs, two or three Indians; used nineteen or twenty dogs at a time, carried between 800 and 1,000 pounds of mail. It took twenty days by dog-team from Nenana to Flat; even today fliers must underbid dog-teams on mail contracts in Alaska and agree not to take longer than "star route" dog-teams did to make the same journey. Now an airplane gets only a little more than half what Milligan did over the same route, but the high cost of carrying the mails is still one of the phenomena of Alaska.

On the way to Ruby a bright red plane kept us close company as far as Tolovana

Flying down the Kuskokwim

Our Alaska car on the Richardson Highway

Cordova has a picturesque situation

I pretend to no Alaska-dog knowledge myself, dog-team-
ing being no summer sport and one of the few forms of
transportation I have never tried. But Fred gave me some
bits of dog lore which I may as well pass on to you:

Pet one dog or show favoritism toward him in any way
and the others will take the first opportunity to gang up on
him and kill him. Don't whip your dogs; scratch them on
the back, jolly them along. Alaskan dogs are incredibly
strong; most of them willing workers. They claw into the
snow and ice like mad to drag a load up a steep hill. You
start working them when they are a year old; try them out
for six months and then shoot them if they are not good
workers. Dog food is too expensive to let drones live.

I understood Fred to say—stop me if I am wrong—that
on the coast one dog is hitched in front, the rest in pairs,
each with an independent trace fastened to the main trace.
In the interior they are hitched together in pairs, tandem
fashion. Inland you must stick to the trail, but along the
north coast you travel by compass. Coast dogs have
shorter legs and longer hair than those of the interior.
The coast dogs have "feathers" on the bottoms of their
feet; interior dogs a bare pad on the foot—snow would
gather in the "feathers" and "ball up," and eventually the
dog would go lame. Milligan used moccasins (6 cents a
foot) on all his dogs, especially after a new snow and
freezing weather, since freezing snow is particularly dam-
aging to dog feet. In April you can travel only at night,
stopping as soon as the sun comes out; otherwise your dogs
will have no feet left.

A dog has better feet if he has some wolf blood; moreover, a wolf is in heat only once a year, a dog twice. The
wolf does not pull his feet together as he walks, but an
Outside dog picks up a snowball on each foot. The malamute is part wolf, unlike the Labrador husky, and husky
and malamute crossed with Siberian make a good combination. No reins are used on dogs; you stand on the

"ouija board," a kind of tiny platform attached to the tug line of the sled, and steer with your voice and a gee-pole on the other side of it. This is better than wearing snowshoes, as you can stamp your feet or drop off and run behind the sled. But woe betide you if you trip and let go! Most dogs will not wait for you and old Jack Frost soon overtakes you.

As cattle in a cattle country will not attack a man on horseback but may one on foot, so the Eskimo dog will not attack a man while he is upright, but may if he trips and falls in the snow. Now and then the lead dog starts up a tree after a ptarmigan or across the white wastes after a rabbit. I met one old-timer who, wearing heavy mittens and with the lead line wound around his hand, lost a little finger when his dogs suddenly saw a rabbit.

In early gold-rush days stampeders brought in any large dog, irrespective of species. Dogs were developed in Alaska just as horses have been elsewhere, for racing. I gathered from Fred that the white Siberian dog, the one with the "glass eyes," is best; good for a hundred miles without a rest, whereas the Yukon malamute travels only from 35 to 50 miles a day and carries a lighter load.

The Alaska musher or prospector still has his pack-dog, capable of carrying about forty pounds, much less than the musher often carries on his own back. We had with us a Bergen knapsack, which I consider the best made. But Alaskans do not think much of it compared with the pack-board, two flat layers of canvas wrapped around a rectangular frame.

Dog-teams still scamper across Alaska in winter, but the airplane has greatly reduced their use and value. They have left behind them at least a useful word: "Mush!" (its origin still in dispute) is the Alaskan command to move on, a word of warning, even to get you out of the way of a baggage truck on a railroad platform.

"Every dog has his day," sobs an editorial writer in the

Fairbanks *News-Miner*, "but that of the Alaskan dog, who perhaps had the greatest day in the world, at least as far as his usefulness to man goes, is approaching twilight. The inevitable march of 'progress' has reduced him from the harness of activity to the idleness of the town and village streets, with the same result as happens to men left idle. Man is not showing toward him, by permitting him to spend the twilight of his declining years quietly and unmolested, the loyalty toward the dog which the dog did to man in his first hard years in Alaska."

CHAPTER IX

To Bethel with Bill Knox

*"W. P." . . . Off at Last . . . Down the
Yukon to Ruby . . . McGrath and Flat . . .
Along the Kuskokwim . . . A Night at Bethel
. . . Cheery Eskimos . . . Back to Fairbanks*

I GOT up at six on Thursday to fly to Bethel . . . at 10
A.M. on Saturday! But if only Rogers and Post had been
as patient and cautious as the Pacific Alaska Airways! It
was a long wait, there in the red room of the Nordale,
with nothing to do but watch old-timers making paths from
the streamlined, red-leather chairs to the ice-water tank.
But smiling Alaska Moody could keep any one cheered up,
not merely across a ticket counter but on a desert island.

If "W.P." is not Alaska's favorite slogan at least it is
better known there than WPA. It means "weather permitting" and applies of course mainly to air travel. The
Alaska pioneers of today are its aviators. But though they
are bold, hardy and enterprising, none of those left are
foolhardy enough to set out without "waiting for weather."
And in Alaska good weather reports all along the route
you wish to fly are sometimes a long time in coming.

Ten years ago there were eight planes in Alaska, which
flew 25,000 passenger miles. Last year 155 planes flew
5,634,461 passenger miles. They say the Territory's per
capita air mileage is the highest in the world. Alaskans
call an airplane as we Outside do a taxicab. Flying suits
the Alaskan temperament as well as the Territory's physical characteristics. I forget which of the many enterpris-

135

ing aviation companies in Alaska advertises: "Time flies. So should you."

The Territory is full of small airplane companies and individual fliers for hire. More than thirty planes are based at Fairbanks alone; half a dozen companies make their headquarters there. The most important of these is Pacific Alaska Airways, subsidiary since 1932 of Pan American Airways. Unlike its many rivals it does no charter flying and operates entirely on a cash basis—something its sponsors were told simply could not be done in Alaska. It even refuses to carry drunks. Independent operators who need the money, or have old friends who drink, cannot always be so hard-boiled—and once in a while have a peck of trouble. The only company with a fixed schedule, Pacific Alaska covers little of the country, in one sense, just a trunk line clear across it and one long branch down to the mouth of the Kuskokwim. Its freelance rivals, ready as bees to hop anywhere at a moment's notice, give it some competition even on these routes.

Alaskans believe the via Fairbanks, Nome and Aleutians air route across the Pacific is bound eventually to supersede that via Hawaii. For one thing it is 1,400 miles shorter. Meanwhile the airplane has changed the mining picture in Alaska completely. Mines are discovered by air which can be worked only with the help of the airplane. Supplies and miners are flown in and ore and miners are flown out. Or again, instead of taking the last boat out about November first the miners on the Seward Peninsula, for instance, can get in at least a month's more work at the two ends of the summer and pay only $75 more to go Outside by plane in a hurry.

A dense blanket still hung low over all Alaska on Saturday morning, but we were off at last, with a 2,000-foot ceiling that gradually began to break up. A bright-red plane flew close along beside us for the first half-hour or more, then dived down and landed on the Yukon at Tolovana

. . . to pick up the estranged wife of a man who had shot himself in Fairbanks the evening before. You see, there are no secrets in Alaska.

We landed on a bare field high above Ruby, sprawled a little way along the foot of the north bank of the Yukon. There I chatted with two college boys who had been selling books by rowboat down the Yukon all summer, while Bill Knox pumped his own gasoline from steel barrels opened for him by a pair of local workmen. Aviation in Alaska gets virtually no government help—though some hindrances. There is not an air beacon, radio beam, lighted airfield or any other government help, except weather reports—and along about December there is mighty little daylight. Fortunately it is not very dark up there when snow is on the ground, and once in the air, in winter, things are usually jake, for clouds are rare and you can make a ski landing almost anywhere. But you must build a fire under a plane motor, as we used to under balky horses, to get it started in the wintertime, because airplane motor oil freezes at 20° below zero.

The highway that runs a long way out of Ruby, ten to twelve minutes by air, looks pretty good . . . from the air. They say it goes to Poorman, sixty miles out, where there are mines, and that on the ground it does not deserve the name of road. After that the airway lies among hills growing up into mountains, the country turning pale, so thin are the trees on sandstone plains or sand-hills. By noon the most curious patterns and colors spread out below us.

Straight south to McGrath on the Kuskokwim, already a real river even this near its source, then west by south across a sun-patched, fantastically patterned country. Flat, near the Iditarod River, among bushy rather than wooded hills, is as dreary-looking a place as its name. Yet it is hospitable to the unheralded stranger and has its own civic prides, social rules and local culture. It is proud, for instance, that it still maintains the old but vanishing Alaskan custom of using no coin under two-bits. Distinctly a white man's community, as compared with the hundreds of Indian and Eskimo villages in Alaska. "But a lot of the men go down to the Yukon to get their brides" . . . in other words, squaw-men will soon be in the majority, which is tantamount to saying that eventually the white man will be absorbed and the land returned to the natives.

Along the lower Kuskokwim, second river of Alaska, the color of a Frenchman's morning coffee, is tundra country, and endless yellow-green flats patched with hundreds of black ponds. Close along the edges of what looks from the air like a stream of no great significance is a hint of low-tree vegetation. Then came more and more lakes and ponds, hundreds, literally thousands of them, of every size and capricious shape, as if Nature were trying out all the patterns in her workshop. Incredibly squiggly rivers and black little lakes and ponds wreathed with a green ring of water plants, all in a world carpeted, high-napped, with small evergreens, though there were still considerable patches of evergreen forests. . . . But maybe you get tired of seeing the world below from a plane. I never do.

Sidewalk lounging New Yorkers would mistake Bethel at the mouth of the Kuskokwim for the end of the earth. But I found it interesting. For one thing I saw there my first Eskimos, at least in their native habitat. Bethel has a truck, too, and maybe a mile and a half of road. But there were seven planes parked that evening at the landing field out beyond the many wooden crosses knee-deep in grass and head-high in weeds at the north end of town. Then there is Bethel's boardwalk, a resounding wooden sidewalk that runs the whole length of the single-row town —and beyond, vaulting a minor stream by transforming itself into a bridge, reverberating on into what I suppose Bethel calls its suburbs.

Along it are a Moravian church, the N. C. Co.'s trading-post and its inevitable rival, two roadhouses, the beginnings of an imposing hospital. Smiling, friendly but religiously exacting Eskimos flitted in and out of the church. Of the two roadhouses one apparently had a monopoly of popularity. Lodging $1; meals $1 each are standard Alaskan roadhouse prices, and you need never get up from a roadhouse table hungry. But there were seven or eight men in the room upstairs that night, in case you don't like that. Neither do I, as a regular thing. But it is rather chummy and homelike now and then—and do pilots talk shop!

Besides its planes Bethel has considerable small ocean craft and river traffic. The little steamer anchored far out across the muddy water had brought a new schoolteacher for Akiak up the river. Just the man for such a job, I should say: rural Missouri grammar, sturdy physique, simple tastes. He had brought along a wife, who didn't seem, just then at least, to be one hundred percent for this adventure, and a baby five months old, who did. They had been six weeks getting this far from Seattle, on a government boat that carried all their goods and chattels and supplies for the winter, and they would be at least another week getting up to Akiak, ten minutes away by plane.

The Saturday night movie in a side room of the N. C. Co.'s trading-post, stocked with at least a sample of almost everything under the sun, was three years old—but who minds a little cold storage in Alaska? In fact, seems to me Hollywood improves with a little aging.

That knee-crushing ordeal over, the folding chairs, but not the hearty native smells, were removed and dancing began. Bethel, alas, has no native dancing, but there were plenty of dancing natives. Friendly, likable Eskimos, who made the Indians we so far had seen in Alaska seem sour and surly by comparison, hoofed it in the modern rhythm with the ease of débutantes. An Eskimo man with a face so ugly it was fascinating was, if not the best, at least the most tireless dancer. An Eskimo woman in a bell-shaped gown-over-fur reaching to her ankles and the inevitable baby invisible on her back danced unconcernedly with a white man in boots and lumber-jacket. The whites and natives mixed freely—sometimes too freely, some of the faces in the throng suggested. Or is it better so, perhaps; a new, amalgamated race that may be just the thing for such a land and climate? That pretty halfbreed girl over there, for instance, married to an American, is an excellent typist, and probably as satisfactory as the average American wife, and no doubt can drive a dog-team and skin a seal, if need be, into the bargain. But for the width of their faces and the deep color of their eyes, you'd have needed some sort of laboratory test to prove that several of the halfbreed girls had native blood in their veins. The impression one got was not that the white man is due eventually to wipe out the natives but that he himself will in time be absorbed.

Warm; thirsty work even just watching them. Beer was 25 cents a bottle next door; crackerjack did very well in lieu of pretzels. They will open the beer for you inside, but laws are laws and you must go outside and lean against a post to drink it. Yes, I was glad to have made that trip to Bethel on the Kuskokwim. But the real Eskimo life must be somewhere off to the far northwest. Harry was missing nothing by not being with me here as long as he would be going there with me.

There was just room for me in the plane next morning, also a very low ceiling, so that I got back to Fairbanks only by the skin of my teeth. I might have been marooned in Bethel for a week; Bill Knox has been for a fortnight. For as a mere round-trip sightseer I had agreed to yield that eighth and last seat to any old and important customer flying north on serious business.

The high-booted, Scandinavian atmosphere inside the plane included one of the Olson brothers of Goodnews

Bay. There was a stampede to Goodnews Bay, out beyond the mouth of the Kuskokwim, back in 1911. But prospectors cursed a heavy, grayish substance that interfered with the gold in their pans. Some years later an Indian picked up a nugget of this stuff and sent it to the University of Alaska, which pronounced it platinum—"white gold" now to Alaskan miners. There was another stampede to Goodnews Bay.

But that is not a region favorable to hand-mining methods, so in 1934 the Olson brothers brought in a dragline and other big machinery; now have a $500,000 dredge. No large-scale thawing is required, because only the surface is frozen, thanks to the Japan current. There was no timber to be cleared, plenty of water, no mosquitoes, a good harbor, though only three summer days without rain. At last accounts Platinum, Alaska's latest boom town, four years old now, had forty-eight white men, two white women. There was a native village nearby but they tell me the Eskimos would not build on the sandspit where Platinum now sits, because of some superstition. Legend has it that it was the scene of a bloody battle long ago between Aleuts and Eskimos.

There seemed to be more tundra on the way back to Fairbanks than on the way down. We landed at Flat but might have skipped McGrath had Bill Knox not sent back word: "Anybody want to eat?" One man did, so down we came. "We'll stay about three-quarters of an hour," said Bill, making for the roadhouse restaurant, and that is time enough in McGrath. It was preparing to move across the river, with the successor of the N. C. Co.'s store that had recently burned. Just then it was much worried because it had too few children to entitle it to a school during the coming winter; and one can hardly drive the children to school somewhere else each morning from McGrath on the S-ing Kuskokwim.

That afternoon I had my first inkling of what motor

trouble might mean in a plane. The engine stopped—
just as I killed a stowaway mosquito. All of us reached
automatically for our belts and looked down . . . to see
a thinly low-wooded country. No doubt Bill Knox, who
had been flying this route for years, would know just what
to do in such an emergency. But . . . then suddenly the
motor was purring along contentedly again.

"Sorry if I gave you a scare," said Bill, as we sat down
at Ruby. "I knew the gas was low in one tank, but I was
fooling with the radio and . . ." Two gasoline tanks
would be reassuring on the highway also.

At Ruby, Olson suddenly spoke to two fellow-passengers
stretching their legs with the rest of us. One of them
snarled back at him; the other, who looked as if Death
were stalking on his heels, turned his back and hobbled
back to the plane.

"We don't speak to a fellow like you," said the man
who remained. "You let Hank there almost die on your
damn job and then don't even come down to see him off
when he has to try to get Outside before . . ."

"Why, I didn't know . . ."

"The hell you didn't know. You seen Hank, didn't
you? Does he look . . ."

Their voices, respectively angry and apologetic, drifted
away toward the plane. All the way to Fairbanks the in-
valid's companion glared at the big boss of Goodnews Bay,
while the sick man clung to his injured silence. It was like
a surreptitious peep into what must go on in many an
isolated Alaskan mining camp.

The fantastic scrolls of a river below, a phantasmagoria
of clouds, the incredible pattern of the world spread out
beneath us . . . how can any one call air travel boring?
Not only did the winding Tanana and, later, the Chena
offer constant landings—had we been equipped with pon-
toons—but the flat world was simply patched with water,
like a beggar's coat. Brown patches where some one had

been careless with a match contrasted with larger velvety green patches. Though we were nearly two thousand feet up, the passing of the plane set glassy surfaces of lakelets to shimmering with myriads of little waves. For a little time we followed the hairlike line of the Alaska Railroad, a tiny train creeping at a snail's pace toward Fairbanks.

We flew right over the diggings at Ester and Cripple Creek. From so high aloft placer mining operations look rather like the scratchings of a gardener with a hoe, the "pipers" like upright mice busy with nothing in particular, the second largest dragline in captivity like some baby's plaything. Then Bill sat her down with the ease of a butterfly landing in a flower field and the mild uproar of Alaskan city life quickly engulfed us again.

CHAPTER X

ONCE IT WAS RUSSIAN AMERICA

Alaska Purchase . . . Seward and Stoeckl . . .
Extent and Population . . . Resources . . .
Customs and Characteristics . . . The Indian
and the Eskimo . . . Liquor Flows Too Freely

ALASKA, our oldest and biggest "possession," was called
by many names, some of them profane, three-quarters of a
century ago. The most polite of these was "Seward's
Folly" or "Seward's Ice-Box," to which some social wit,
I suppose it was, since we had no columnists or radio com-
mentators in those days, added "Walrussia." Today it is
called the best example of the remarkable foresight of
the Honorable William H. Seward, then Secretary of
State.

Two men were mainly responsible for our purchase of
what was known, when we first heard of it, as "Russian
America": Baron Stoeckl, the Czar's Minister at Washington, and Secretary Seward, trying for a political come-
back. Only last year, after repeated refusals, did the
Soviet government unearth the documents in Moscow and
allow American diplomats at last to study the Russian side
of the story. They show how a Russian diplomatic sales-
man spent fifteen years getting the maximum price from
the United States for a territory which Russia was only
too glad to have off her hands.

Ever since Vitus Bering, a Dane in the service of Russia,
found it lying around loose in 1741 and appropriated it,
the question had been what to do with it. True, it furnished Catherine the Great the furs she could not live or

love without, but beyond that it was of no great practical value. Its defense was a thorny problem, its upkeep costly, its profits non-existent—or at least they never flowed as high up as the Czar's Treasury. Though Great Britain had finally given Russia undisputed possession of it in 1825, the Czar's government was always afraid American "filibusters," or, worse still, some European power, might seize it. They even feared that the harassed Mormons might turn north for a refuge, thus "forcing us either to provide an army of defense or renounce part of our territory." Perhaps Russia had read some history and run across the story of Texas and our war with Mexico. In short, Russian America had become Russia's problem child, its government's current headache, when one of its loyal sons inveigled Seward into taking over the white elephant.

Russian Minister and Privy Councilor Baron Edouard de Stoeckl, hard-boiled realist—that is, a sophisticated European versus naïve Americans—got the idea as early as 1852, but did not find the task as easy as he at first expected. First of all he had to convince his own government. In 1855, during the Crimean war, Russia offered to sell her American colony, fearing England would seize it. But she neither set a price nor made any other practical move at that time. Two years later the Czar's brother, Grand Duke Constantine, urged its sale. In 1859 Stoeckl returned from St. Petersburg with instructions to accept any reasonable offer. Senator Gwin of California encouraged the initial discussion, but just about then our Civil War broke out.

Stoeckl struck again after the war was over. He went back to St. Petersburg in 1866 and continued pressure until the Czar called a meeting of his best minds. Russian interests had clashed again with the British and the Russians were only too glad to welcome any solution that might reduce their problem in the Far East. The recently discovered papers show that the conference was careless—the

Chief of the Copper River Indians

Peter McKay of Ketchikan

The gravedigger of Cordova, Judd Harris

That million-dollar bridge between glaciers on the now abandoned Copper River Railroad

A bit of Alaska from the air

They are still washing for gold on the beach at Nome

Czar's advisers probably wanted to get back to their vodka and their mistresses—so they casually mentioned $5,000,-000 as a minimum, defined the boundaries only vaguely . . . all of them no doubt being weak on geography.

Back with instructions to sell Alaska for at least $5,-000,000, Stoeckl outsmarted Seward from the start. Being a shrewd trader, he saw to it that the offer was first made by Seward, who sadly needed something like the Alaska purchase to reestablish his waning popularity. Stoeckl stressed the cordial relations that existed between the two countries because Russia had remained neutral during the Civil War. Curiously enough, there was no thought or mention of minerals or fish on either side; the only resources discussed were coal, forests, furs, shipping and ice —for refrigeration. (San Francisco cooled itself on Alaskan ice for years.) Seward offered $5,000,000 but the minister held firm for $7,000,000. Negotiations were swift and the sale was consummated at 4 A.M., like any other poker game, on March 30, 1867, in Washington. The treaty text was so brief that it could be cabled to St. Petersburg on the newly successful transatlantic cable. Stoeckl even made us throw in an extra $200,000—some say as an exchange differential between dollar values in New York and London, some that this was to liquidate the rights of private property owners. The impatient Seward also footed, or at least permitted the taxpayers to foot, the $9,000 cable bill Stoeckl had run up in his transatlantic chats with St. Petersburg.

Alexander II gave his approval and we seem to have taken possession at once, as if Alaska were already ours— and then Congress went hog-wild and fit to be tied. For the deal had been one of the most secret ever conducted in American history. It took an angry Congress, not hand-fed in those days, more than a year to appropriate the money. Russia even considered sending us a proud note telling us either to pay for Alaska or to take it as a gift, with her compliments. That plan was dropped like a hot cake, however, when some one in St. Petersburg suggested that those unsophisticated Yankees might, instead of seeing that it was merely a subtle bit of European sarcasm, accept the offer.

But at last "Walrussia" was ours, for $7,200,000 *in gold*—oh, yes, and those cable charges. We paid by check on August 1, 1868, no interest being charged. I don't see how Stoeckl came to overlook that. Alaska was the first non-contiguous territory to become a part of the United States and remains the largest of them today, with an area of 586,400 square miles. We paid about two cents an acre for it, being shrewder, evidently, in those days than when we paid $287 an acre for our latest and most nearly worthless possession, the Danish West Indies—and left the Danes owning nearly all of those. Though for that matter Seward offered what we finally paid for our Virgin Islands. Many of Alaska's acres are probably not worth two cents, but as Seward's Folly has produced $2,000,000,-000 to date since 1867 it was not a bad bargain after all.

Stoeckl was a tired old man by the time the job was done; and the Czar gave him 25,000 rubles, then about $10,000. One Gunther, some sort of real estate man, seems to have got a $40,000 commission out of the deal, but most likely from the naïve buyer. There is evidence, too, that Russia distributed considerable sums to individuals in the United States where it would do the most good. Another persistent story is that Alaska really cost us only a million or two, because we already owed Russia some five millions for sending over her fleet, as a demonstration of friendship with us against England, and that she included that indebtedness in the purchase price. Stoeckl's official despatches and public correspondence are full of flowery utterances, but he told a friend that, especially as he got the top price and had passed up a post in Europe in order to stick on among us western barbarians, he thought the Czar was not very generous—which from a diplomat is close to violently profane language.

Russian America up to the time we bought it had been badly administered by the Russian-American Company, patterned after Canada's Hudson's Bay Company. We renamed it Alaska, which is a corruption of the Aleut words "al-ay-ek-sa," meaning great land or mainland. Though it has only one-fifth as much area, it is as long and almost as wide as the United States proper. A favorite means of bringing home this astonishing fact is to superimpose the map of Alaska on that of the United States and show that if you place Point Barrow at Duluth, Alaska's southeastern point touches the Atlantic just about at the South Carolina-Georgia boundary, while Attu, the tail tip of the Aleutian Islands, encroaches upon the suburbs of Los Angeles. It is more than twice as large as Texas, or Germany (at last cablegram account), larger than the Union of South Africa, larger than Bolivia, or Peru, or Colombia, or the United States in 1787, that is, the thirteen colonies.

Alaska's census begins early this year and the returns will probably not all be in before we have counted heads in the United States proper the following year. So it is anybody's guess just how many people are rattling around in our immense northwest territory of today. The 1930 census gave the population as 59,278, or about one human being to ten square miles. Of these 28,640 were reported as white, 18,460 of them native born. "Indians" numbered 29,983; that is, the census enumerators lumped Indians, Eskimos and Aleuts together. "Others," of whom there were 655, include quite a number of descendants of Russians who chose to remain after the purchase.

Until the new census returns are in, the guess is that there are about 60,000 people in Alaska, half of them white and half natives, 19,000 of the latter Aleuts and Eskimos. Four-fifths of the whites are males, though you do not notice that discrepancy as persistently as you do, for instance, among the Filipinos on a Hawaiian plantation. The predominant white strain is from Norway and Sweden; in fact, even Alaska's Legislature has a strong Scandinavian accent.

Its optimists claim that Alaska could support 12,000,-000—some say 18,000,000—inhabitants. The Soviet Union, they say, is showing us that agriculture and the far north are not incompatible. They point to Norway, Sweden and especially Finland, in almost the same latitude and much like Alaska in many respects. All three of them, with Denmark and Iceland thrown in, would still leave room for Wyoming in Alaska. Yet they support nearly three hundred times as much population and give them a high standard of living. Finland, for instance, cultivates an area of 6,000,000 acres, supports a population of 3,750,000—and pays her debts. Alaska, say men who should know, has 65,000,000 farmable acres and 35,000 square miles of good grazing. In other words, Alaska wants it understood that her resources are not confined to mining and fishing but that she is capable of becoming a great agricultural country.

Alaska is our last frontier, in the sense of a free land where any man (or woman) may carve out a future. It is the only place left where Uncle Sam will still give you 160 acres for the asking! The valleys of the Yukon, the Tanana and the Kuskokwim are cited as places with great agricultural possibilities. The Kenai Peninsula, said to have the best farming land and climate, is already getting settlers and homesteaders. The colony at Homer is made up of sturdy individualists, who call the Kenai Peninsula "The Garden Spot of America." "Don't confuse these people," says the old-time Alaskan, "with the governmental parasites at Matanuska."

Though the winters may be too severe for the best results in some of the regions Alaska calls tillable, even if the

ground is forever frozen a few feet down, the long summer sun thaws it deeply enough to grow excellent crops.
Any farmer in the States, they contend, would quickly
recognize the agricultural advantages of a sun that hardly
sets during the growing months.   Moreover, the ice beneath provides water, a kind of irrigation, in the summer
as it thaws, so that crops will grow almost irrespective of
rain.   The farther north wheat, like fur, grows the better
it seems to be.   The few farms around Fairbanks are said
to produce more wheat to the acre than Illinois.   Oats, rye,
barley produce more abundantly in some parts of Alaska
than in the States; hay does itself proud.   A Swiss old-
timer tells me that most vegetables, cabbages especially,
will grow more magnificently in Alaska than in his own
country, if you plow the ground deep as soon as the surface
has thawed and give the plants plenty of water when they
are set out.   After that, he says, water seems to seep up as
the ground thaws farther down, so that most of the things
he plants do well—unless you weaken their drawing powers
by watering them.

There are very good gardens as far north as Bettles and
Wiseman, site of Alaska's most northern mines, where the
thermometer drops below 80° in winter.   Huge root vegetables, immense cabbages; yet Alaska grew almost no
vegetables for sale until Matanuska was opened to colonists.   Probably there is as much good farming land in
Alaska, conclude its optimists, as in all the North Atlantic
States down to the Potomac.   But there are barely a thousand farmers—unless you want to count gardeners growing only their own flowers and vegetables.

A group of Denver business men recently filed incor-
poration articles for an organization that is to attempt
colonization in Alaska with European refugees and American unemployed.   Mormon leaders visited Fairbanks and
vicinity last summer with the idea of starting a colony
there; they plan to send up a few families the first year,

eventually perhaps as many as a thousand families. "Alaska's Dictator," our current Secretary of the Interior, recently suggested, perhaps with his tongue in his cheek, that we open Alaska to Jewish refugees. Well, it's already wide open to any one who can get there; all they have to do is go up there and dig in, as other Alaskans have done. But with all their multifarious virtues Jews are hardly the people Alaska needs, unless you put a ball and chain on them. The problem of course would be how to keep them from abandoning the farm work Alaska needs most and hurrying back to the cloak-and-suit business in New York City; and if they do remain in Alaska, to make them stay on their farms instead of offering disastrous competition to the local Alaskan merchants.

Alaska has more coal than Illinois and Pennsylvania combined, experts tell us; and late reports say there is an almost unlimited amount of oil. But Alaskans continue to burn mainly wood, though wood "costs expensive" in places like Fairbanks. And by the way, there are millions of acres of peat in Alaska; huge hills of sulphur . . . oh, yes, Russian America has turned out to be well worth what we paid for it.

Somehow we carried home from our mere summer there the perhaps quite erroneous impression that there are more he-men to the square mile (or at least to the hundred square miles) in Alaska than in any other place under the Stars and Stripes. Jack London, Rex Beach *et al* gave us for a generation the notion that Alaskans are constantly engaged in hand-to-hand fights and tests of physical strength, gambling away fortunes on the throw of a card, regular movie heroes and villains. There is, or has been, some of that. But if you take your Alaska from Alaskan novels and movies you'll have about as false an idea of it as even Hollywood, with all its advantages, could manufacture. As a matter of fact Alaska has always been a peaceful country, or at least Alaskans never were tough

in the Wild West sense, and your true prospector or fron-
tiersman often has a quiet and gentle way about him which
makes city people seem noisy bullies by comparison.

All Alaskan (and Yukon Territory) towns are so conscious of their wicked past that they now have, or at least
strive to have, some of the atmosphere of an old ladies'
sewing circle, remind you a bit of the reformed sinner who
shouts of his past sins at a Salvation Army meeting. Luckily there are lots of hard drinkers and the like to wipe this
vapid smile off the communal faces. It is still a virile,
able-bodied land, where spacious spittoons and ribald jokes
have not lost their vogue—though some of their heavy
witticisms have a painfully inept Outside tang. Here's
one, for instance, told in all solemnity over cards and
whisky in the backroom of a saloon: "D'ye hear about the
tourist lady whose hat blew off between Seward 'n' Curry?
So next morning she jest ordered flapjacks and saved one
of 'em and pinned it on—an' nobody ever noticed, for she
was right in style—no, not even when she couldn't find
here in Fairbanks what the ladies nowadays call a hat an'
wore the flapjack back down to Seward an' Outside."

You've missed most of—the only point to this little
anecdote unless you noticed that talk of the other sex in
the backrooms of Alaskan saloons is likely to be highly
respectful rather than bawdy. In Alaska women, white
women, that is, are all "ladies," until they simply have
forfeited that title to the point where the use of it would
seem sarcastic. After that they drop to the bottom; they
are "sluts" or "broads."

Yes, it is even today a stalwart, he-man place, though it
is gradually improv—I mean changing, tending little by
little to become more and more like everywhere else, God
help us. Like most frontiers it is no place for those with
overrefined sensibilities: no Alaskan, as far as my experience goes, ever closes a door without slamming it. To do
that would, I assume, verge on being a "sissy." Dish-

washing, at least in public eating-places, falls just short of
smashing each dish as it is set down. Hobnailed boots
thump down the hotel corridor in the small hours like
a squadron of cavalry. It is a fine place to go for those
with hardy muscles, nerves, tastes; others do not always
find it quite so entrancing.

I never saw a tuxedo in Alaska—though for all I know
Sourdough chests may be full of them. Another delightful
thing about the place is that there are no secrets. You
know almost every one and all about him, because the
population is so thin. The telephone operator tells all.
"Yes, they have a bathtub down there. It's been crated
five years." You may suddenly hear repeated verbatim
the whole conversation between a new husband and bride,
and that sort of thing. Entertainment is scarce, and tid-
bits of gossip sometimes take its place. Better perhaps
to pin back your ears and listen rather than talk—which,
incidentally, is good advice, at least to the traveler, almost
anywhere.

Alaskan hospitality and good cheer seem to be catching.
Even men recently from commonplace towns in the East
take on an open-handedness, a frontier spirit, an expan-
siveness which they would never have developed at home.
Alaska stands for solitude, freedom from competition, or
at least is fairly free from the blinding speed and shat-
tering noise and painful overcrowding of modern "life."
There is a certain independence of job slavery; depressions
and other distresses of large cities are scarcer there; Alaska
has real American energy and initiative, yet the senseless
rush of our East is not in the Alaskan's philosophy.

Given any isolated community of intelligent people and
they are so anxious not to be considered backward that
they are usually a little more given to intellectual pursuits
than people Outside. I have already mentioned that
Alaska seems to have an above the average vocabulary;
people you would not expect to in other climes, read good

Walrus-skin blanket tossing is a popular Eskimo sport even in Nome

On the beach at Nome, where scrap iron is abundant

King Island children in summer garb at Nome

Once this beach relic at Nome graced the now defunct Seward Peninsula Railroad

books, listen to good music. The long dark winters, the lack of other entertainment, the scarcity of wives or even less agreeable companions, seem to make men educated who might have ended their days much less so Outside, where distractions are legion.

Alaska is still the land of wooden matches, and he-men snap 'em alight with a thumbnail. It used to be a communal insult to put a padlock on your house, cabin, cache. If you were hungry or cold you could go in anywhere and help yourself; the worst crime was, and in some parts still is, to use a man's firewood without cutting more. Now locks are almost universal in places like Fairbanks. Still, "people are not always after your money the way they are Outside. When Alaska gets that civilized I'll move on north"—the speaker was already sixty-five, both in age and latitude.

I wish I could say baldly and categorically that there are no social lines in Alaska. It is a first-name country; a "lady" may dance with a man who digs sewers without damage to her social standing. But the character of Fairbanks at least is changing, and they say that Juneau "is as cliquey as Washington, D. C." The universal hospitality of earlier days is beginning to wear thin even in villages, and social distinctions are tending to become as ridiculous as they are Outside.

I have been speaking thus far of course of the whites; the natives and the "breeds" are a class apart, except among those who work for their advancement, or in isolated places where they are in the overwhelming majority. "Siwash" (fish-eater) means any one with native blood, in any degree, and there is a sneer in the word. To "go siwashing" means to live off the country, to subsist on what the natives eat. Natives of higher rank resent the term, which in the olden days was applied only to their lower classes. But the whites are as free with it as they are with the word "squaw man," which also always has a contemptuous connotation.

Personally I am not so horrified at the "squaw man" as some Alaskans purport to be. If you were up here for years without seeing a white woman . . . and seems to me a native wife would be preferable to an incompetent and discontented white wife who scorned this kind of land and climate and existence. Not that there aren't lots of competent and satisfied white women in places to which it hardly seems fair to bring one, women immensely superior to some of their sisters Outside. But there are by no means enough of them to go round. So . . .

But halfbreeds are no good, the typical Alaskan interrupts. The native mothers are too proud of their children with white man's blood in their veins; think they "have something" over other children—which they usually haven't—so they spoil them. Won't let them learn native jobs as native children do, so that in the end they are handicapped for life compared with the full-blooded natives. "The government rushes them to Eklutna by plane —they won't do that for my children; it's up to me to get them to school—and they come flying back again a few weeks later, also at government expense, because 'I didn't like it there.'"

The halfbreed girl at least, seems to have a problem on her hands as to whether she shall look up or down the social line for a husband. The Bishop of the lower Yukon cited the cases of two half-Indian girls in his congregation as examples of what they are up against. One, married to a white man, was bitter at not being accepted as his social equal, at lack of the luxuries she had known in school Outside. The other married an Indian, goes trapping and hunting with him, accepts life as she finds it and is happy.

Mathilda Holst, half-Indian, of Juneau, is a magnificent singer. Nutchuk (Simeon Oliver), an Eskimo from Unalaska, has made a name for himself in the United

States as a pianist, gatherer of folklore and folk-songs, lecturer and writer. Eskimos who have gone to the University of Alaska have brought with them just as good minds as the whites. But for the most part even the half-breeds seem to revert to native life.

Indians and Eskimos long fought each other in Alaska. On the whole they still do not mix, are said to hate and fear each other, though they are friendly enough where they do live together, as at Beaver on the Yukon. "Eskimo," by the way, is an Indian word meaning eaters of raw flesh; Eskimos call themselves Innuit, which is merely their word for "men." Old-timers tell me that in his native state the Eskimo is superstitious and afraid of all strangers; used to shoot them on sight, "because they might be bad men." All that of course is over, but the two native races of Alaska (Aleuts and Eskimos being closely akin) are very different in many ways. The sour-looking Indians are a contrast to the smiling Eskimos; there is sadness and disillusionment in Indian faces, not in Eskimos'. The Indian is impulsive; the Eskimo is slow to make up his mind, but once it is made up he sticks to it. Eskimos are friendly, cheerful, intellectual, industrious, hospitable, kind, unhurried, compared with Indians, say Alaskans who know them both; morally, intellectually and physically superior, a fun-loving people, fond of music and games, good-natured, peaceful. "Eskimos do not quarrel; if they don't like what is said or done they pick up their hat and beat it. Traders skin the Eskimo, as they do the Indian, but the Eskimo never holds a grudge. Whisky, however, makes him a brave man, and with a few shots of that under his belt he can even barge into a white man's saloon with the sign 'No Natives Allowed' staring him in the face."

Natives still have their pride, but the Eskimo is more likely than the Indian to swallow it on occasion. When some one sent word to an old Indian chief that it would be nice of him to pay his respects to President Harding the chief sent back word that Harding should come and see him; that, after all, he and his family had been chiefs centuries longer than this white man's chief. The nearest approach to that retort courteous attributed to an Eskimo came from a woman. A teacher sent a boy home one day with a note asking his mother to please wash him, as he smelled of fish. He came back with the note, bearing the endorsement, "You are supposed to teach him, not to smell him."

You should take time to see in the Juneau Museum, or in the lesser ones most other Alaskan towns of any self-importance maintain, how the Eskimos jumped overnight from the stone age to modern ways with the arrival of the white man. They used jade, stone, slate, ingenious skin-scrapers, made all sorts of ceremonial masks. Today the good-natured Eskimos are no longer self-supporting; can't live by their own wits, as their fathers did. But they have not yet attained all the finesse of civilization. Eskimos now chew gum instead of blubber, and gum becomes communal property, to the delight of the tuberculosis germ. But do our chewing-gum millionaires care? Eskimos still tan skins with urine—and do they smell! In spite of self-sacrificing doctors, nurses and teachers under the Bureau of Indian Affairs, child mortality is high among the natives of Alaska, because most of them still live uncleanly. Epidemics decimate them. In 1918 two out of three natives in a large section of the country died of the flu; the natives of Tonsina *all* died. Where there were seven villages on the lower Yukon (or was it the Seward Peninsula?) there were so few survivors left that they were gathered together into one village. To look at the round, oily faces of the Eskimos you would expect them to survive almost anything. But looks evidently are deceiving.

Tuberculosis was unknown among the Eskimos, Father LaFortune told me, and they were very healthy in most

other respects until the white man came.   Then they died
of his simplest diseases: whooping-cough, measles, even
chickenpox.   There is still no tuberculosis among those
who live by themselves.   Contrary to popular belief, there
are no igloos, that is, no snow houses in Alaska, never have
been, as far as records show.   The Eskimos of Alaska do
not even know how to make them, though they may man-
age something of the sort when caught out in a blizzard.
Over to the east of Barrow, on the Canadian side, on
Herschel Island, for instance, and out on the ice on the
shallow Arctic Ocean, the snow house of popular fiction
does exist, but not in Alaska.

Uncle Sam is far more solicitous of his native wards in
Alaska than of his nephews Outside.   But he is still letting
the trader skin them, say missionaries and others who have
the good of the natives at heart.   Drink, they specify, is
ruining the Indian and the Eskimo, except in the few places
where they cannot get it.   The Bishop of the Catholic
mission along the lower Yukon told us Indians were increasing there, until the government allowed them liquor—
and when an Irish Catholic talks like a prohibitionist
things must be bad indeed.

"There are three kinds of people who should never
drink: Us Irish, the Indians and the Eskimos.   Liquor is
to the Indians what 'coke' is to the white man.   Once he
gets to drinking, an Indian or an Eskimo sells all his skins
for liquor.   Now that they have liquor they are doomed.
But the government says they must have all the rights of
citizens, including the right to drink themselves into the
grave—though it doesn't give them other citizenship
rights, widows' pensions, for instance.   Women and children die because their men trade their furs for drink
instead of feeding their families, and undernourishment
soon brings on tuberculosis.

"Traders have no conscience.   They want to get rich
quick and go Outside.   One of our traders at Nulato

boasts that he can nearly always pay off his native workers in liquor; won't hire those he can't. Traders threatened the Indians who signed the anti-liquor petition. Politicians and the liquor interests go hand in hand. Too many liquor dealers are commissioners; there is an ex-bootlegger in the Legislature."

I was laboring under the impression, until I came to Alaska, that it was a penal offense to sell or give hard liquor to Indians, at least on reservations, in the United States, as it still is in Canada. But it seems that on June 2, 1924, Congress granted citizenship to all Indians (which of course includes Aleuts and Eskimos) born in the United States, if they gave up their tribal customs. Thus the repeal of prohibition automatically gave them legal access to liquor; or, where local prohibition prevailed, once they had the vote they promptly voted themselves liquor. Now Alaska's natives are signing petitions asking the Territorial Legislature to please make them stop drinking; in some villages the entire adult population has petitioned the law-makers to forbid the sale of liquor to natives.

The Legislature is considering granting the natives their petition, even at the risk of such a law being ruled unconstitutional. For as the natives of Alaska are Uncle Sam's wards, as we shall all soon be, many contend that only Congress can take liquor away from them. In his latest message to the Legislature, Governor Troy, on the spot between traders and Indians, says that requiring natives to get permits to buy liquor would solve the problem, whether or not the Territory establishes Territorial Liquor Stores. But as many of the commissioners who, obviously, would have the power to issue such permits are traders and liquor dealers that plan has a slightly brassy ring to it.

"This liquor trouble is overestimated," said the Governor's Secretary, as we flew from Fairbanks back to Juneau. "Probably a big majority of Indians and even more of the Eskimos never drink. They know 'that stuff

is not for me.' Take a place like Tanana Crossing down
there, or Lake Tetlin or places like that; the men are out
fishing or trapping most of the time and seldom if ever
get liquor."

Word comes just as this summer tale goes to the printer
that the "liquor interests," abetted by the influence of the
hard-drinking Indians in southeastern Alaska, managed to
keep the Legislature that has now ended its biennial session
from outlawing liquor to natives.

I like a nip myself now and then, but there is no doubt
that there is too much drinking in Alaska, even among the
whites. The Territory, statistics show, consumes eight times
as much liquor per capita as the United States as a whole.
Hard liquor can now be bought only in liquor stores and
cannot be consumed on the premises—the worst possible
plan, some Alaskans say, as men get several bottles each
and go to their cabins or their hotel rooms and drink all
night. Solitary drinking is worse than convivial drinking
anywhere, but particularly so among people inclined by
temperament or pioneer conditions to like their own company best. Once a man is drunk or a habitual drunkard,
it is illegal to sell him any more liquor. But in Alaska a
man visibly under the influence of liquor is given that
kindly toleration common in frontier society. I see by the
papers that now and then a man gets ninety days for being
drunk and disorderly; but on second look the names sound
suspiciously like those of natives.

Some of Alaska's law-makers want to change the present
$300 carry-it-away license to a $1,500 consume-it-on-the-
premises license. In fact, the latest report is that they
have done so. But that will bring back the old saloon,
protest those opposed to the plan. There are plenty of
saloons in Alaska now, but they call themselves beer parlors and can sell only beer and wine. Some restaurants
take out a beer-parlor license, but in most places you must
bring your hard liquor with you or go without.

Nearly all stores and all saloons are open on Sundays in Alaska. Good-looking gals behind the bars may look like immorality to newcomers from the States. But there is more than a mere Swedish accent up in Alaska, and the point of view on women in saloons, either as guests or barmaids, is more European than American. Besides, more often than not they are the pretty daughters of the proprietor and no one would dream of treating them as anything but ladies—at least in the presence of Papa and Mama. You can see the same thing in Wisconsin. But the American prejudice is creeping in upon them: Fairbanks has refused licenses this year to saloons—pardon me, beer parlors—employing barmaids.

Alaskans of course are great gamblers, as who isn't nowadays? It was a gamble that brought them there in the first place. The Territory, unlike every country, state and province south of the United States, cannot run a lottery. But—well, for instance, virtually every saloon has a gambling device known as a punchboard. Behind the bar hang a great collection of prizes, all manner of things, ranging from screwdrivers to radios, rifles, even an outboard motor, all wrapped in cellophane. Usually, too, ranged within a space fenced off from the rest of the room, there are several tables at which old-timers seem always to be playing cards, but overlooking the opportunities for wagers in the accuracy and distance of their spittoon marksmanship. Signs warn non-players to keep out of this restricted preserve. One might be back in the Middle West of my boyhood, except that now the noisy nickelodeons play the masterpieces of great masters like Irving Berlin instead of "Doris, My Doris" and other songs popular in '98.

Father Bernard LaFortune of King Island

Inside the Russian Orthodox church at St. Michael

On the boardwalk at St. Michael

Eskimo argument

Father Hubbard and Ed Levin threaten to subdue Harry, Jr.

Abandoned Yukon River steamers at St. Michael

CHAPTER XI

THE RICHARDSON HIGHWAY

We Hire a Car . . . There are Roads—and Roads . . . Paxson Lodge . . . Through the Gorge to Valdez . . . Bob Reeve . . . Copper River Indians . . . A Railroad That Was . . . Cordova . . . Tire Trouble, to Say the Least . . . Rescued by the Sourdough Express

WHAT used to be the Richardson Trail, laid out in 1905 by General Wilds P. Richardson, then president of the Alaska Road Commission, is now called a highway—shame on Uncle Sam! Still, Alaskans consider it quite a road. They say the government built it as a military precaution, but so far its chief function is to compete with Alaska's government railroad.

There are bi-weekly buses from Fairbanks to Valdez, 372 miles, and growing competition had brought the fare down to as little as $10 in one instance. But would we see all there is to see, have time to photograph all there is to photograph, by public conveyance? The answer is "Yes," but hindsight is only an annoyance. So we rented a car from the Fairbanks undertaker at a mere . . . but people tell me no one nowadays is interested in costs. The car was ten years old, lacked this and that, such as license plates, windshield-wiper, horn, brakes and a few other nonessentials, but who wants to be mistaken for a millionaire? Besides, a car in style would have cost nearly twice as much—which perhaps would have been cheaper in the end.

Some wit, I assume, rather than the Alaska Road Commission, put up the sign just out of Fairbanks: Radio City, 4699½ miles. Perhaps a road builder could explain why the Richardson Highway winds so incessantly, just to keep beside one river or lake after another. That summer Alaska had 2,292 cars, 1,176 trucks and 32 buses, not counting, I suppose, those that carry no license plates. But we met very few of them on the road to Valdez. Only fifty-one miles out of town is a fox farm; then came another forty miles of entrancing solitude. Once a road scraper all but sent our humble conveyance slithering into the forest-jungle alongside, but the driver looked as if he camped out by night. Once we came to a fork—and no sign, no house or other car for many miles. There were bright-yellow sheet-iron road signs almost every mile to cheer a struggling car and driver on, except that it had been some exhilarated Sourdough's funny idea to shoot the figures off them, and as usual there was no sign where one was most needed. We guessed right and ten slippery miles farther on found that the other fork would have taken us to Harding Lake, where the élite of Fairbanks goes to escape its deadly summer heat.

Mile after mile of scrub woods, broken here and there by even less vegetation. An aged kitchen stove stood rusting by the roadside. Now and then an eagle volplaned overhead. One man, they say, makes a living shooting eagles, on which there is a $2 bounty. The soil looked fertile in places; we heard that a tract of more than 10,000 acres somewhere along this northern end of the Richardson Highway was soon to be opened to homesteaders.

Some ninety miles out thoughtful Uncle Sam maintains a government ferry across the swift Tanana River. It is run by the current, ingeniously harnessed to an overhead cable, sparing the sad young man stationed there unnecessary exertion. Sign your name, pay a dollar—and no one seems to mind the lack of license plates. Gasoline was 40 cents, and there were leaks in both the tin pitcher and the funnel. There was a big log roadhouse, but no groceries or other portable supplies for a good many miles beyond. And some of the road between here and there was . . . "but there's a cat to pull you out if you get stuck."

Alaskans beg of you to remember that a road in Alaska is not the same thing as a road Outside. Alaska's 2,000 or so miles of roads (there are some 11,000 of government trails) cost Uncle Sam only between $6,000 and $7,000 a mile to build and not more than $10,000 a mile including maintenance to date. Compare that, they say, with the cost per mile of a good concrete highway Outside.

This far the road had clung tenaciously to its habit of following rivers, the one beside us now spreading out in half a dozen channels across a wide sandy bed. But soon it caught sight of lofty snowclads ahead and set out to climb them, bidding the river good-by. We ate canned beans in the wide open spaces, the sun burning our backs, though patches of ice in the ditches beside us showed that it would be uncomfortably cold there at midnight. The snowclads looked down upon us with something between a friendly welcome and a warning as our ancient car purred blithely past Pillsbury Dome, Black Rapids Glacier, Rainbow Mountain, then over the summit—what, only 3,310 feet above sea-level!

Tents obviously occupied at night by road workers stood at another unmarked fork, but there was no sign of the workers now, much less of the "cat" we came perilously near needing to get ourselves out of the slough that had once been the road. The unfinished new one descended to a highway almost worthy of the name, close along the green but treeless bluff shores of Summit Lake, six miles long, then of another lake. Here the road was thickly bordered with fireweed, on and on, endlessly, beautiful deep-pink flowers, often shoulder high.

Paxson Lodge, 180 miles from Fairbanks, might seem no day's run at all to Outside motorists, but they have not seen the Richardson Highway. The fishing, grayling especially, is so good there that Fairbanks has difficulty in keeping its dentist where ailing teeth congregate. Good living, rowboats thrown in, costs only standard roadhouse prices, and how one can sleep at 2,800 feet above tidewater in mountain solitude! The massive log walls of Paxson Lodge are half hidden by trophies: bear, moose, sheep and other heads and skins . . . somehow I was reminded of the head hunters of the Amazon. Excellent hunting thereabouts in season, said the proprietor; just the place for grizzlies, and he was corroborated by a chewing-gum millionaire with massive jaws who strode in after dark with fish enough to feed his multitude of consumers.

The Road Commission lodges, every log house along the way, had moose, or at least caribou, horns thrusting forth from the gable peak. Three miles north of Gulkana a road marked Nebesma, 105 miles, struck eastward toward one of Alaska's big mining centers. There are lodgings, meals, and in most cases groceries and gasoline at Gulkana, Copper Center, Tonsina Lodge and Tiekel Roadhouse, if weariness or mishap should overtake you. But the thirty miles or so between them is unadorned scenery. The last fifty miles into Valdez is through glorious mountain gorges with waterfalls leaping in suicidal fury, abysses at your left elbow, startlingly sharp turns at both ends of a bridge, the Devil's Elbow roaring at you from below . . . then what Valdez calls her Keystone Canyon opens out into a wider valley. Bigger and better fireweeds line the road for miles; the last few minutes is a procession of more bridges than I have ever seen so close together anywhere else: twenty-three of them, say those whose minds run to statistics, and six more beyond the town. For the glacier behind it comes down in many different channels as it melts, and has also forced Valdez to protect itself with a million-dollar dyke.

At first glimpse of the town you may wonder whether its preservation is worth any such sum. Valdez is not quite a ghost town, but it does give you for a moment the startling impression of having seen a ghost—town. It faces the Gulf of Alaska, in the form of a great fjord-like bay that opens out into Prince William Sound, and sits on the moraine of the glacier four miles back of it. In certain lights, or fogs, it is beautiful in an impressionistic sort of way.

Ten thousand seagulls—no, not by actual count, but I'll swear to it if you wish—circle in clouds over the broad mud flats in front of it, when the tide is out. Its mosquitoes hold high carnival even out at the end of two long plank-rumbling piers, but its scenery is grand. The mainly aged frame and not often painted houses of Valdez are a trifle better kept, perhaps, and the weeds not so high and omnipresent as in Skagway, the wooden sidewalks a little more continuous. But it is no longer one of Alaska's boom towns. Dan Wilcey is ready to sell his two-story store building, proudly inscribed with his name and a date early in the century. But civic pride has by no means died out in this town out on the toes of a glacier.

Like Skagway, Valdez has no shoemaker, and Harry sadly needed one. Here, surely, is a good opening for some one. Jimmie Fujii, who came to Alaska not long after "my good friend" Yasuda but went back to fight the Russian-Japanese war, runs one of the three not particularly epicurean restaurants. "They can't get me back to fight any more, though," says Jimmie. "Anyhow I'm too old. Yes, four Chinese in town; all my good friend."

Old-timers and a distinct Scandinavian accent hang about the Pinzon poolroom in Valdez. It was pleasant to sit close to the roaring upright-barrel stove—and hear the radio announce a great heat wave all over the United States. The local U. S. marshal, built like a steel post filed down to the essentials, sat watching a four-hand game which flourished noisily at his elbow. The stakes were higher than the garb of the players seemed to warrant; the marshal would have been a perfect illustration for a rip-roaring pulp-magazine sheriff of New Mexico or Arizona. He had worn his star for forty years, I believe he said. An old-timer of as hard-boiled mien sat at my other elbow, reading the book review section of a San Francisco paper and now and then displaying unerring marksmanship at a sawdust box some three yards away. At the pool and billiard tables the click of balls never ceased.

"Bill, you ought to go out and see Vancouver," said one of the stove circle to another.

"What fer?"

"It's changed a lot in thirty-five years."

"I'd be killed by them autymobiles."

"But you're already seventy-fi . . ."

"Seventy-four, an' good fer a lot o' prospecting yet. No, Alaska's good enough fer me. They can have their cities."

The sufficiency of Alaska for the average Sourdough is —I was going to say pathetic, but it is really the opposite. And Alaska's ex-foreigners are nearly all ardent Americans. Much as I have seen of the world and aware as I am of the faults of American life, this transfer of patriotism has always been incomprehensible to me. But in Alaska it is taken as a matter of course.

Anecdotes rambled on, broken by interest in the jackpots.

"Remember the man in the blue parky, the only hold-up man ever to come to Fairbanks? I'll never forget that marshal walking up to him where he sat on the end of the bridge an' takin' his gun away from him, walking him off to jail like a boy'd run away from school. Got twenty-five years, didn't he, Marshal?"

"Yeah. But he escaped every time they shut him up and finally, during the war, from Leavenworth."

The subject changed too fast for me to find out who or what the man in the blue "parky" held up, why his parka was blue. . . .

"Remember the two Swedes, didn't know pay-dirt from muck, that came along up the creek [what creek didn't seem to matter] and asked where there was a good place to prospect. An' the fellers that were panning sent 'em to a tree on up the creek, as a joke—an' bust my suspenders if they didn't get rich there!"

"Wonder what ever become of Kendall, who turned down one claim way up his creek because he thought there was nothing there and a greenhorn took $10,000 out of it and got rich with the saloon he bought with it Outside. Kendall never heard of it until years later, when he was marshal and the greenhorn, up here bulging with diamonds, told the bar about it without knowing who Kendall was. You should have seen Kendall's face!"

Some one else called up from the past two partners who quarreled on the trail, killed each other, or at least both died, and their dogs came back without them. Another reminiscence concerned a young prospector who told the men crowded around him at a bar, as a joke, that he had washed out a pokeful of gold in half an hour somewhere or other, which started a stampede there. The stampeders found no signs of gold, but on the way back they met a bigger crowd on the way up—and among them was the original joker! He had heard talk of a new strike and had forgotten where he had located his mythical pokeful of gold.

The stories came too thick and fast to set them down. One concerned a man who, given the job of digging a grave in stony ground at 45° below zero, sawed both the corpse and the coffin in two. At Dawson in the rush days "Two-step Jake" (Hirsh, if I got the name right) gave Sweet Marie, a shockingly well-built blonde, $10,000 to teach him the new-fangled two-step. Jake, it seemed, was still living at Tenekee, a cabin resort some miles out of Juneau, a sprightly lad of eighty-four summers, flowing Buffalo Bill-ish hair on both his head and face. Wild about Mae West, some one said, though he had never had his picture taken with her, as Martin Itzen of Skagway did.

Some one mentioned Miller Gulch on Slate Creek, some distance from Valdez, I gathered, as distances go Outside, but right next door in Alaska. It was named for the father of Nancy Anne Miller, who, you remember, married an Indian rajah. She was born and her father made a fortune up here in Alaska, it seemed—and maybe up here where squaw men and their descendants are numerous she absorbed less than the average American prejudice for other races.

"The filthy old cuss!" said the Swede landlady of the Seattle Hotel, one of two in Valdez, as she came out of his room with a covered receptacle next morning. "But he's an old-timer and sick, and somebody has to take care of him until the judge can send him to Sitka. If he wasn't an old-timer . . ."

There is a sort of unofficial brotherhood of old-timers of both sexes in Alaska that is engaging. She hadn't been Outside in thirty-five years herself, the landlady added, as she hobbled on down the not exactly immaculate hallway.

At the other Valdez hotel I met Gordon Bettles, hale and hearty at 79, for whom a town on the upper Koyukuk is named. Born in Detroit, Bettles came to Alaska in 1886 and is the only one left of the seventeen early white men on the Yukon. There he had trading posts; printed the first (1890) Yukon newspaper; now priceless; lost the usual fortune. He has lived not only at Bettles but at Akiak, Bethel; lives now on Chanega Island, on the coast, where his wife is a community worker and teacher.

"There were four hundred of us came up in 1886, but two hundred of them got cold feet and turned back. Forty of us came here from Montana, and forty went to Africa.

We were all offered a good job on the Rand, Transvaal, at good wages, but I was afraid of the heat. So I stuck up a stick and it fell north. . . . And you know, nearly all the forty who went to Africa came back rich; ten to fifty thousand pounds apiece.

"The *Ancon* and the *Bruno,* old sidewheelers, were the only boats running to Alaska when I came in. There was one store in Juneau. When you outfitted you had to have two canoes to carry what you couldn't get along without. Six weeks in an open canoe, with an Indian at a hundred dollars a week, to get from Juneau to Dyea; fifteen dollars a pound for an Indian to carry your stuff only to the summit. Then you hauled it yourself, 'by the neck,' to Lake Bennett—no dogs then; no one knew about dogs—and built a boat. Took three trips to haul your outfit to the lake. . . ."

"There's no fixed sleeping time in Alaska in summer," explained Hal Selby, dean of Alaska editors and the one-man staff of the Valdez newspaper. I had remarked on the emptiness of the morning streets. "I make myself get to work on the linotype at eight, regular as clockwork, but nobody else gets up until ten, least of all in winter." Perhaps it is because he gets up early in the morning that most of Alaska dotes on Hal's pungent editorials, served with a sprinkling of humor, but straight from the shoulder and no holds barred.

In the Valdez museum guns large and small, covering almost the whole history of firearms, testify how many different nationalities wandered along the coasts of Alaska in the early days: Spaniards, Englishmen, Frenchmen, Russians, Captain Cook, LaPerouse, Arteaga, Golivin, von Kotzebue, Fidalgo, Malaspina. . . . The brutality of the Russians is attested by a huge ball and chain such as once adorned natives working in the mines on the Kenai Peninsula. In those days the natives now and then struck back at the white men they now accept without visible protest.

One Russian party of twenty-three was killed during the night by native women whose men they had captured.

It used to take a week and cost $600 to $700 a ton to get supplies to miners up on the glaciers behind Valdez. Now Bob Reeve flies them up at one-tenth that, though his rates are a hundred dollars a day. The hardy aviators of Alaska carry anything and fly anywhere, but Reeve makes a specialty of landing on glaciers. In Valdez he is called the "human ptarmigan." He estimates that he has flown a million pounds of freight to those tough babies who mine up there *under* the glaciers; has lost count of the number of sick men, dead men he has brought down.

The airplane makes possible eleven mines up there now, where there was only one when Reeve came to Valdez. Old-time prospectors would be amazed at the places now being mined by the use of airplanes. Up there behind Valdez quartz knobs protrude here and there above the perpetual ice and in these men dig horizontal tunnels, run narrow-gauge tracks back into the very rich mountain (up to $100 a ton in "values"), cut the white-streaked stuff out in man-made caverns with pneumatic drills, work stopes from the bottom with compressed air.

Reeve uses skis even in summer, flying from the mud flats just a bridge or two west of town to his glacier landings. He says mud, at least this mud, makes the best of take-offs. But his skis with stainless steel bottoms are very expensive, at least by Outside standards—"cost only $300," is the way he puts it—when he makes them himself. They slip in the mud as if it were greased, take off in a surprisingly short distance, though he must rock the "ship" to overcome the suction. He has made two thousand landings on glaciers, bringing iron pipes, bulky machinery, drums of gasoline, anything you can get into a plane. Sometimes he drops his cargo instead of landing: he has dropped thousand-pound loads of dynamite, at least 30,000 pounds by now, in bags. The boxes burst open, sometimes are reduced to kindling-wood (most welcome to the miners) but the sticks are intact. Once he dropped a Diesel engine—by parachute; and it was working two hours later.

Reeve once flew for Pan American Airways down in South America when passengers by air were pioneers. He has two Fairchild monoplanes—though one was cracked up just then—no mechanic; does all his own work. He's that kind of man, the sturdy individualist type that finds Alaska still a happy hunting ground. The plane he was using now was ten years old and had once cracked up before he bought and repaired it. One must circle round and round to get altitude in the mountain pocket where Valdez sits. In winter it takes hours to thaw out the oil and get a plane started. It was hard to judge snow landings, at first. Blinded by sun glare he dived headlong into the snow against the mountain the first time, was stuck in soft snow for five days. He carries no radio, though he has a wife and child, not to mention a mother-in-law, down in Valdez. The rule is that he will be home again when he gets there. His twin brother, in government service, was killed by lightning not long ago while flying a plane in the States. But to Reeve, if not to his family, it is all in the day's work.

It was Bob Reeve who flew Bradford Washburn, of Harvard and the National Geographic Society, over much of that part of Alaska for the pictures he was developing in Valdez when we were there. Flown by Bob Reeve, Brad had discovered a glacier at least a hundred miles long in a place marked simply "mountains" on the map, stretching from Mount St. Elias to the Copper River. A fringe of mountains hides it and the glaciers we see along the coast are mere tongues of it, minute by comparison.

Reeve offered to fly me up onto a glacier. But there was heavy fog next morning; a great blanket of clouds had wiped out all that panorama of mountains that encircle Valdez. I got Reeve out of bed, but it might be hours, days, even weeks before any one could land on a glacier; and Time is inexorable with the most vagabondish of us.

The journey inland through the Keystone Canyon and over that 2,722-foot pass is, if anything, more graced with nature's beauties, and difficulties, than the trip down to the coast. An hour out of town the sky was so clear that I could practically see myself landing on a glacier. Ninety-two miles above Valdez a fork leads southeastward to Chitina, thirty-nine miles farther on. Chitina is a railroad town, built for the railroad, like Anchorage, though in this case the government was not the builder. The railroad should have been built from Valdez, not merely its own citizens contend. But in 1907 half a million dollars was raised to keep the Guggenheims from getting the right of way up Keystone Canyon. But they called in Michael J. Heney, builder of the White Pass Railroad, and he ran a railroad up from Cordova kitty-cornered between the two great glaciers of the Copper River, where experts said it was impossible. The fight over that enterprise is one of the most vivid in Alaskan history. Even critical old-timers say that "The Iron Trail," by Rex Beach, in spite of being fiction, is very nearly a true story of that episode.

The Copper River Railroad cost the Kennicott Copper Company $17,000,000, they say. And now the mine was about to be abandoned. But don't rush out and sell your Kennicott Copper stock on the strength of that tip. The mines at McCarthy, 195 miles inland from Cordova, 65 above Chitina, are but minor holdings of the company as a whole, which is said to have taken $200,000,000 worth of copper down this railroad in thirty years.

Chitina claims less rainfall than any other inhabited place in Alaska. The sunshine fairly flooded it, in its little hollow among the mountains, both times I saw it. Resi-

dents say it is just the place for a health resort, and that
this district should be kept open as a national park. Let
the Alaska Road Commission take it over and if the railroad is abandoned all you'll have to do is to put flanges
on your automobile tires, pull your steering wheel out by
the roots and you'll have a train of your own. Chitina's
main hotel will be boarded up, in the hope that the government will take over the railroad (and cut the fares in half)
or at least make it over into a highway up to McCarthy,
Kennicott Copper's mining town. But Congress probably
won't authorize that half million dollar dream.

Time was when the Copper River was thick with Indian villages. Now there were only 123 Copper River
Indians left, all in a village barely a mile out of Chitina.
Already they were getting ready to move away, convinced
that Chitina is doomed to die. There are those who believe that the Copper River valley offers better opportunities for pioneering farmers than Matanuska. But the
Indians of this region "are on their way out; low types
now, especially the young ones." William Delehant and
his wife, from Colorado by way of similar work for the
Bureau of Indian Affairs in New Mexico, had been here
ten years now. They have filled in the sloping fringe of
the mountain rising high behind them to make a garden;
have built a greenhouse; give tomatoes to the Indians,
two a week to the sick. They smoke salmon; can them
in their own canning plant; coax the Indians to tend their
fish wheels, spasmodically, and to go trapping. The women
sew and make moccasins, now grow vegetables and can
them, too, as well as berries. They put away these things
in the cellar of the school for the winter, each marked with
the owner's name. But when one family's stock runs out
the rest is common property to them; an old Indian custom.

Missionary backwoods type, the Delehants, but sincere
and hardworking beyond Outside understanding; the salt
of the earth. They keep orphan or misused Indian chil-

dren in their own home at one end of the school building. "Some of the children are bright, but none of them will ever go very high and they would revert to type if they were taken Outside.

"Our Cordova Indians are the worst drunks on the coast; they would drink whisky if they saw you putting strychnine in it. They are unmitigated liars. They will do anything to get a ride. But that's the Indian of it. Down in New Mexico a man sent us word that an old woman was dying at his village. We rushed out there in our Ford, dust thicker than clouds. 'Oh, she's all right now,' said the old man, when we got out there in the hills. 'But can I ride back with you? I want a ride to town.' Here a man shot himself through the hand just to get a ride in an airplane."

The Delehants do not use profane language, of course, no matter what the provocation, but . . . "the dog-skinned rascal!"

Almost all the Indians were still asleep when I came out again at ten next morning. Uncle Sam has provided them with good houses, but they are still Indians in their house-keeping. They have electric lights from the Chitina power-plant; piped water (by gravity) in that Indian village. Yet it is hard work to get them to carry two buckets of water an hour to the icehouse. But . . . "oh, yes, the chief here is a fine man. He's as distressed as we are at the way the young people—and they don't often live as long as he has, you know—are going to the dogs."

The chief himself was big and sturdy, with the look of a man who could face difficulties single-handed. His wife, too, had a self-reliant air that recalled the old days when the Indians of what is now Alaska needed no man's help to win their constant battle against nature. But there was lit-tle left of this spirit, unless looks were deceiving, among the late-sleeping young men and women and the puling infants living in discomfort of the Indians' own making in the adequate framework village Uncle Sam had provided for them. Many of the population had only begun to stir when I left the place at noon.

The fare is (or was) ten cents a mile on the Copper River Railroad, which is why Harry stayed in Chitina while I went down to Cordova—with a corpse. The train was of three cars, one of copper ore in bulk, one of concentrates in sacks, one a combination passenger and baggage car, with five living passengers. The baggage compartment door stood open, perhaps to give the corpse a feeling of fellowship. Flowers in tin cans—but why leave the labels still on them? Some of them read a little incongruously beside a coffin.

It had been one of those freak accidents. A boulder ten or twelve feet high had been left standing upright on bedrock years ago. The dead man, 62, was cleaning the bedrock seams with a trowel, a hose playing on those around him to loosen the valuable deposits. The boulder suddenly toppled; the man ran. But as the boulder struck bedrock a piece of it flew off and struck him. . . . "He wouldn't have lived eleven days if he hadn't been tough," said one of his four Scotch, Canadian-born brothers. "Only two of us left now." The weeping younger brother had flown from Los Angeles to Seattle and from Cordova to the mine in that little red plane we had seen over Chitina yesterday. But he had been too late to say good-by.

They say a flourishing Arctic glacier underlies all this semi-tropical vegetation along the Copper River Railroad. Trees have no tap roots, the Delehants had told us, radishes grow half above the ground, as if they were trying to get away from the ice underneath; and they are crooked and misshapen from this cringing from the ice only two to four feet beneath the surface. Telephone poles sink out of sight as the ice melts beneath them. Huge holes that must be filled in often appear suddenly close beside or even under the railroad.

Three hundred to three hundred and fifty railroad men, including bridge, maintenance and other gangs, were all to lose their jobs. They had a union; the company tried to dominate it, so eighteen months before, they had joined the CIO. But what can you do, even with the help of a union, if your job drops out from under you? "I'll stay here and fish rather than go Outside on the dole," said the old-timer who posed as conductor.

Another of the world's remarkable pieces of railroad engineering, this line is a little less acrobatic, perhaps, than some sections of the White Pass or that first fifty miles out of Seward on the Alaska Railroad. But Heney must have had his work cut out for him. When there are tourists along, the train stops between those two mountains of ice while trainmen holler off pieces of the glaciers for them. Huge masses of Miles and Child glaciers fall off by themselves, too, making veritable tidal-waves, endangering that million-dollar bridge between them.

A gang of hard-bitten, angular faces got on at a tent-camp stop, shouldering their bundled belongings. Huge old machinery, big iron plates were rusting away in the "jungle" alongside. But a carload of ties on a siding, waiting for us to give them the right of way up-country, hardly looked like abandonment. There were still men in Cordova who thought the company was bluffing.

Cordova is a lively town, at least compared with Valdez. (It's bad enough to have to mispronounce those two Spanish-named towns, as all Alaskans do, without having also to misspell one of them.) Valdez is grown up to weeds; Cordova less so—though now that the railroad has actually been abandoned it may become more so. It has a picturesque, perhaps a practically strategic, situation on a low neck of land between the sea and a long lake, roads in several directions. Rushing glacier water like the outlet of Gargantua's wife's washtub comes down to the sea. Flocks of seagulls sit patiently on huge boulders, watching

Harry adds an Eskimo pal to his collection

A home in Teller, waterworks, dog-sled and all

Unloading supplies for the winter at Teller

At Tin City walrus-skin boats with outboard motor brought us four tons of tin ore each

for dinner; the eyes of the salmon are a favorite dish with them.

Some of Cordova's public buildings are imposing, its hotels and eating-places numerous, many of its homes more sumptuous, inside at least, than those who have never been to Alaska would expect. Filipinos, Indians and Scandinavians roam its one short business street. It was wide open on Sunday, the saloons until late at night; long well-patronized bars, girl bar-tenders, spittoons, busy gambling tables. There seemed to be commercial love for those who wanted it.

There is at least one ex-slave left in Alaska, a small limping Indian with almost no power of speech, whom a charitable chain-store clerk keeps in cigars. It seems that even after Alaska became American territory illegitimate children among the Indians were beaten on the head until they were half silly and given to the chiefs as slaves. Their tendons were cut so that they could not run away, and apparently in some cases their tongues were mutilated so that they could not talk too much. I met, too, Judd Harris, the local grave-digger, from Belfast by way of the coal mines of Pennsylvania, who insisted on showing me that grave-digging may be more certain but is less easy than prospecting. Rock and frozen ground and trees make $15 to $18 a grave no sinecure. Then, too, with an average of only eighteen graves a year . . . "and some bad years there are hardly a dozen."

Harry had gone on with a Road Commission truck, with the privilege of driving another from Gulkana to Paxson Lodge, where he hoped to get in some fishing. I should have joined him there by ten that night but for the fact that nails are sometimes dropped even on the Richardson Highway. It took me an hour in the half-moonlighted road to change so old-fashioned a tire. No one at Paxson Lodge knew any better than I how to patch a tire of that vintage, especially with no materials with which to do it.

So we went on next morning hoping for good luck, which we didn't have. Hardly ten miles north we were left with only three tires, and not a sign of humanity except the road during an hour of waiting and hoping in the rain.

I had heard the expression "riding on the rim," though I had never tried it until now. I don't recommend it. For even the rim began to show signs of disintegration hardly two miles beyond. I walked another slippery mile in the rain, but even the foreman of the road camp had no luck with the spare tire. So we abandoned our ancient conveyance, still 150 miles from Fairbanks, got a hop in a Road Commission truck to another tent camp and a road-makers' dinner, coaxed a road man to drive us to a place called Rapids, where there is a roadhouse, but could coax him no farther.

All this would have been trivial but for the fact that we were booked to fly from Fairbanks to Nome the next morning, just in time to catch, we hoped, the Alaska Steamship Company's only cruise to Siberia that summer. The young couple keeping the roadhouse could offer us nothing but food and lodging and condolences, a very welcome hot stove and the use of their telephone. We discovered that it costs nothing to telephone up and down the Richardson Highway—unless you call Fairbanks. From there, none of the roadhouses to the south having any knowledge of north-bound trucks, we got a promise that some one would be sent to our rescue. But the promise never materialized. Weeks later we learned that "just as we were getting ready to send a car for you somebody phoned us to come and get a man who had shot himself and" . . . naturally a dead man took precedence over two impatient live ones.

Finally, tired of looking at the black glacier across the way and the heavy rain and heavier clouds that made it useless to call for a plane from Fairbanks, Alaskan fashion, we had about decided to go to bed and forget Nome, or Siberia at least, for this life—when that day's one and only north-bound truck turned up at 9:30. But the driver refused to take more than one passenger! He said, as he ate a leisurely Alaskan roadhouse meal, that the road was too dangerous with a crowded cab, and that anyway he always had his dog with him.

Kept out of Siberia by a dog! We couldn't blame him for feeling that way about the road, but—well, world wandering does at least develop one's powers of persuasion. Hours later Frank White, the driver, confided to us that he was an avid travel-book fan and had guessed my identity before he had finished his meal in the roadhouse, otherwise . . . thus do a man's past sins now and then come to his rescue in the nick of time. So at ten we were off in the rain and mud, all cramped in the cab of a Sourdough Express truck more or less loaded with groceries, the dog definitely resenting trying to sleep on two laps (and he was no lap dog) instead of his accustomed three-quarters of the seat.

The ferry across the Tanana goes on a strike from midnight until dawn, but we made it at 11:59. Here we got first-hand information on one of Alaska's grievances, at least of Fairbanks and beyond. The truck was weighed, first the front wheels, then the back ones, on a little weighing machine, by a man who very much resembled a customs officer whose duties obliged him to get up in the middle of the night and in a heavy rain. After a long calculation he collected toll on the weight of the groceries—and of our baggage. That could pass free only in a private car. Toll is 2½ cents a ton-mile, which works out at about $9.28 a ton. It has been collected ever since freight coming in over the highway began to compete with the Alaska Railroad. Nothing is charged on truckloads coming as far north as the ferry, but only on those crossing it; which is Fairbanks' chief grievance against "the colonel" in particular and Uncle Sam in general. They say that if toll were charged on all trucks, or all cars, using the highway it would be all right with them (I wonder), at least if the toll income were spent on up-keep of the road. "But Uncle Sam gets it and no one knows what he does with it."

An hour beyond the ferry the road got more slithery and narrow and winding than ever and I volunteered to go back and sleep with the groceries. Luckily they were all in cartons instead of wooden boxes. I had almost dropped off to sleep once or twice when the truck came to a definite halt and my two fellow-travelers lifted the back curtain. We were right in front of the Nordale Hotel in Fairbanks and the time was 6:30 A.M. Barely time to shave and bathe and repack and re-dress and dash to the airport—for this time of course the plane was not held up "waiting for weather."

CHAPTER XII

ON ACROSS ALASKA

*West of Honolulu . . . Nome After the Fire
. . . The "Midnight Merchant" . . . They're
Still Panning the Beach . . . King Island Eski-
mos . . . Father Hubbard and His Bodyguard
. . . Fathers LaFortune and Cunningham*

THERE were thirty-four gadgets by actual count on the dashboard of that Electra on which we made our aerial pierhead jump. It carried eight passengers to Nome, most of them one-day round-trippers. When I looked out again we were flying 9,300 feet up, over a complete eiderdown blanket of clouds. We regassed at Ruby and were off again . . . came at length out of the clouds above a treeless, though bushy, brown and yellow-brown landscape of Alaskan tundra, with probably more water than land area. Twice clusters of reindeer in corrals slipped past beneath us. Otherwise I saw no evidence of animal life, and only a rare village along the southern coast of the Seward Peninsula. Sledge Island rose in the sea dead ahead. Both King and Sledge Islands were named by that Captain Cook who came to so violent an end on the island of Hawaii. We circled low over what looked rather like the ruins of a never very important city and sat down at the airfield a mile outside it. A dog-team from Fairbanks to Nome costs $1,000 and takes eleven days. Now one flies it in four hours at less than one-tenth that expense.

Nome is 250 miles *west* of Honolulu. We were one-fourth the way around the world from home, six (in summer seven) hours behind the Atlantic seaboard in time.

Luckily, for it takes time to find lodging in Nome. You may remember that Nome nearly disappeared from the map a few years ago. Fire started in the Golden Gate Hotel on September 17, 1934, fortunately in the daytime, and destroyed half the town, especially the business section. Several persons were burned to death. It left nothing several blocks wide along the sea-front, almost the full length of the town.

Though some of it has been built up again Nome is still the world's worst city in which to get hotel accommodations. The few rooms in what purports to be the best and is certainly the cleanest hotel were full; the other, overlooked by the fire, was anything but inviting. But the lapping of the waves on the beach just below us helped to make up for that grocery truck ride. In fact, the room Harry drew had an all-glass western wall through which we could see only the Bering Sea, giving the impression that we had reached the end of the world.

The Nomites were nearly all caught without insurance when their big fire came and the town, they say, would have reverted to a native village but for that 70% rise in the price of gold. Once it had 2,500 inhabitants; now— well, the last census credited it with 1,213, but the guess is that there are 1,500 people there now in winter and nearly twice that number in summer.

Nome is not a handsome city, though on the whole we very much liked its people. Its big new Federal building, covering a block, was nearing completion; it has a larger and no less modern school than any city of equal size Outside. Its very wide main street, alternately muddy and dusty in summer, is lined more or less continuously on both sides by more one- than two-story frame buildings, all in the architectural style of a Nevada frontier town. But its stores are adequate and just then at least well stocked. Prices are not quite so high in Nome, where steamers come in summer, as in Fairbanks. The best citizens wanted no

shops on the sea side of the main street, which would have
given the place a vista across a very wide beach all the
way to Asia, as far as atmospheric conditions ever permit.
But merchants had real estate holdings and private property is still private property some parts of the world.

Nome is a great junkyard, perhaps the world's greatest
dumpheap, per capita. Its beach for miles is strewn with
all sorts of rusted old machinery, everything from tin cans
to abandoned locomotives, including whole narrow-gauge
trains of the defunct Seward Peninsula Railroad, everything all the steward departments of the seas throw over-
board. It is as if a tidal-wave had once wrecked the town
and strewn the indestructible parts of it along the beach,
after which its hardy citizens had rebuilt it . . . except
that many of the buildings surviving the fire look too old
to support so easy a theory. Here is one, for instance,
still plainly marked, though not functioning as such:
"HOTEL; Accommodations for Dogs." Everything imag-
inable lies tumbled along that beach. Perhaps a coroner's
jury could decide whether the locomotive on its knees in
the sand right under Harry's window came to grief in
trying to run away from the land or was swept out to sea
and back again in one of those storms that have made
Nome insist that she must have a breakwater from the
mouth of the Snake River all along the front of the town.
But it would take more than that to explain why Japan has
overlooked this magnificent supply of scrap-iron.

Men ride bicycles; horses drag wagons shod with automobile tires; children with little evidence of white ancestors
tie ropes high up on a telegraph pole and swing back and
forth across the narrow wooden sidewalks on them.
Mangy, disgruntled dogs, chained for the summer to their
wooden houses, to the débris of that apparent tidal-wave
or to anything else handy and solid enough to hold them,
howl dismally in tune with the noonday whistle of a dredge
so near town that its thumping can be heard all night by

those not fortunate enough to live facing the swashing sea.

George Blanchard, who helped found the first newspaper in Alaska, finds native boys helpful even on the linotype machine in getting out the Nome *Nugget,* once the Nome *News,* a little four-page, three-times-a-week newspaper that is mainly advertisements but which still costs two-bits. It is worth that to be able to read all the world's essential news in ten minutes. The Lomen Brothers are perhaps the largest, certainly the most widely known, of several important Nome business houses. The Railway Express maintains an agency, under an agent whose anecdotes are more worth hearing than easy to start going. The A. T. & T. (in Nome that means the Alaska Telegraph and Telephone Company) shares an office and manager with the Northern Power Company, which furnishes Nome with electric light, getting power from the dredges in summer, supplying it to them in winter, when they are inhabited only by caretakers. Rates, in case you are thinking of moving there, begin at 20 cents per kilowatt hour and show no great speed in climbing down from there. You can telephone seventy miles inland from Nome, forty more by relay messages. There is a total of 125 miles of roads in various directions out of town, not counting an ex-railroad. Nome not only uses silver dollars, like all Alaska, but its bank won't even give you dollar bills, though you plead too weak a back to carry a pocketful of cart-wheels. Tourists of course bring in paper dollars, but the bank gathers them up and ships them Outside, as unfit for human consumption.

There is a sketchy sewer system, but it works only in summer. In winter people run their sink water out on the ground, and there are no flush toilets back from the beach. For while Nome is not built on rock, as so many Alaskan coast towns are, the ground is perpetually frozen underneath, so close underneath that when it thaws houses go awry. Since it is too frozen to dig them, there are no cel-

lars inland; and those down on the beach often fill with
water from the melting ice underneath and your nice new
oil-burning furnace sinks! The storm that half-wrecked
the town a year or two ago flooded all cellars on the beach,
ruining furnaces—and there are lots of automatic oil furnaces in Nome.

But in spite of these drawbacks and on the whole not
very luxurious outward aspects Nome is a real American
community and many Nomites live in houses just as full of
modern comforts, even luxuries, as any town of similar
size in Iowa. The lack of running water (since pipes cannot be set down in the ground and would be of little use
above it some seven months of the year) has brought
Nome long tank-wagons drawn by pairs of stout horses
and attended by men with gasoline tins, who parade between the wagon and the back door, if any, of most houses.
The lack of sewers, too, has given rise to another prosperous business; in fact, they say it has made several "millionaires." Or at least, more cautious Nomites put it, the
"midnight merchant" is the wealthiest man in town, with
the possible exception of the banker; has two daughters
in college Outside—which just goes to show what opportunities the world has for a man without finnicky preju-
dices.

The "midnight merchant" is a Greek, an old-timer who
prides himself on being his own boss. During the night
his wagons come and in the morning the pails that sit beneath the seats to which one retires alone are miraculously
empty again. ·Some of the spoils are burned; the rest of
them are deposited on the beach at the far end of town, in
summer. In winter they simply drive the stuff out onto the
ice and in the spring it goes to the North Pole.

A big business man, runs one anecdote, just arrived in
Nome with orders to show those languid Alaskans how to
operate a corporation, called in the Greek and told him his
price was too high. "Mister," the Greek is said to have

replied, "that's my price and if you don't like it you can carry your own . . ." but he used a good old Anglo-Saxon word that has long since been abolished from even semi-polite society. An Idaho sheep man, eager to improve his calling, underbid him and at last accounts there was competition in Nome's second best business; but the Greek has seen that flare up and die down before.

There are still quite a number of sandpile prospectors along the beach at Nome. It was the discovery that gold could be washed out of the sea sands that gave rise to Nome in the first place, you know, and men, even women, are still shoveling it into sluices and rockers. Some of them shovel it with a tin can on the end of a stick, using a wash-tub and a long sloping trough with riffles much like those of a washboard. Water is pumped to them by little gas-engines or motors from a creek a few yards inland, through large fireman-like hose stretching across the road out along the beach. Old men, young men, boys, even girls, at least one sour old woman who did not want her treasure-field intruded upon even by passing eyes, were slowly shoveling sand that afternoon, in the constant cold wind. Most of them were very friendly men, willing to take time off to explain their methods, prospects and hopes. But some of them were suspicious or don't like company, which seems to be rather a common old-timer ailment in Alaska.

The gold fever is incredible! Men who admit they do not average a dollar's worth of gold a day go on shoveling, day after day, the sands of the littered beach into their grizzlies, a kind of coarse sandscreen, hoping for enough gold to pay their grocery bills, if not for wealth. The riffles have copper bottoms covered with a thin coating of quicksilver, which catches the gold, if any. Yet even here one can understand why old-timers who go Outside to stay hurry back.

It was comfortable walking, that mid-August day, with the sun shining full blast, in a winter suit, a light overcoat and a moderately heavy sweater. When the sun was hidden you wanted more than that in facing that cold wind, perpetually blowing with a force that made it feel like leaning against a wall. Out along the beach in the direction from which it comes is a shack town known as the King Islanders' village. Each summer they come from their island in a complete exodus and settle down here, Eskimos all, except their living patron saint, Father Bernard LaFortune, who has lived with them unbrokenly for thirty-five years now. Here they gather under their umiaks, or walrus-skin boats, turned upside down on stilts on the beach, their kyaks on frames beside them. Blankets or canvas or walrus hides form three walls against the incessant cold wind and here they sit, hoods drawn over their heads, and carve ivory.

It was Father LaFortune who taught them, or at least had them taught, to carve ivory, which until then was mere walrus tusks to them. Now they carve all manner of ivory things, from chessboards to knitting-needles, salt-shakers to comic-strip figures. Smaller things cost more than the larger; that is, work is more costly than materials, which is rarely the case among primitive craftsmen in other parts of the world. In Alaska even the natives have, compared with natives elsewhere, an exaggerated idea of what their services, their handicrafts and tourist souvenirs are worth, due no doubt to contact with miners to whom two-bits is the smallest coin worth using. Nor do the King Islanders undersell one another; they indulge in neither sales pressure nor price-cutting; stick together and stick to their prices, perhaps at the instigation of Father LaFortune.

To bore holes in the ivory the Eskimo uses what looks like a small bow and arrow, holding the top of the arrow or bit in his mouth, pulling back and forth the bowstring wound around it. "Green" or new ivory, white or creamy in color, from recently killed walrus, is less valuable but easier to work than old or "beach" ivory, from the tusks of mastodons and the teeth of mammoths that died no one knows how many thousand years ago. "Beach" ivory peels off in layers, like an onion, and what is left solid and intact inside is so hard that it is difficult to work, but ranges in color from a beautiful gray to a velvety brown.

The *Denali* came in the morning after we reached Nome and anchored well out, as steamers must at Nome. Until then the open sea before us was broken only by the *North Star,* in the revenue cutter service, which makes a yearly trip to Barrow for the Bureau of Indian Affairs, and by a small naval craft, miles offshore, the first U. S. armed forces we had seen in Alaska. Landing at Nome means being swung over the side, half a dozen at a time, in a cage or even on a mere platform without sides, onto a barge, like the rest of the cargo. But little by little the streets of Nome took on the aspect of any isolated port that is visited by only a cruise ship or two a year.

Until we reached Nome Harry and I had no means of knowing whether the *Denali,* making the only Siberian cruise of the year, would pick up stray passengers who wished, or at least only had time, to make the Nome-to-Nome part of the cruise. But genial Joe Harnish soon relieved our misgivings, even to the landing-cards we would need to get ashore in Siberia. Good friends in New York had managed to procure those for us and had cabled him that they would be in the hands of the purser on board.

The Eskimos at the King Islanders' village left off their ivory carving to put on a show for the tourists. First there was what they call a dance, with hoops covered with walrus-bladder-skin as drums. A complete circle of round, brown faces, framed in fur parka hoods in the case of the women and girls, an invisible baby on almost every woman's back, surrounded the performers. The men were in ordinary cold-day clothes, which each dancer modified only to the extent of donning a very prominent pair of snow-white gloves. Eskimo women and girls wear calico or cotton slips over their fur garments, to keep the snow out of the fur in winter and to keep it clean in summer. But while Eskimo men wear white shrouds in winter as a protective coloring, most useful in hunting the walrus, for instance, the males in this congregation might have been mistaken, but for their faces, for wharf workers on a strike.

The dancers half crouched, throwing their white hands dramatically this way and that. Half a dozen of them took turns in telling stories of war, of the walrus hunt, of capturing a whale, in gestures that were as comprehensible as understandable words would have been. Then the chief started to dance, as if it were his duty but he resented it, much as the mayor or the big business man of a small town in the States might resent having to perform solo, to play the clown before his neighbors to amuse a crowd of distinguished but not particularly reverent strangers. He wore, until he warmed up, an ordinary cap on his head but was dressed in a white smock and mukluks. As the dance proceeded, he took off the smock, stripping to his bare arms in a white undershirt, donned a mask and heavy dark gloves. His seemed to be the whale dance and the applause of his fellow-islanders had that sincere ring of actors applauding a star among actors. Finally a woman, oldish and with the embroidered band of her parka snatching at her ankles, brought the dancing to a conclusion.

Then came blanket tossing, in an immense walrus hide with handholds cut in its edges. Eskimos were thrown as high as any of the small houses roundabout, yet remained perfectly upright and almost always came down so. Harry volunteered to be tossed—and didn't come down so upright. Too late to dissuade him I heard that necks, especially of tyros, are sometimes broken in this hardy sport. Eskimos are famous also for their high kicking, with both feet, half again their own height being no unusual performance; but before we got to that, cold rain with a hint of sleet put an end to the afternoon games.

If the waves are at all high cargoes cannot be landed at Nome, and by this time the sea was crashing ominously on the beach. The *Denali* moved offshore until it was almost lost in the mists, leaving its tourists marooned ashore, sans toothbrush, comb or night clothes, which quickly emphasized the lack of hotel accommodations at Nome. Its business men had just met to plan a modern hotel, of perhaps fifty rooms, but that did not help the situation that night. After a dance, modern style, in the spacious high school gymnasium, the Nomites took the strangers in, housing them in every house that had a spare room and still leaving some, unless what they had to say next morning of their night's adventures was mere boasting, to bed down on billiard tables.

Father Bernard R. Hubbard, S.J., the "glacier priest," was in town, not to mention his two assistants, Ed Levin and Ken Chisholm. We had expected to find Father Hubbard older and a trifle . . . well, not didactic exactly, but perhaps faintly impressed with his own importance. I've no idea where I had picked up this completely erroneous impression. For it turned out that the privilege of going with him on that Siberian cruise was one of the most delightful experiences of our summer's adventure. But with all due respect to a man whom we liked immensely at the first meeting, Father Hubbard looked rather like a lower-grader in awe of his betters, between Ed and Ken.

As to Ed Levin . . . the first time we saw him, as he came barging into the Alaska Steamship Line's new office with agent's home attached to ask Joe Harnish the same question we had come to ask, I had an inclination to slip out unnoticed. For at first glimpse you'd think Ed, with his prize-ring-battered nose and his weather-beaten face, a man to be avoided by other men of merely average physical prowess—whereas we soon found him a magnificent boy of thirty-three, with a heart as big as his brawny arms and with that delightful naïveté, that entrancing sim-

plicity in its most complimentary sense, of the wholesome
outdoor man. Ken Chisholm was taller, but his aspect was
less redolent of the prize ring.

Ed and Ken and Father Hubbard had spent the winter
on King Island, where Ed had taught the Eskimos to play
basketball, to box . . . had found them natural boxers
and excellent athletes. What they, especially the King
Island boys, thought of Ed was obvious from one glimpse
of him striding through the streets of Nome like a giant
surrounded by adoring dwarfs.

It was worth coming all the way to Nome, too, for a
chat with the man who has given his life to the King
Islanders. Father LaFortune came to that rock in the
Bering Sea in 1903; has never been east of St. Michael
and Kotzebue since! Yet he is a graduate in chemistry and
mathematics of the Sorbonne in Paris. Born in Montreal,
he still speaks his very fluent English with an accent, but
is said to be the best Eskimo speaker on earth. He knows
all their dialects; corrects the natives in their own speech.
He is a little man, impervious to such things as clothes and
personal appearance, but it was easy to understand why the
King Islanders, who made little use of ivory before he
came to them, now sit under their bottom-up skin boats and
carve ivory all summer.

Father Cunningham, on the other hand, is a tall, handsome young man with a very weather-reddened face, who
has come even farther to offer his services to the Eskimos.
Son of a farmer of southern New Zealand, who went out
there on account of trouble in Ireland half a century ago,
he had been two years on Little Diomede, where there was
no missionary before he came. Before that he had been
running a boat and "skinning the cat" on the Yukon for a
year, and knew almost no Eskimo when he first took up his
new duties. Like Father LaFortune, he was spending his
summer at the Catholic mission in Nome.

Unlike those of King Island, only some of the 140 inhabitants of Little Diomede come to the mainland in summer. Little Diomede is bigger than King Island, and higher, rising 1,200 feet above sea-level, and is very rocky; the village is part-way up one side of it. It has no wood except what is picked up along the shores, and the currents carry only small stuff there, though big logs drift up to Herschel Island north of Alaska and the Yukon Territory. But Father Cunningham now has all the comforts of home, including two oil burners!

There are no white foxes on Little Diomede or on King Island but plenty of them on Big Diomede. They are hard to shoot, being white as snow. They used to be worth only $2 when Father LaFortune came in 1903. But today a white fox skin is worth real money. That was not the reason, however, I gathered, why Father Cunningham and some of his Eskimos had gone over to Big Diomede one day during the past winter. There are only seven or eight people on Big Diomede, which belongs to Russia and is a day ahead of its smaller neighbor and namesake. Eskimos of the two Diomedes are friendly; they used to go across the ice frequently to visit each other. But this time Father Cunningham was promptly arrested by two Russians, one of whom turned out to be a big man in Sovietland; at least his face adorned one of our news weeklies not long afterward. To cut short a long but exciting story, the Russians seemed bent on taking the priest of Little Diomede back to Moscow with them. But Father Cunningham heard his Eskimos on the roof of the sunken igloo planning to kill the two Russians if they did not turn him loose, and the Russians, who understood no Eskimo, were finally made to understand that they were hopelessly outnumbered.

Why Russia pays so much attention to Big but insignificant Diomede is a mystery to Westerners. So, apparently, do the Japanese. The water is shallow between the two Diomedes, though a ship did once make the passage between them. Imagine Cunningham's surprise, then, when

Deering is typical of Eskimo village sites—on a sand spit between ocean and river

The dogs of Deering look with a hungry eye upon next winter's supply of dried salmon

The turn-over in baby carriages is slight in Northwestern Alaska

The boys of Deering show a visitor from Outside one of their cozy dwellings

not long ago he saw a Japanese war vessel steam full speed through a channel not even marked on U. S. maps! "They land without asking any one's permission; know everything there is to know up here." Preparing, perhaps, for world conquest?

CHAPTER XIII

Our Siberian Cruise

Run-down St. Michael . . . American Tin Fields . . . King Island Ahoy! . . . In Sovietland Again . . . Brief Shore Leave . . . Back to Nome

THE storm abated at last and the *Denali* came back within reach of the shore, so that tenders could go alongside and plow their way inside the miniature model of a harbor at the mouth of Snake River. No wonder lighterage charges are high at Nome, and its best-known firm prosperous. We went out with a tender that evening in time for dinner and beds above the Alaskan average. The stewards aboard ship at once recalled the crowded, competitive, quarrelsome, CIO life in the States; emphasized the friendly, hospitable, room-for-all atmosphere of Alaska, at least of the interior. I came ashore again next day, to splash about in rain and mud in quest of interesting Nomites, while Harry confined his questing to fair faces among the tourists. Late that afternoon I was swung aboard once more like a sack of meal and some time in the small hours between Saturday and Sunday we were off.

We anchored well off St. Michael next afternoon and lay there until morning. For it was Sunday and missionary influence, I understood, rather than union rules left us with nothing to do but talk and read, until Father Hubbard came to the rescue with the first of his nightly informal chats, illustrated with choice bits of the many motion pictures he had taken in Alaska.

Late Monday morning St. Michael's docks came out to the ship—or so it seemed in that semi-fog, rather than that the ship moved in toward the docks—and the passengers were rope-elevatored into a tug and sent ashore. Once an important town at the "mouth" of the Yukon (it is really a hundred or more miles from it, but the delta can hardly be navigated by ocean steamers), St. Michael is now a half-abandoned town of tumble-down houses and loose-board sidewalks climbing away across rolling, high-weeded country. The rain was incessant during our three hours there and most tourists got no farther than the trading post, where ivory trinkets, skins, furs, baskets and the like were still not cheap, nor plentiful, but distinctly less expensive than we had seen them elsewhere.

There had been constant rain, "unusual" weather, all summer. The population of about 150 included six whites, among them a good woman teacher. St. Michael was once all natives; may soon return to that status. The Indians seemed a little more friendly, or at least a bit less unfriendly, than those up along the Yukon. Soggy wooden sidewalks climbed down to Indian shanties on the shores of the bay at both ends of town, where wrecks of old stern-wheelers, their engines sold to Russians for use on Siberian rivers, lay in rotting clusters. The big gymnasium of the former military establishment here, abandoned after the world war, is still largely intact, the bowling alley completely so, even to ten pins and balls, but won't be so much longer.

Many old wooden houses are gone completely; others are boarded up or falling down. The trading post has its inevitable smaller rival; there is a Catholic church. St. Michael's chief tourist attraction, the old Russian church, was showing distinct signs of disintegration, but it still had its gold chalice and other valuable religious trinkets; safe here even with broken windows. After the Bolshevik revolution no more money came from Russia, so the church began to fall in ruins and "the Catholics took over all our people." The Russian priest who still now and then comes to St. Michael from somewhere else in Alaska takes away a few ikons or vessels at a time. But the inhabitants would not let even the captain of the revenue cutter *North Star* take anything out of the church, though he claimed (and I verified his statement later) that Father Kashavaroff, who might be called the head of the Russian Orthodox Church in Alaska, had asked him to bring out what was left of value.

As usual the Bering Sea weather got worse instead of better. But we made our way across Norton Sound again to Golivin, then up along the southern shore of the Seward Peninsula, passing Nome in the night, to Teller and Tin City. There walrus-skin boats brought us four tons of ore in sacks each. An old Eskimo in skins, who looked as if he had been there before the first white man came, sat at the tiller. An umiak seems frail, large as it is, carrying such heavy cargo, and looks incongruous with an outboard motor. But apparently it is as sturdy as any wooden boat.

A young American engineer and his very pretty wife in boots and pants came out for a ship's dinner. He said they thought they had huge deposits but could not be sure yet. American Tin Fields is developing back of Tin City (which is far from being a city) what is at present the largest placer tin mine in the world, I believe the young man said, and the only tin mine under the Stars and Stripes. There was a crusher lording it over some shack houses on the beach, a road winding away around a bare hill into the unknown. But they have to ship their ore to Singapore, because there is no commercial tin smelter in the United States. So far these deposits have been worked about two years. There were about twenty whites ashore and, according to the young engineer, the Eskimos thereabouts are good workers.

We had passed close to King Island and heard much about it from Father Hubbard and his party. Fantastic pillars of rock, like statues of prehistoric people, stand on top of King Island. The rest of it is worn down, sway-backed, being 900 feet high at the ends, 800 in the middle. There are no trees, though considerable driftwood. King Island houses, made of hides and driftwood boards, are really little more than porches on stilts and lashed in front of the hillside caves or rock openings in which the people live. This led one writer badly in need of a head-line to call the King Islanders Uncle Sam's cave dwellers, which is rather overstating the facts.

The village in which all King Islanders live is part way up the steep, rocky eastern side of the island, which has cliff shores all around it. There is excellent water where the village stands, but nowhere else. Up the slope back of the schoolhouse is a big half-level space on which the people would like to build, but can't, because it belongs to the government. Father Hubbard now has a comfortable community building there, in addition to Father LaFortune's church and home. On our return to Nome I met a fat Mississippian who, with his wife, had been assigned to teach school on King Island when the population returned, but teachers do not usually learn Eskimo.

King Island has about 180 inhabitants, all good Catholics—though none just then. Its population has slightly increased since 1918, when entire villages were wiped out by an epidemic of flu which killed 70 percent of the natives in northwest Alaska, 5 percent of the whites. King Islanders are smart people. They will not leave their island, permanently; perhaps feel it is one place too unimportant for even Hitler or the Mikado to covet. They pick up their annual meat supply as the ice brings it down to them, right past their door, in the form of walrus herds and seals. They keep the meat in a community cave, a perfect icebox. But though each family's supplies are marked, in case of emergency the meat is common property. They have been offered reindeer, which would mean moving to St. Lawrence Island, but prefer to remain where they are and go on raising only dogs and babies. King Island has never had a murder, or a divorce. The chief, whom we have already seen dancing at Nome, has officiated at 1,200 births without a single—later Father Hubbard said only one—casualty. Latest hospitals please copy.

All King Islanders go to Nome in June; come home again in September. They leave behind only their dogs, which can howl unfettered and uncursed all summer. The dogs catch birds on the rocks sprayed by the sea, puffins and the like, cleverly, and are fat and tail-wagging when the people come back in the fall. They still use their umiaks in their annual migration, but propel them with outboard motors now. They load their skin boats to the gunwales; cook all their food, of which walrus flippers are a great delicacy, that has been kept frozen all winter, and take it to Nome. They bring over the ivory they have carved during the winter and walrus tusks enough to last through the summer, then carve all summer long. The icebreaker *Northland* takes them back in the autumn, when the seas are too treacherous to let them risk the trip alone in their umiaks. In fact, in 1937 a Coast Guard boat, finding the weather tricky, brought them over to the mainland. Uncle Sam's white nephews may risk their lives to their hearts' content, but not so his dear Eskimos and Indians.

Once the King Islanders were very unclean; now you could eat off their floors, to quote their Catholic benefactors. The men, wearing white clothing over their furs, stalk behind blocks of ice and shoot walrus, then go back to their boats and dash after the herd, harpooning right and left. The least bit of bone prick causes blood poisoning unless attended to at once. With a triangular knife the King Island women remove the whole carcass of a seal through the nose, without cutting the skin anywhere else. The men use kyaks, are thrown in them from the cliffs into the sea. When a kyak ships water it is sucked out by the gourdful and poured over the side.

You cannot get to King Island even by plane in winter, though you can to Little Diomede. St. Lawrence Island, farther south, is very much larger, with some 300 inhabitants, and "the best machine shop in the north," established by the St. Lawrence Island teacher. It does not have the warble fly, so it is a good place for reindeer. Only the other day nervy little Hans Mirow flew to St. Lawrence Island and brought back to Nome a woman suffering from appendicitis. Hans had never been there before, and the only other man to perform this feat had spent weeks on the island in preparation for it. Wrangell Island, farther north, belongs to Russia—though one of our Congressmen recently took issue with the Soviet Union on this point and recommended that it be fortified as a part of our national defenses.

Alaskans smile at the doubt many people Outside still have as to the origin of the people found on the American continent when the white man discovered it. Did the Amerinds come from Asia? "Of course they did," laughs Father Hubbard. Only last summer he and his men proved that it is quite possible for an umiak to make the trip between the continents—by doing it themselves. Alaska and Siberia are only 56 miles apart, with several stepping-stone islands between them that can be seen from one to another on anything like a clear day; and the continental shelf between the two continents is only 180 feet deep, implying that it may once have been dry land. You can see the islands from Siberia, and Alaska from the islands, and early man was just as curious as his modern successor as to what lay over beyond the horizon. Until Bolshevik times Eskimos from Alaska and Siberia crossed on the ice to visit and trade with each other; there is no reason why they should not have done so ages ago.

Scientists believe and Alaskans "know" that the American Indian (and of course the Eskimo and Aleut) were originally Asiatic. There are plenty of artifacts in Alaska to prove it, they say; and mastodons and mammoths probably came from Asia about the same time as man. Father Hubbard found relics of stone-age villages near Point Barrow, gradually being uncovered by the ocean waters. Pleistocene artifacts and microliths found on the campus of the University of Alaska are identical with those of the Gobi dune dwellers. Many Indians so closely resemble some of the central Asiatics in physical characteristics that any one with half an eye, who has been in both places, can hardly refuse to come to the same conclusion.

If you still have doubts you will be overwhelmed with more arguments: The Tenah Indians of central Alaska, for instance, speak the same tongue as the Navajos and Apaches of our Southwest and northern Mexico. There is evidence that the great river basins of the northwest were more likely routes of human migration than the rugged coasts of Alaska and British Columbia; linguistic evidence that man spread from the Mackenzie area to the south and southwest in the far northern part of the continent, then swung toward the southwest and on into the United States and down to Mexico.

Our tin ore loaded, we went out past Cape Prince of Wales. Why the western tip of the western hemisphere, of the United States, except for islands, should be named for an Englishman I don't know; seems a good chance to glorify one of our own politicians. Next morning found us close off the coast of Asia, a Siberian town faintly visible high up on a steep shore almost lost in the mists. What I understood to be Dejenew was quite a town, well protected by forbidding cliffs, their tops hidden in clouds, the wind blowing half a gale. As he could not land us, the captain took us on north until he could truthfully deliver certificates attesting to the fact that we had crossed the Arctic Circle, then wandered down along the Siberian coast again.

Once more the waves were too high before the town where our permits allowed us to land but where the sea still denied us that privilege. The *Denali* went on around a point into a cove, where there was a much smaller town, a mere hamlet of hardly a dozen buildings, close down on the shore, with a bare but green rising world behind it, and came to anchor half a mile or so offshore. There were huge patches of dirty snow hanging down to the water's edge on the lower face of the low cliffs at East Cape, though it was August. They had obviously been there all summer. The wind from offshore as we lay at anchor cut through the heaviest clothing like a knife.

It was then nearly noon and the captain, evidently mistaking this for just another port, at which he could land when he saw fit, made what seemed to some of us the tactical mistake of waiting until after luncheon before doing anything more about carrying out his orders to set his passengers ashore in Asia. Then one of our lifeboats was sent ashore with half a dozen members of the crew in charge of the second mate.

There were fourteen or fifteen buildings on a bare neck of land, between treeless brown hills with a hint of green is them. A sheet iron building with radio spires and bearing large faded letters that looked like RKO stood much higher than the others on the foreshore. Half the buildings, which appeared through the glasses to be round, were up on a knoll, and the place looked at least equal to the average Alaskan river or west coast town—until we got ashore and saw them close up! A motorboat that looked as if it had been used by Vitus Bering—who had nothing to do with St. Vitus dance but who first discovered the Alaskan mainland in 1741 and died on the bleak shores of the sea now named for him—was anchored part way out, but it was a long time before there was any sign of life on it or on the shore. They were for all the world like bandits crouching in their hideout until they were sure the invading force was friendly—or not strong enough to subdue them.

At length our boat returned, followed by the ancient motorboat, from which stepped a big Russian in the familiar Soviet army uniform, red star and all. He was in full winter garb but wore no insignia (later we heard that his rank was similar to ours of major). A very large automatic was strapped in plain sight at his waist outside his heavy overcoat. As he stepped on deck he saluted the little cluster of passengers and a steward or two who had assembled at the top of the gangway. His motorboat withdrew to some distance from the ship, as if fearing contamination or, more likely, the danger of being thrown a ham bone or a cigarette and being liquidated for lack of strength to refuse it. The two boatmen in ragged uniforms were visibly shivering, visibly hungry, for that matter, even from where we stood.

But that did not hurry the important young man who had come on board. We had with us a former Russian now employed at the radio station in Nome—and there is a slight significance in the fact that, now he had become an American, his new citizenship was honored by the Soviet authorities. But it seemed that he had no qualms on this point, having been at East Cape as ship's interpreter several times before.

But this time he was evidently not having much success in his mission. Mere passengers were of course not allowed to attend the epochal meeting in the captain's office, but bit by bit we were able to piece together, before the trip was over, the details of that international conference.

The Commissar or Major was, after the time-honored custom of the sea, invited to dinner. He regretted; said he had already eaten. But at least he would have a drink? There was on board good English whisk . . . No, he never drank! Then a cigar? No, he only smoked cigarettes—Russian cigarettes, he hastened to add, when some one thrust toward him a pack of American fags. Obviously he was scared pink of being caught hobnobbing socially with or accepting gifts from foreigners, the penalty for which, one gathered from his hunted-fox face, was liquidation.

Nor could he give us permission to land! Documents, in Russian of course, giving us permission to do so were laid before him; he took refuge first in the statement that he could not read! When he was smoked out of that sanctuary he said, "Yes, but you see, this permit is to land at Dejenew" (or whatever is the name of the larger town back along the cliffs) "not for this place." One gathered that he had explicit orders, or at least a personal resolve not to risk his rank and perhaps his life; no doubt recent Japanese border trouble had tightened things up.

Last year, too, the commander would not eat on board; refused a drink; put up a long resistance before accepting a cigar—and maybe had been liquidated for that; for this man would not even accept matches! As they were leaving the year before, the Americans had whispered to the man in charge or to one of his trembling aides that they were leaving them a crate of apples and another of oranges on the beach when they pulled out. "You mustn't; we can't accept them!" the Russians had cried. "Then give them to the natives," said the Americans. The natives came surging forward—but the last view from the departing boat was of the Russians chasing the natives away and grabbing the fruit themselves.

The report was that the authorities at East Cape had refused landing permission, earlier that summer, even to our Coast Guard cutter *Northland,* in spite of a permit issued by the Soviet Embassy in Washington. They had even driven off an American naval vessel which came to salute them after the United States recognized the Soviet Union; so we hadn't very verdant hopes. It was only four years since I had traveled almost freely in Sovietland, but Stalin no longer wants tourists, they say; considers them more trouble than they are worth. Probably it made him unhappy to have people, no matter how few, in his country whom he could not liquidate when the whim came upon him. Another theory is that he woke up once in the middle of the night and decided that all so-called tourists were really spies in disguise, or at least enemies of Communism.

At last our distinguished visitor accepted a compromise. He would telegraph to Moscow! With that his cold and hungry boatmen took him ashore and went back into hiding some distance out from the beach.

The cold afternoon blew itself into the past tense. We had all, as far as I could find, given up any hope of being able to land when, lo and behold, the aged motorboat again showed signs of life. The major, automatic still prominently displayed, mounted the gangway again, saluted once more, and was conducted with much respect to the captain's quarters. Yes, he had heard from Moscow. As Moscow is almost on the other side of the world from East Cape, some one, probably not Joe Stalin himself, must have got up in the middle of the night to answer his inquiry. Evidently we could land, after all. That is, the men could land, but not the women! Though I was not present at the interview I can picture every one who was, striving to impress upon this strange fellow the fact that the leading sex in the United States does not have the Russian point of view and that to refuse them privileges granted the other might cause all trouser-wearers in sight to be liquidated. At any rate he modified this dreadful order; granted landing permission to any who had the requisite $5 permit, bearing his photograph and other pertinent, in fact, some impertinent, information as to his past, present and plans for the future.

But to recapitulate—now that the major had capitulated: First he wouldn't let any of us ashore; then he wouldn't let women ashore; finally all those could go ashore who had the official visa—which did not include Father Hubbard and his brawny assistants. Moreover, cameras, most important of tourist playthings, were strictly forbidden. Of course we could have licked them all, Ed Levin with his revolver—yes, with only his fists and his battle-scarred face—leading us, but I suppose that would have resulted in what dapper diplomats call an international incident.

And just when everything seemed hunkydory the passengers paraded past the door of the conference cabin in their most ridiculous costumes and idiotic mood. Hadn't Cruise Director Cross chosen that very evening to hold a Hard Times Dinner! Europeans no farther away than the west coast of Great Britain have difficulty in understanding Americans in their playful moments. What then would this Tatar-minded man from the other side of the world think of us? He gazed in something like awe mixed with incredulity and seasoned with a suspicion of having unwittingly come on board a floating madhouse—or was all this bedlam a camouflage, a prelude to seeing his bailiwick invaded by an armed force?—as that insane gang, that incomprehensible riot of lunatic savages paraded right past the door in which he stood just after he had been coaxed into letting us land. I marvel that he did not at once withdraw his permission.

We had of course to use our own lifeboats to go ashore. Some twenty of us climbed into the ship's motorboat at the bottom of the gangway and we were off at last—for some twenty feet, when the motor balked and continued to do so for so long that we began to wonder whether we were not going to be carried out to sea. But whatever it is that happens to motorboats at crucial moments was finally more or less cured and we putt-putted toward the shore. There we ran our prow up on the stony beach and were lifted to dry land by our sailors in hip boots, or jumped at the right moment to escape an incoming breaker, depending on our sex, prowess, or sense of self-sufficiency. Our $5 "passports" were taken up almost while we were in midair. None of our crew except those required to perform this hip-boot service were allowed to land, and they had to stay down on the edge of the beach.

Luckily days are long at East Cape in August and though the sun had gone into hiding behind the clouds, it was still above the horizon. Just above the reach of the incoming combers stood a couple of soldiers wearing the red star, their uniforms a bit dirty, or at least faded, and in one case patched; long light-brown shoddy overcoats. We gathered that they had been stationed in this God-forsaken place for three years! There were also several sailors, perhaps a bit less soiled or faded and with a hint of not feeling so hopelessly marooned. A soldier told us in gestures to climb the knoll on the right, where stood the round Eskimo houses, which of course made us assume that the rest of the mushy "town" was forbidden ground. But it turned out that they were merely determined to show us that traffic could be properly regulated even in this outpost of Bolshevism.

The half dozen round Eskimo houses on the knoll were made largely of driftwood, pieced out with bones of walrus and whales. They were covered with skins, mainly of the walrus, held down by faded and frayed ropes with huge stones tied on each end of them, thrown over the house. The houses were perhaps fifteen feet in diameter. Some had aged cloth or walrus-skin partitions and all were earth floored. Inside, they were an inch or more deep in mud and filthy beyond anything an untraveled American imagination can picture. Misery personified; far more miserable than the worst Eskimo huts I ever saw in Alaska, as much more so as the fear in every face, manner, attitude of these Eskimos was from the gaiety and constant grin of the Alaskan Eskimos.

Women and children were incredibly dirty, fearful and dead silent. One Eskimo man knew a spoonful of something resembling English; one other was bold enough to keep talking to us in Russian, louder and louder, as if he was sure we could understand him if he shouted loudly enough. But they all seemed perpetually and deathly afraid of something or other, in marked contrast to Eskimos on the American side of Bering Strait.

The hill slope was a muddy swamp and there had been no attempt at bridging it, except a two-by-four here and there, tossed there by some individual for his own use and used, communist fashion, by any one else who came along. In one spot there were some large reddish bricks or pieces of bricks imbedded in the mud. They came from Vladivostok——no, from Kamchatka, the soldiers finally seemed to agree. We sloshed along at random, invariably finding the route we chose as wet and muddy as any other. Down at the bottom again, we were motioned and told in Russian to go to the "Russian house," which turned out to be a store or trading post run by a white civilian with a distinctly pretty but entirely speechless wife, both real Russians. She acted as if she had heard somewhere that to speak to a foreigner meant the firing squad, and not the faintest sound could any advance wring out of her, though her eyes showed wonder and great curiosity and at least average intelligence.

The store was obviously Russian and about as well stocked as the average Alaskan trading post would be if its supplies were cut off completely for two or three years. There were quite a lot of very bad shoes, some crude brooms, but not much else, at least in sight, except a plentiful supply of medallions, portraits and posters of Stalin

An Alaskan trapper's cabin is no place for a covetous lady of fashion

The Pied Piper of Hamelin had nothing on Ed Levin when the boys of King Island spied him in the streets of Nome

Mr. and Mrs. Paul Davidovics and a daughter. Kotzebue

An Eskimo woman scraping a sealskin on the beach at Kotzebue

and Lenin and other precious Soviet things like that.
Tourists must of course buy, whether there is anything
worth buying or not; and apparently the taciturn young
man with the speechless wife was mildly willing to sell.
But he could take only Russian money—though he must
have known that it is against the law to bring Russian
money into Sovietland, even to be in possession of any of
it outside.

"Rubles," he kept saying. Yet neither he nor we had
any idea what a ruble was worth in American money—or
rather, American money was worth exactly nothing there.
One man finally offered a $20 bill for something or other
obviously not worth a dollar. Maybe he was only foolin',
but at any rate the storekeeper wouldn't touch it. One of
our younger and more vivacious women did talk a broom
out of him, one of those handfuls of coarse broom straw
tied to a stick with which European housemaids flick off
the front steps each morning. But nothing but a smile
would he take in return. In the end we were reduced to
carrying home as souvenirs stones picked up from the
Asiatic beach.

Even the soldiers and sailors would not accept cigarettes, not even matches! One passenger, wanting to exchange a pack of American for one of Russian cigarettes,
finally got the idea across . . . to the extent that a soldier
ran somewhere and came back with a large pack—only
twenty in that one, too, of course, but those long tube
mouthpieces take up a lot of room, so that it looked like
a very poor deal for the Russian when the American
handed him the package of Camels. Handed, did I say?
He wouldn't touch it with a ten-foot pole—well, at least
not with the tip of a finger. It was all worlds apart from
Alaska . . . and just like the other end of the Soviet
Union, where I had been four years before: complete indifference to, or at least complete lack of, comfort, life
in the rough in every particular, and above all that mantle

of fear hanging perpetually over everything and every one.

The Siberians or Eskimos would take anything offered them, but even they remained solemn and scared-to-death-looking as long as we remained. Several of our most nearly young and good-looking gals got the soldiers and sailors almost gay before they were through with them, so amazed them with their free and easy American manners that they seemed almost to forget their fears for a moment. Even the chief of the Soviets, the village commissar or army major or whatever he was, began to smile under this treatment before we left—all, that is, except the storekeeper's good-looking wife, who never for a moment took off her expression of speechless amazement as long as we remained.

We saw nary a polar bear, no walrus, not a single oogruk, not even a seal, on our Siberian cruise; if that is what you want to see you'll have better luck in your home zoo. But our Siberian visit was well worth while for all that. The major gave us until nine o'clock to leave USSR waters; had forbidden us to use our ship's radio until we were ten miles offshore. As the brief August Arctic night settled down over the cold Bering Sea we felt as if we had by accident been momentarily transported to another planet—from which we were only too glad to escape so easily and promptly.

There are now some 200 inhabitants at East Cape, I gathered; excellent reindeer country with good moss. They say the animals are fatter and the meat better than in Alaska—which, as you know, first got its reindeer from Siberia. In the days of the Czars the Eskimos were entirely free, as far as the government was concerned. They wandered without let or hindrance across the Bering Sea. Lots of them moved over to the United States when Russia went Bolshevik. Even now Eskimos are, at least in theory, free to go back and forth. But they have been told that even a shack, the very stuff in a cache, belong to the Russian government.

In Czar days there was almost free trade between Siberia and Nome. Huge quantities of furs came across; buyers from New York and way stations came to Nome with choke-a-horse rolls of bills, dealt out shovel loads of silver dollars, which fur traders took back to Siberia in the same small boats in which they had brought the skins. Russian gunboats, Japanese vessels, all manner of foreign boats came to Nome and their crews or passengers went up and down the street buying anything, everything, no matter how out of fashion (which made them particularly a godsend to the merchants) to take back to Siberia and trade for more skins. But, alas, those happy days are very much over, perhaps forever.

CHAPTER XIV

SOME ALASKA WE DIDN'T SEE

The Pribiloffs . . . Fur Seal History . . .
Beachmasters and Cows . . . Unlucky Bache-
lors . . . Milady's Sealskin . . . The Long
Aleutians

IT is a bitter law of physics, and of travel, that you
can't go in two directions at once, and our route lay north-
ward when we were set ashore at Nome next morning after
leaving Siberia. What we envied our fellow-passengers
most was not the glimpse they would get of Unalaska on
the way back to Seattle but their day at the Pribiloff
Islands on the way up. But strange as it may seem, pump
even a tourist, or a lot of them, and you will get a fairly
clear and coherent story of what they have seen.

The Pribiloff Islands are, with two minor exceptions,
the world's only fur seal sanctuary. Ninety percent of the
fur seals of the world summer there. The Pribiloffs were
discovered in 1786 by the Russian Gerassim Pribiloff and
were first called the Mist Islands, because the meeting of
the Japan current and Arctic winds leaves them almost always covered with fog in summer. They are a cluster of
rocky, barren islands with some thick tundra, volcanic,
treeless, almost bushless, impossible of cultivation, yet
growing wild flowers and luxuriant grasses. Aleuts were
brought to the uninhabited Pribiloffs by the Russians. Of
the five islands only St. Paul and St. George are now inhabited; and that, if we understood our tourists, only in
summer. Then there is a village of some 275 population
on St. Paul, 100 on St. George, all of the Greek-Russian

faith; eight white families; a dentist, a doctor and their
wives, a Russian Orthodox priest, the engineer of the
steam plant and his wife, a foreman who supervises the
killing. . . .

Tundra, scowling skies, whining winds, rarely a day of
sunshine. The skies are clear in winter, but the islands are
uninhabited then, the population moving 250 miles south
to the nearest land, Unalaska. St. Paul village is modern,
immaculate, with electric lights, running water, a big
school, a native recreation hall. The natives are all wards
of the government, which furnishes them everything: food,
shelter, clothing, even medical care, so that their share
of the fur sale is all velvet. They work at sealing, foxing
and village maintenance. The Aleuts, divided into five
classes, as far as sealing is concerned, earn an average of
$500 a season, and mail order houses in the States get most
of that. There are many blue foxes (and white, the same
litter) on the Pribiloffs. The top men get $1 per fox skin
and 65 cents per seal skin. There is no dock, no harbor
to give shelter from the strong winds; lighterage is by
skin boats. Twenty-five miles of lava road served sixteen
trucks at last account; everything is under government
supervision, including the seals.

Two million pelts were taken the first year after the
islands were discovered, and the price fell to $1. By 1834
only 8,000 skins were taken, so then Russia stopped seal
fishing for thirty-three years, and when we took over in
1867 the herd was estimated at 4,000,000. Pelagic sealing soon brought the number down to 75,000. The United
States tried to claim jurisdiction over the seal herd even
on the high seas, by International Law, but it took an
international treaty to stop pelagic sealing. This treaty
was signed on December 15, 1911, between England (that
is, Canada), Russia, Japan and the United States, and has
since been renewed. Japan, Russia and England get 15
percent of the take; Japan in cash, Russia in unpaid debts,

England in skins, so that her workers can get work curing them. Strange as it may seem, the Japanese reciprocate, at least in theory, and give us 15 percent of the take on their small seal sanctuary, Robben Island—sent us 214 skins a season or two ago. The natives can hunt fur seals, even outside the twelve-mile limit, I gather, but only with no-power boats and with spears, so they get only about 200 a year.

There were fewer than 50,000 fur seals left when the government took over in 1912; now it is estimated that there are 1,900,000 of them. For twenty years 100,000 seals were taken yearly by a commercial company and Uncle Sam got $13,500,000 in taxes and import duties. Now he runs the business himself, and this is one branch of the government on a paying basis; it helps to keep up the Bureau of Fisheries in the rest of the United States. The Coast Guard follows the migrations; no one is allowed to land on the Pribiloffs except with a Department of Commerce permit. For fur seals stampede like cattle; tourists scare them worse than they do the natives, and a stampede may do much damage.

These are fur seals, really sea bears; the hair seal and sea lions we see in zoos and circuses are different. At St. Michael I bought a large hair seal skin for a dollar, but that is only fit to be a bedroom mat. Fur seals are never seen on land except in the Pribiloffs and those two other small islands. The males, bulls or beachmasters, contrary to the custom in summer colonies along the Atlantic seaboard, come up first, arriving about the first Sunday in May—probably having shut their desks for the summer the previous Friday. Each bull takes a pitch, a point of rock on which he has probably summered before. Rocks worn smooth by generations of seals begin to be spotted with fat, belligerent bulls, roaring, fighting, waiting for their harems, regular Brigham Youngs, battle-scarred and bellicose. The beach is marked off by numerals, but the bulls do not seem to be able to read them. There are, however, invisible boundaries which they respect. Tripods twenty feet high have been erected from which to count the seals. The islands have miles of shore line of mammoth tumbled rocks, as if an earthquake had tumbled them or a broken world had ended here; and seals and rocks are so nearly the same color that you can hardly see them, at first, until they move.

The females or cows come up late in June or early in July, having no doubt stayed behind to put the house in order, and surround their favorite bulls like chorus girls around a Jewish comedian. The cows are much smaller, dainty little things compared with a bull; some are a kind of silver-gray in color—and gentlemen seem to prefer blondes. A bull may weigh 500 pounds; the graceful creatures that surround him hardly average a hundred. One bull to forty cows is the usual proportion, though a big strong self-assertive beachmaster may have far more than that. A group of harems makes a "rookery," of which there are about fifteen on St. Paul, covering some eight miles of shore.

There is no fighting except in the breeding season; then bulls will attack you and lash you to pieces unless you make yourself scarce. Bulls have huge scars, use teeth and flippers and sometimes kill each other. Females breed at three but bulls are not graduated from the bachelor estate until they are six or seven, even eight years old, though it is not quite clear whether this is because they are not mature enough before that or whether, like young men in modern civilization, they haven't yet the strength to butt in and take the females away from the established old-timers. It is a definite case of the survival of the fittest, and the bull who can no longer protect his harem from an aggressive bachelor has to give up his marital pleasures and perhaps his life.

Cows pamper conceited bulls by caressing and "kissing"

them; that is, rubbing noses. (Is that where the Eskimos got the custom?) But they are often rudely "flippered" for showing their affection openly. Cows flirt with neighboring bulls and now and then one of them makes a dash for a nearby strutting beachmaster—in human relations we call it going to Reno. But if she is caught before she gets across the invisible boundary her bull takes her in his teeth by the nape of the neck, beats her with his flippers and slams her back into his own harem; no Hollywood stuff for him. Bulls rarely move more than three or four feet all summer long after they pick a spot, except to retrieve a coquettish cow or to lunge at a less strong bull, tirelessly trying to break into his harem. Then they can go over the rocks faster than a woman in high heels can run. If the cow makes her getaway, manages to cross the boundary, the two bulls often fight to the death. Cows fight among themselves for the attention of the bulls—in short, fur seals are distressingly like people.

All bachelor seals keep away from family groups, however, which makes life easier for both bulls and sealers. They have a corridor through the married lines, like the Poles through Germany, by which they constantly go to and return from the water. But woe betide the celibate who even casts a covetous glance or so much as a sniff at a harem! Yearlings come back with the mother and join the segregated bachelors, remain with them until they are big and strong and old enough to fight for their marital rights.

Each cow has one pup (rarely twins) which she brings back to the islands with her the next summer. The gestation period is eleven months and since the female has a double uterus she can conceive either before or after the pup is born. Pups of last year's mating are fuzzy, cute little fellows, who will snap at you but wait patiently while the mother goes out to sea for three or four days at a time to get food. Only the females go to sea in the summer.

They eat squib and small fish but bring back only milk. The cow comes back and finds her pup, recognizes it by smell or some sort of magic—as puffins do their rows upon rows of blue eggs on the rock ledges of King Island, as workmen living in English rows of houses recognize their own house among a thousand others identically like it. Cows will suckle only their own young, so if a mother dies or fails to return it means a dead pup; there is no adopting, contrary to the custom among Eskimos. Other cows will knock it over, even kill it, if it tries to suckle them. Hence the wanton waste of pelagic sealing, which not only killed most of the females but left their pups to starve.

By mid-summer the pups become very vocal and a rookery sounds like a flock of lambs bleating; shut your eyes and you might think you were on a sheep ranch in Wyoming. The pups begin their swimming lessons when they are six weeks old, but find it as hard to learn to swim as children do. When the mother thinks her pup is old enough to take up natation she hustles him to the water's edge and pushes him into a shallow pool with her nose—and finds she has quite a job on her hands. The pup is frantic and sometimes she has to carry him out, as a cat does a kitten. But by fall he can dive gracefully through the surf, flap awkwardly over the rocks at amazing speed; he has been weaned and taught to eat fish and is ready to go south for the winter. Mothers and young leave in November. Some go only to southern California, like Iowans; some, they say, to South America. Most of them reach the Santa Barbara Channel in December and winter off Santa Barbara or around the Catalina Islands, more or less leaving their young to their own resources, above all never trying to foist them upon Hollywood.

Bulls never eat or drink (or even smoke) during the breeding season; confine themselves to their marital duties. So by August the beachmaster is worn out and starved and goes away in quest of food, his attitude toward life having completely changed. Some bulls go south, most of them spend the winter in the Gulf of Alaska, as befits hardy characters.

Meanwhile disaster has overtaken the merry bachelors. "Killables" are the three-year-olds, as their furs are old enough but not as yet scarred up with fighting. As your boy with a limp escapes going to war and becomes a war profiteer, the three-year-old seal that has been a scrappy youngster and been scarred escapes killing and becomes a beachmaster. When killing time comes in June the Aleuts herd the bachelors like cattle, at night or early in the morning, when the grass is wet, cut them off from the beach by clapping sticks and shouting, drive them by thousands as easily as sheep. They must go very slowly, for an overheated seal means a poor fur; move at about half a mile an hour, like a funeral procession. Even then they must be allowed to cool off before they are killed; sit and fan themselves with their flippers while the killers go to breakfast. The herd is really conserved by killing, for there are too many males and their wars are not severe enough to keep them down to the available food and harem supply.

Confused and sleepy-eyed, the youngsters arrive at the killing field, where they are dispersed into small "pods." The "killables" are deftly hit on the head with a club like a long baseball bat. All women who wear sealskin should be obliged to see the pitiful look in the seal's eyes when it is clubbed. The herders try to kill only the three-year-old males, but now and then make a mistake and are bawled out. One crew knocks them on the head, another bleeds them by sticking a knife into the heart, a third crew drives iron rods through the skulls, flipper men expertly cut around each flipper and nose and slit the belly, and still other men strip off the pelts with tongs, with one tug; 600 are skinned in an hour.

The killing leaves a huge field covered with white carcasses, like a battlefield on which the corpses have been stripped by the advancing army. Seal oil is made from the blubber and meal from the carcasses, for fox food and fish hatcheries in the States. All hides are salted for twelve days and partly tanned, or at least cured, then shipped to St. Louis, graded, prepared and sold at auction. It takes two months to dress, dye and prepare furs for auction; many of the processes are jealously guarded trade secrets. Before the world war all fur seal skins went to London, but that is one of the many things England lost by getting mixed up in that mêlée.

Buyers come from far and near and the average skin in St. Louis brings Uncle Sam $27. The Pribiloff crop last year was 58,364 skins, the most in 49 years. But of course it takes more than one seal skin—or one rabbit skin, for that matter—to make a lady fit to be seen at the opera.

Our fellow-cruisers, as I have mentioned, stopped at Dutch Harbor, Unalaska, on the way back to Seattle. Not far east of there the Alaska Peninsula breaks up into what we know as the Aleutian Islands. Six hundred miles of land mass with volcanoes about every 35 miles, the Alaska Peninsula was once nearly all islands, a series of volcanic peaks that have gradually sand-drifted to. gether. Today sand bars are gradually tying Unimak Island to the mainland; that's why one former channel is called False Pass—even the salmon cannot get through it any more. As John Muir said, "In Alaska one learns that the world, though made, is still being made; it is still in the morning of creation."

The Aleutian Islands stretch twelve hundred miles westward, to the longitude of New Zealand. In summer the sun is just setting on Attu, half way to Japan—except that Attu never sees sunlight—when it is rising in Maine. So maybe we also can say we have an empire on which the sun never sets. There were 25,000 Aleuts when the Russians came; now there are about two thousand. They

used to live well on the sea otter, now virtually extinct.
Today they are famous for their baskets; even the natives
of Attu Island make splendid baskets of grass, roots and
a kind of scrub willow—but are they expensive! Large
ones, such as you would pay $1 for, perhaps, in Mexico,
cost $12.50! There are buried villages of great numbers
of aborigines on the Bering Sea side of Unimak Island.
But today there are only ten or twelve small villages on
all the Alaska Peninsula, including its adjacent islands, of
which Kodiak, the first Russian capital in Alaska, on the
island of the same name, is the largest.

Shishaldin volcano on Unimak, the latest of the islands
to join the mainland, is almost as perfect a cone as Fujiyama. All but two of Alaska's volcanoes are on the Alaskan Peninsula or in the Aleutians and together they form
the longest volcano chain in the world. There have been
eruptions there greater than Krakatoa or Pelee have ever
staged, but as no one lives near them to get hurt they
suffer from lack of publicity.

The last major eruption there to date was in 1931,
when Aniakchak, said to be the largest active volcano in
the world, blew its head off, forming a crater twenty-one
miles in diameter, a hole three miles across and no one
knows how deep, sending flames 7,000 feet high and raining ashes for twenty-five days over hundreds of square
miles. The previous eruption of importance was on June
6, 1912, when Katmai, after being dormant for so long
that there were no records, not even legends, of its being
active, burst forth in one of the most violent explosions
known to history. It was heard not only at Dawson and
Fairbanks but at Juneau, 750 miles away. Midnight darkness reigned over Kodiak, a hundred miles from the volcano, for sixty hours; dust fell in Juneau, Ketchikan, the
Yukon Valley; Vancouver thought something on the stove
was burning. Rivers became undrinkable; bears were
blinded; ashes wrecked many houses on Kodiak by their

mere weight; ashes were hip deep, like snow in mid-winter; ashes lay on trees like snow and ice for a year, even for years. For violence, quantity and distance of ashes thrown this seems to have been an all-time world's record.

It was this eruption that formed the Valley of Ten Thousand Smokes, a wonder of a generation ago. But don't plan to include that in your Alaskan itinerary. Father Hubbard tells me—showed us on the *Denali* screen, in fact—that the region is desolate and difficult, even dangerous, to reach, and there is not much to see when you get there. For today the Valley of Ten Thousand Smokes has so nearly died down—they were never smokes, anyway, but only steam—that it is very disappointing.

Father Hubbard, too, credits this part of the world with controlling our winter climate. For only when the Aleutian storms do not form for a continued length of time, he says, do we have cold winters in the eastern United States, because then the Hudson Bay cold slips down upon us unmolested. Climatologists say we need weather stations, 400 miles apart, in the Arctic, to make long-range forecasting for the United States possible. Oh, I don't know; do we pay enough attention to weather forecasts now to warrant heavy expenditures just to have more weather to talk about?

CHAPTER XV

OUR FARTHEST NORTH

Flying to Deering . . . On to Kotzebue . . .
Eskimos and Old-timers . . . Up the Noatak
. . . Too Far Away Barrow . . . Back to Nome

CLEAR weather brings all kinds of transport in together at Nome, so we made perfect connections there that almost cloudless September morning and were off at 11:40 with John Cross (Northern Cross, Inc.) in his bright-yellow plane. Cross comes from our southwest and at first meeting strikes you as anything but an airplane pilot, more like an easy-going, unexcitable boss cattle rustler on the Texas plains. But he drives out to the airfield in his aged half-truck, warms up his plane just as nonchalantly as a Texas pecan grower does his Ford . . . and off we go, Hans Mirow just in from Fairbanks setting his new Travelair down right behind us.

Cross flies his Waco Standard with an oversize motor, factory overhauled only last April, mainly between the six trading posts of the Magids Brothers, now in charge of his wife. But like most Alaskan aviators, he will fly anything anywhere at the drop of the hat, if it fits in with regular business. Rates, in case you are interested, are, or were just then, $30 from Nome to Deering; $45 to Kotzebue, ten percent off on round-trip tickets. Nine dollars a ton is the lowest Nome-to-Kotzebue freight rate, $19 a ton for groceries, $23 a ton for first-class freight.

It was the first time, except perhaps on my very first flight, from Weimar to Berlin in 1919, that I ever sat beside the pilot—and I found a plane has a brake, just like any other vehicle. For all my flying I never knew that before, though it should have been obvious. But after the Boeings, Sikorskys and Lockheed Electras I had been hopping about in the past few years this bright-yellow, single-motor plane—why, you could pick up the tail in one hand and swing it around!—gave you the feeling of being several thousand feet aloft in an orange crate, or wafting along high above the earth on the dining-room rug posing as a magic carpet, but likely to fold up and return to its natural calling at any time on a moment's notice. Not that I had even a twinge of fear, rather a thrill that mere human beings much like the rest of us had conquered the elements so easily, dared airily go aloft in so frail a con-traption—though I admit that when I asked John how he governed his altitude and he suddenly shot us up from 8,000 to 9,000 feet by a mere touch on a spade-handled lever. . . . I wouldn't particularly mind myself, having had my share of an average lifetime of fun, but I did want to bring Harry back to his mother intact.

I had always wondered what the pilot or some one in his entourage always unwound in a take-off and wound in before landing. Thought it had something to do with the elevation, whereas this time I found John was letting out fifty turns of an aerial wire—weighted on the end with an empty beer bottle! Every few minutes he slipped on his earphones and talked with the radio operator at Deer-ing, who happens to be his wife, still best known on the Seward Peninsula as Bess Magids (or, with a hint of affection like that in a Spanish diminutive, "Queen Bess").

Man-made streams squirm around rolling valleys behind the dredge-maltreated ground just back of Nome. Ditches seventy miles long meander the hillsides, keeping on the level by such meandering. They say U. S. Smelter alone has 110 miles of ditches in the hills back of Nome, dug by an ambitious but unlucky old-timer who was forced to sell out cheap. Keeping up ditches is one of the chief expenses

Nap-time on an Eskimo porch

Half a century ago there was not a reindeer in all Alaska

An Alaskan potato field in blossom

Alaska would like you to remember that it grows magnificent vegetables

of mining on the Seward Peninsula; in the Fairbanks district, you remember, we saw the water brought down in huge pipes, but it also has open ditches, and ditches must be treated with more respect.

Seward Peninsula soon climbs into brown, treeless high hills, dotted here and there with patches of reindeer. Sawtooth Range on our left was spotless with the first new snow of the year; Mt. Osburn, highest point of the Seward Peninsula, about a mile high and never long free from clouds, was completely so that morning. But soon we were above a sea of white clouds, though Nome had been clear. Cross amused us by making circular, perfectly round small rainbows, on the clouds below us, as other men make smoke rings. It seems the only reason we don't always see both halves of a rainbow is that the ground interferes with it.

The delicate patterns of a generally soft-brown earth below are beyond mere words. We flew over an old lava field, then over a really huge lava field; the gold is below the lava, Cross says, also below the last glacial ice, which makes it hard to get—but you have to dig for your gold wherever you get it. It was smoother on top of the clouds but they were nearly solid ahead. So Cross preferred to go lower, even though it was bumpier, to trying to find an open spot in the clouds over Deering when he got there. We flew right over a little mining camp to which Cross often brings supplies or plays taxicab—it looked like mice clawing mud along a thread-like winding creek, just where it comes down toward the bottom of the hills.

"Now I'll have to play hide 'n' seek with the clouds," mused our pilot. "No, I can't make it through there. I'll have to go around. . . ." Perhaps it is just as well not to be too close to the pilot and too intimate with what is going on; it rather interrupts your own thoughts, always ebullient so high aloft.

Soon a road began clawing its way along a creek and

mining camps that were almost towns grew up. Farther back we had seen the lone white tent of a prospector. Cross still phoned his wife every five or ten minutes; was saying now, "I'll be a little late to dinner," just like any businessman. The road, twenty-five or so miles long, escorted us on into Deering, over which we made an immense circle, like a communal salutation, before we sat down—to find we had lost the beer bottle!

Deering has a typical Eskimo village setting on the southern edge of Kotzebue Sound, on a long and narrow sand spit with a lagoon behind for boats and near the mouth of a river, where salmon can be taken in the running season. At Magids Brothers' store "Queen Bess" and cute little Patsy, just back from convent school in Seattle, had dinner almost ready. There was one church, Okuda, the Jap's, roadhouse, about eight white people, three of them women. Driftwood igloos half buried in the ground and covered with sod and earth were almost invisible, but cozy and comfortable within. Gasoline-drum stoves; more sod than frame houses along the main and only street, which is the road for Cross's car from Magids' store to his airfield. More split fish drying in grass-roofed racks and more tethered, restless, howling dogs than we had ever seen anywhere else.

Eskimo boys found excuses to ride with us back to the airfield, which Cross had a few men lengthening by picking up stones and leveling off hummocks. Boys hung about the plane—safe enough from depredations and vengeful acts here in his home town, Cross said, at least so far. Back at the store Thomas Ahtilak, ninety-three according to the best village memory, abetted by both legend and looks, got his fifteen big silver dollars by making his trembling mark on his monthly social security check; promptly spent $3 of it for a pair of pants to bridge the gap between this early fall weather and the snow drifts soon to come. Oh, yes, and a package of chewing-gum—what, with those

birthday gums! But no doubt he has grandchildren, great-
great grandchildren they ought to be by now.

We flew across lots of water and along only a string of
land between Deering and Kotzebue. The plane high
above rippled the surfaces of otherwise mirrorlike lakes.
The corpse of a walrus lay on the beach below, farther
on another one. They are killed at sea and only the tusks
taken! Northwest Alaskans say that if the government
doesn't regulate walrus killing they also will disappear.
Two or three abandoned houses, if that is the word, almost buried in the sand—places of refuge on dog-team
journeys in winter. Nothing much else, except incredibly
wide open spaces of sea and tundra, until Kotzebue, a big
village on another long sand spit. Queer that people who
have never seen an automobile, or a train, or for that matter a horse, don't even look up at a plane.

There was real Eskimo dancing at Paul Davidovics'
roadhouse that evening. Frank Stoker, of Philadelphia
and Noatak, and Walter Blankingship of Kiana were
there, and of course Paul himself—what an expert at line
drawing Time is in writing a man's history on his face!
Paul is half Hungarian, half German, born on shipboard
at Pola, now Italian, when it was Austrian, so, as he says,
who knows what he is? Mary, his Eskimo wife, must
have been pretty when they were young; is not bad-looking
even now. That of course makes their children rather a
mixture, which didn't hinder Angelina, now in Fairbanks,
from winning a beauty contest Outside. Another daughter
was working in the Kotzebue hospital; the youngest, fed
up with Eklutna's native boarding school, does her share
of the cooking and serving of Paul and his friends and paying guests and guests who never get around to pay, all in
the roadhouse kitchen. Get Paul to talking between serving drinks to white men in the bar-room and pushing natives out into the general room with theirs—how he saw
an Eskimo shoot thirteen polar bears from one spot . . .

how even his own Eskimo wife wouldn't believe that he, a white man, had killed a polar bear.

But I started to tell you something about the Eskimo dance. It took place in the big general room of Paul's roadhouse, more and more of the natives drifting in, wearing their mild-winter-weather furs, nostrils steaming even this early in the fall, too often leaving one of the two outer doors open behind them. Eskimos usually use drums like barrel hoops with taut walrus-bladder skins stretched across them. But there being none of those on hand, a gasoline drum lying on the floor before the welcome stove made perhaps even more noise. Oil and gasoline drums cost $2 plus freight when they come up here as containers. Seattle pays $1.50 for empties, but the freight charge on an empty is $1.75! So places like Kotzebue use oil drums for every possible purpose: as stoves, water barrels . . . Kotzebue's new CCC main street, gravel and beach stones three feet wide, was lined on the beach side with oil drums laid end to end for a mile or more, and still abandoned gasoline drums lie all about the place.

But I seem to have trouble in keeping my mind on the dancing. The three or four performers (one could hardly call them musicians) sitting before it beat the drum rhythmically and loudly with sticks, singing a doleful chant, now in a low nasal monotone, now in a higher key; never stopping. There is some similarity between Eskimo and Cambodian dancing. Dancers posture, feet wide apart, knees bent, jump about stiff-legged, raising their arms and stiffening their muscles in an attitude of defiance and defense. They stomp and cavort as if imitating an angry reindeer, at the same time keeping up a patter in Eskimo which now and then draws roars of laughter. You can call these "hops" advisedly.

An old fellow would start a ballad, and the audience gradually took up as much of it as they knew. But the best of them had to be coaxed to sing or dance. Like a

Quaker meeting inspiration some man would suddenly leap
to his feet, strip to the waist, or at least as nearly so as
missionary influence allows these children of nature to go
back to the good old healthful days, pull on a pair of canvas working gloves and begin a pantomime dance. Maybe
others, even women, would join in. At first the tempo was
slow, gradually quickening to frenzy, bringing every
muscle into play. As excitement increased the beating of
the oil drum became louder and louder, the bodily contor-
tions more vigorous, facial grimaces fiercer. Dancers
stamp, jump, grunt a mighty "Ugh!" at every foot-to-
floor, now and then shout in their rough guttural tones.
It would be a fine workout in a gymnasium for "tired"
businessmen.

The men seemed always to be involved in some mighty
struggle in their dancing: hunting the whale, the walrus,
fighting crunching ice and raging seas; women, on the contrary, floated about the room with rhythmic grace, their
arms alone telling the story. Eskimos grew rusty on dancing when the missionaries talked them out of that particular kind of wicked sinning—which was their way of
keeping fit through the winter. The busy-body men of
God as usual monkeyed with the buzz saw of nature before
they knew anything about it, and Eskimos are far fewer
today than they might have been without this white in-
vasion to save their souls at the expense of their bodies.

Jap-like faces gleamed from parka hoods. Most of the
village was constantly coming in or going out and always
banging the outer doors, though never shutting them both.
Natives sat on the floor in an ever-thickening circle against
the walls, the musicians forming one end of the ellipse.
Wide-eyed boys and girls began to fall asleep around the
room. More parka-hooded faces appeared, sometimes
bringing a shout of welcome and a vociferous invitation to
dance. Eskimo parkas come down below the knees, but
our modern leg-free women from Outside find this too con-

fining. So they have evolved from it a lovely short jacket, of reindeer fawnskin, with or without the hood—but of course without a mikaninny, which is an Eskimo child, asleep in the back of the jacket, stark naked if it is small.

Blankingship at least of the white men tried to join in; but though he had seen Eskimo dances nearly all his life, even in his own home, white men do not seem to get the swing of it very well. It's queer I can't tell you how much longer it lasted after we went wearily upstairs to our hardly luxurious beds; for we were right over the room in which the dancing raged on and on. There had been dancing Eskimos but nothing like this at Bethel. Here we had seen all there is to see, they said; no need for us to go on to Barrow.

Eskimo dining etiquette is as inflexible and unexplainable as our own. All squat on the floor around food in one dish—that is old stuff, of course. But there are some Eskimo eating customs which, it seems to me, we might copy to advantage. For example, the host starts right in to eat—to show his guests that the food is not poisoned. Guttural, throaty speech, or as if they had a mouth full of saliva; I came to the conclusion that Eskimo is spoken more with the vocal cords than with the lips and tongue, as we talk. Here is a sample of Eskimo, from the Bible, in case you are interested in learning to read it:

"Tenotei vittekwichanchyo kakwili kwut sut zyeh nunh ha eltsui.

"Ako nunh kwitechin kettun tigwedi chyoako kwizha; akp tsegga techiltyin chekh kkwa. . . ."

Out along the stony CCC beach road, Kotzebue's main and almost only street, next morning the permanent houses soon gave way to tents on the beach. For miles there was a cheery "good morning" with a smile from every one, men, women, even timid children. Fish drying; they catch more trout than salmon this late in the fall. Seal skins full of seal oil; an old woman scraping the under side of a seal skin with a triangular knife much like a trowel had time left to grin broadly. An obviously part-Negro Eskimo getting on in years implied that rampaging sailors of whaling days were not all white men.

I met George Washington that morning, grinning from ear to ear. When I asked him his name he answered very proudly. He had asked mine first and made no open comment on it, as if implying that I hadn't much of a name after all. Abe Lincoln, Thomas Jefferson, Dan Webster and other famous people live in Kotzebue and vicinity. It seems the Friends, who have the missionary rights in this district, sold names to the natives, at graded prices, so that a really famous name costs money. I wonder they have not tried peddling those of Hollywood stars—though perhaps there would be a smell of the sinful about that.

The Friends—Quakers from England by way of Indiana, as nearly as I could pin them down during a brief call at their church and parson house and on their first man in the field—first had Juneau; but they swapped with the Presbyterians. The Kotzebue district is, they contend, exclusively theirs by right of conquest—well, at least of amicable division of labors among the Protestants. The Southern Lutherans have such rights in Nome; south and east of there belongs to the Swedish Evangelicals; Barrow and Wainwright are Presbyterian; Point Hope and Point Lay, Episcopal; the Congregationalists have their own field, the Moravians theirs, down toward Bristol Bay. The Friends complain that the Catholics "trespassed" upon their field eight years ago—but so far have almost no native adherents except the progeny of Catholic squaw men. The Catholics, they contend, had no right to intrude; but I found a broader view of the whole controversy in my chat with the intelligent young Spanish priest who had just taken over the Kotzebue Catholic church and parish house from a far less meticulous old man.

Mr. Laws and his wife came up forty-some years ago and took over this section evangelically—and materially, adds non-Quaker Kotzebue. They say the Friends claimed a lot of land in Kotzebue by right of settlement, though they never used it; that even the Magids Brothers' store pays, or did until recently pay, them $50 a month rental. Tom Berryman and his far from diaphanous Eskimo wife seem to be the most ardent Quakers among Kotzebue's laymen; Tom doesn't even open his store on Sunday, for instance, which is unusual piety for Alaska even where there is no bitter competition.

Mr. Laws and his co-workers in the Lord's vineyard say that the traders are a curse to the natives, so short-sighted that they induce them to get drunk and lay off work, even though it hurts their trade and interests in the end. The traders reply that Mr. Laws himself is not without black spots in his record. I merely report, without any attempt at a judgment. The Quakers, their non-conforming fellow-residents continue, mulct the natives with their tithe, take one-tenth of all they earn; every fisherman, every trapper, they say, even every old woman coming in with a bundle of willows is stopped and forced to leave one in ten for the church, or compelled to tell the storekeeper to give the church credit for ten percent of what they trade in. The Friends retort with the statement that they got only thirteen skins out of all last winter's trapping, and if that be exploiting the natives whose souls they work so hard to save let the worldly make the most of it. More than 95 percent of the natives in this section, they add, are Friends—though there has been some back-sliding of late. The missionaries do not find it possible to hold the traditional Quaker meeting of silences broken by bursts of inspiration, but hold regular services. There are lots of native pastors. But the Eskimos are very superstitious and fear many things which there is no cause to fear; take their religion much as Negroes do.

Steamers anchor sixteen miles out at Kotzebue, which makes it even more of a frontier. Just then the Coast Guard cutter *North Star* was lying offshore on its annual trip to Barrow, with a doctor, seems to me a dentist, and supplies enough to last these isolated communities through the winter. The captain and his second mate were even then hobnobbing with old friends ashore, but refusing to predict when they would be back from Barrow. It is a game of hide and seek with the ice up here, and woe betide the ship that is tagged.

Government nurses check up on the health of all natives semi-yearly and send them to hospital by the *North Star* —or even by plane in an emergency. Natives are so much better taken care of than the whites, the latter complain, who cannot (officially) come to the Kotzebue hospital. A nurse named Gaddie is at least properly named, among those who spend their lives, or such part of them as they give to Alaskan service, in traveling hither and yon throughout the Territory, amid many hardships. But why the head nurse in Alaska that summer speaks with a strong Russian accent, when many American girls in the States need jobs, is more than I can tell you.

Half a dozen of us started north in Blankingship's un-luxurious motorboat on Saturday morning . . . verbally only; then at noon, at two, three, four—and were finally off at six across the corner of the bay and up the Noatak River. "Doc" Smith's conscience was the chief cause for the delay. He felt it wrong to leave his hospital even overnight; slept upright like a man utterly worn out most of the way up and all the way back next day. "He's skookum, that man; he's all man, salt of the earth," runs Kotzebue's opinion of Doc Smith. Constantly with operating cases demanding his immediate attention—natives only; the white man can shift for himself. There are other hospitals for him in Alaska; this one is meant for natives. But Dr. Smith has so fine a reputation both as a surgeon and a man that white men fly to Kotzebue in the hope that he will find their case, as he often does, so acute that he'll have to operate.

Dr. Walter R. Smith, stationed at the Bureau of Indian Affairs hospital in Kotzebue, has more territory medically under his jurisdiction, from Unalakleet on the Yukon to Wainwright, than the British Isles—though only about 5,000 people. He is unique and cannot be replaced, say the people of Kotzebue; needs an assistant, if only because there is so much paper work in a government hospital and the department will not allow the nurses to do all of it. A very conscientious man who is wearing himself out for little material return. He loses fewer cases than the average U. S. hospital, where the doctor comes through with a whole retinue of internes, nurses and assistants and has unlimited apparatus and all the latest scientific aids to help him.

Our farthest north in Alaska was Frank Knapp's fox farm, about 67° North. It was three or four in the morning before we splashed through the night to Logan Varnell's log house, with his wife still cheerfully up to feed us and bed most of us down comfortably on the floor; verging on midday when we waded up the hill to the fox farm. Knapp is an ex-army sergeant who has been here ten or fifteen years. Blue foxes are cute—and suspicious. Most fox farms seem to fail in Alaska, if not elsewhere. They tell me the skins are much better if the animals run wild, even better than if they run wild on an island owned by a fox farmer. It is the same old story: evidently because they are fed and not forced to grub for a living they become WPA in energy, initiative and general philosophy of life. If it rains for a couple of weeks just before pelting time—and especially in southeastern Alaska the chances are excellent that it will—the fur can't be combed out and it is ruined. If the animal is kept over until the next year it costs $25 to feed him, and fox farmers got less than that per average fox skin, last pelting time. By the way, Alaskan fur farmers kill foxes by kneeling on their chests—soft-hearted ones use a two-board clamp—until the heart stops beating.

Knapp grows excellent vegetables; big blueberries and cranberries, both growing on tiny plants that hug the ground, were in their prime there that first Sunday in September. Ancient arrowheads and ivory trinkets are found in this region, implying that it was once well settled. Now there are 3,400 natives, 250 whites in this Kobuk district, centering about the synthetic town of Noorvik on the Kobuk River, and it produces 35,000 furs a year. "It seems so good to see trees again," said our fellow-visitors; Noatak village is the northern limit of trees in Alaska. Delightful weather, even in the rain; the delicacy of the vegetation is entrancing, the ground like beautiful colored rugs stretching on to the north and east. You want to go on farther and farther north, even to the Pole.

Or at least I wanted to go on to Barrow and see Charlie Brower, but that's what killed Post and Rogers. More to the point, it costs $450 to fly from Nome to Barrow and back . . . and Mrs. Wiley Post had waited all summer in Fairbanks for weather in which she could fly there, or in which fliers would consent to fly her there, for the dedication of the Rogers-Post memorial, and finally came to Nome and took the *North Star,* which gets back—when it gets back.

Barrow is still 1,200 miles from the Pole! The only actual Arctic region in Alaska is north of the Endicott or Brooks Range, a great chaos of treeless peaks and ridges. There is no such town as Point Barrow, though nearly every one even in Alaska calls Barrow, eight miles inland from the uninhabited point, that. Perhaps Barrow gets more than its fair share of attention because it is farthest north, whereas . . . after all it is just another Eskimo village. The revenue cutter U.S.S. *Bear* made annual cruises to Barrow beginning in 1890, then went to the Antarctic with Admiral Byrd. Now the *North Star* has taken its place, and any one with the ghost of an excuse to go to Barrow can talk the captain over and go along—which is no doubt quite as it should be. Barrow now has 587 people, which makes it, they claim, the largest village north of Nome. The school had five teachers and 200 pupils; a new 24-bed hospital that cost $100,000 was to be opened soon, to replace the one that burned down more than a year ago. Charlie Brower, "king of Barrow," is its only permanent trader and the father of many half-Eskimo children—and worth coming far to see, say those who have seen him.

Both the Hubbard and the Bliss parties said they roasted on the Arctic ocean in mid-summer, but Barrow reported 28° early that September. There are no glaciers on the Arctic ocean. In fact, except around Mt. McKinley they are all in southern Alaska, sending fingers down to the sea on her southern coast. But there is a big church on the Arctic sea, all built from driftwood logs. If you are interested farther north than I have taken you, read a most delightful book mistitled "Daylight Moon," by Elizabeth Chabot Forrest, who spent two years in Wainwright with her husband as teacher—and all that goes with that job in northern Alaska.

Rogers and Post were killed on August 15, 1935, fourteen miles from Barrow, evidently in taking off after landing on a too shallow lagoon. Impatience was their undoing. Joe Crosson and others told them vociferously that they, with years of Alaskan flying experience, would not think of trying to fly to Barrow under such weather conditions. But one or the other or both of them were too impatient or too sure of themselves. . . .

The Rogers-Post monument is fifteen feet high and includes a pink granite stone from Claremore, Oklahoma. It is on a cliff overlooking the lagoon where they crashed,

and has conduits so that it can serve as an airplane beacon
—if Alaska ever gets any.

The flight from Kotzebue back to Nome was never
below 7,000 feet, in order to top the clouds, and the temperature on the strut outside was 20° in bright sunshine.
We had to skip Shishmaref on account of those billows of
clouds—probably there would not have been much new
there, but the name intrigued me. Clouds banked like
immense wind-whirled snowbanks lay below us as we sped
along at 155 miles an hour. That Labor Day hop was
bumpy under the clouds, smooth above them, so all we
had to do was merely stay above in the sunshine. Now
and then a velvet earth like fawnskin far beneath peeped
through at us.

"See that cloud over there pouring down rain? But
these lakes will soon be paved over," mused Cross. In
Alaska the best flying is between freezing and heavy snow.
You can go up 18,000 feet safely enough in such a plane,
Cross mentioned, but you ought to begin to use oxygen
before 20,000. High altitude affects passengers and often
the pilot, who feels depressed—just as people unaccus-
tomed to it do in Bogotá or La Paz. Man has certainly
conquered the elements—with reservations. Pop along
high above the clouds from place to place in a contriv-
ance two strong men can lift!

CHAPTER XVI

ALASKA'S REINDEER

*A Private "Train" Ride . . . Reindeer History
. . . Uses of Reindeer . . . The Reindeer
Controversy . . . Lomen Brothers . . . Duffy
O'Connor . . . "Wolves!" . . . The Great Trek*

THIS time we got a room in Nome's best, or at least
cleanest, hotel. But behold how modernity has its own
drawbacks! The older hotel had at least the soft noise
of the sea to lull us to sleep, while this one throbbed all
night with the clamor of the mining dredge just outside
Nome. Moreover, we not only had to share a room but
a bed—at twice what we had paid for two single rooms
down on the beach. The bed was the latest thing in spring
perfection, so springy, in fact, that whenever one of us
turned over the other bounced high in the air; and the
heating plant was so New Yorkish that even with the one
openable window leaf ajar to its full capacity we spent
the night kicking each other for having unwittingly come
to the tropics. It just goes to confirm the old saw, that
the grass is always sweeter on the other side of the street.

Next day O. S. Weaver, manager of the A. T. & T.
and the Northern Power Company, took us for a ride on
the defunct Seward Peninsula Railroad, in his private car.
This was an old-style Ford chassis fitted with a roomy
Nome-made body so nearly all glass-walled that it recalled
the old adage about not throwing stones. Just the thing,
however, in which to view the passing landscape.

The Seward Peninsula Railroad, built in 1906-8 by private interests, is now a public highway maintained (I use

the word with reservations) by the Alaska Road Commission; that is, any one with the requisite equipment can use it free of charge—which is probably what all railroads will come to some day. As soon as it was caught making a profit the government taxed it $100 a mile and put it out of business, as it has several shorter lines in Alaska. Travel on it, at least in winter, is mainly by "pupmobile," a car drawn by dogs on its billowing narrow-gauge track.

Alaska's public railroad runs, if that is the word, from Nome to Bunker Hill, about eighty miles inland, and now they are building a truck road from there on into the Kougarock district, which may in time be continued clear across the Seward Peninsula. The Kougarock means all the interior, the mining center, of the peninsula, of which Bunker Hill is one of the chief towns. It is a revived placer district, thanks to modern machinery, including planes, and to the present price of gold. Nome, or at least the placer miners on the Seward Peninsula, with twenty-one dredges at last account, had a profitable season, with a total output of $5,000,000 in gold; and look ahead to fifty years of dredging.

We went out only fourteen miles, up the Nome River to its second bridge. It was a beautiful, almost cloudless day, a landscape glorious with autumn colors, even without trees or for that matter high bushes, though there were some willows along the river. Like a Persian rug of beautiful unstudied pattern, it had some patches of green left amid dull reds, but the color now was predominatingly brown, a glossy, velvety brown which would be the despair of a painter. Old abandoned houses, one a famous ex-roadhouse, rotten and rust-eaten machinery, some of it evidently home-made under difficulties, even an enormous fly wheel, or at any rate a wheel, made of wood, joggled past us. Weaver pointed out a bare little valley and said, "More than a million dollars was taken

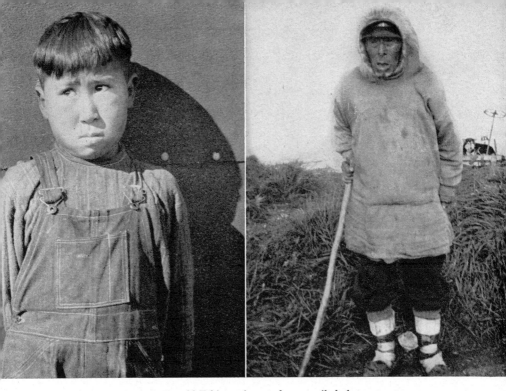

Very young and very old Eskimos do not always smile before a camera

Harry marked our farthest north with a
burst of chivalry

Maybe you'd be serious, too, facing your first
camera lens

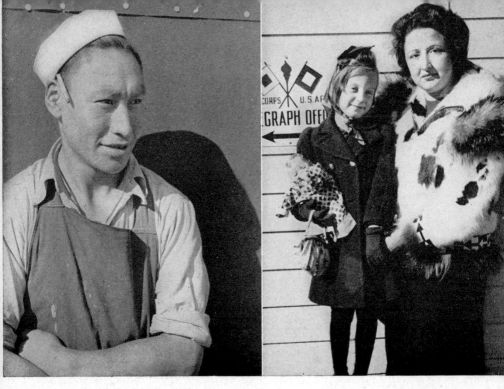

A carpenter of Kotzebue

Just to show you that Kotzebue is by no
means all Eskimo

His cache is as important to the rural Alaskan as his cabin

out there." There was again new snow on the fantastic Sawtooth Range, and Mt. Osburn looked as if it had been caught in the act of shampooing its head.

We saw some mulberry pickers; shot at but missed a big flock of ptarmigan, fished for grayling and trout in a stream, along which many salmon, their spawning over, had crawled or been washed ashore to die. They lay by hundreds among the stones, now mere dried skeletons that crunched beneath our feet. On the way back our capering conveyance suddenly jumped the rails, filling it with broken glass windows. "No harm done," said Weaver; "I was going to fit it with shatter-proof glass, anyway. We may have to walk home, but" . . . but we didn't, for it was just the hour when miners from the dredges were passing by the score to or from their work and they set us back on the rails as easily as if we were children playing with a toy train. "You can give us a ride for that, next time we need it," said one of the miners, with a hint in his voice that these plutocrats with private trains were not always that obliging.

No, we got no ptarmigan, but Weaver and some of his friends had taken advantage of their Labor Day holiday the day before and jolted nearly the whole length of the line, bringing back scores of them. So we ate ptarmigan —and what a treat!—that evening, anyway, Mrs. Weaver having sent a pair of them to the restaurant in which she had advised us to dine. You cannot sell game in Alaska, not even a reindeer steak, though that is hardly game; but you can give it to your friends.

But we had seen no reindeer, except from the air, in all Alaska. Harry, at least, had expected to have to push his way through them, especially up here on the Seward Peninsula. Fairbanks gets a great laugh out of a statement by even as careful and trustworthy a publication as the World Almanac, that "the interior (of Alaska) is a great inland plateau rolling gently north and inhabited chiefly by huge herds of reindeer, guarded by their native owners." There are many reindeer in Alaska; they graze from far east of Point Barrow down to Kodiak Island and well out on the Alaska Peninsula. But they never visit Fairbanks. In fact, I doubt whether one out of ten people in Fairbanks has ever seen a reindeer.

Yet reindeer have caused trouble in Alaska, have pitted natives and whites against each other, have created animosity beneath friendly social intercourse, have brought forth accusations of dishonesty and bad faith on both sides. What is known in Alaska, and in Congress, as the reindeer controversy is too complicated for the brief visitor to try to judge it. Government officials sent up for this specific purpose have not been able to do so. Probably, as usual, both sides are fairly sincere and honest according to their lights. Meanwhile government appropriations hang fire and there is no eventual settlement in sight.

To go well back for a running start: Time was when whalers from New England invaded the Arctic and began to clean up on the whales and the walrus. The first whaler passed through Bering Strait in 1848. Within three years half the whaling fleet was going there, by 1852 two hundred and fifty sail had gone through. They swept the whale and the walrus from the Arctic Ocean until by 1889 they were having to go all the way to Hershell Island to fill their oil tanks and get a supply of ivory and so-called whalebone. By 1890 the Eskimos of the Bering Straits region, their sources of existence drained, were in sad straits. The native food supply of seal, walrus, whale, fish and game, even the raw materials for clothing and other living necessities, was depleted to such an extent that whole villages were almost wiped out by starvation. To make matters worse, the wild caribou were disappearing from the coastal areas.

About this time Dr. William Thomas Lopp, at last

report still living in Seattle, got the idea of importing reindeer from Siberia to Alaska, "as an insurance against famine during the periodical depletions of wild game and sea food." He interested Captain Michael Healy of the U. S. revenue cutter *Bear,* who had himself seen the large herds of reindeer owned by the Chuckchee Eskimos on the Siberian side of Bering Strait. Healy passed the idea on to Dr. Sheldon Jackson, missionary and by then the first general agent of the U. S. Bureau of Education in Alaska. Between them they convinced Jackson, who was then looking for some means of saving the formerly vigorous Eskimos of the far north who had been brought to such a low ebb, that herds of reindeer would do the natives more good than all the schools he was making so much fuss about.

Dr. Jackson in turn took the idea to the departmental heads in Washington, but in those days Uncle Sam had first to be shown. Largely through Dr. Jackson's efforts in the churches, private contributions totaling $2,000 were raised and Congress authorized the use of the *Bear* on a trip to Siberia to buy reindeer. No reindeer existed on the North American continent at the time, only the wild caribou, which is of the same family but has never been domesticated.

But the Siberians didn't want to sell (social rank there depends on how many reindeer a man owns) and the *Bear* sailed 1,500 miles along the Siberian coast, picking up one animal here, another there, until they had all of sixteen reindeer, which they took to an island in the Aleutians. This having proved at least that reindeer do not die of seasickness, Congress came across with money as well as approval and the next year 171 reindeer were landed at Teller (named for a Colorado Senator who interested himself in the matter) and at Port Clarence, ninety miles above Nome. Between 1892 and 1902, when a Russian ukase put a ban on exporting them, 1,280 deer were brought from Siberia to Alaska, at a cost to Uncle Sam of $300,000.

The Act authorizing this expenditure specified that the reindeer were for natives' food and clothing. The Bureau of Education made contracts with the various missionary denominations in northwestern Alaska, providing that about a hundred reindeer be transferred to each specified mission, on condition that the mission would, over a period of years, train a given number of young Eskimos in the care and management of the deer. At the end of the specified period the missions were to return to the government the same number of reindeer loaned them. The increase was to be divided between the reindeer apprentices and the missions as foundation herds.

This apprenticeship system called for a four-year training, during which promising young Eskimos were to receive food and clothing to the value of $300 a year and a certain number of reindeer annually, so that by the end of the four years each successful apprentice had some fifty reindeer and had become a qualified reindeer herder. At first they brought over Lapps, Finns and for a time Siberians to teach the natives—one smart guy got a free ride from Europe to Alaska for a party bound for the Klondyke out of it—but by the end of five years there were enough trained Eskimos to make the system self-supporting.

Dr. Lopp drew up most of the reindeer rules and spent the next thirty-five years in the reindeer service, until he was "released" by the government in 1925. The original government regulations provided that no female deer should be sold or transferred to any but natives of Alaska. They allowed the loan of deer to missions for the purpose of distribution to their converts and dependents, the mission itself to have a certain number of males with which to feed their adherents and, if necessary, to market. Though reindeer bulls do not keep harems they are as promiscuous as Hollywood, and the average herder keeps one bull to twenty females. But the females were to be so distributed that the deer would be spread all over the country, that is, wherever reindeer moss grew. Land that will support reindeer is virtually useless for any other purpose, but only one-tenth of Alaska's 37,500,000 acres is reindeer tundra.

The Eskimos use all parts of the reindeer. Not only does it furnish them meat but most of their clothing. Mukluk uppers, parkas, mittens, trousers, inside parkas (usually made of unborn fawnskin) all depend on reindeer skins for materials. The reindeer furnishes milk, transportation, food, clothing; sinews make thread for sewings, legs make boots, skins make parkas, the marrow is used as butter, the hoofs (and antlers) make glue and knife handles, the hair is used for mattresses (in Europe for filling life-belts)—and the tails as shaving brushes! The skins would make good leather, especially for gloves, but for the warble fly, which lays its larvæ in the skin, especially along the backbone, and leaves a scar which appears when the hide is tanned, scars so numerous that many a hide is almost worthless. Fawnskins at about three months are choicest; later they have longer hair and are warmer and are mainly used as sleeping-bags. Even the Lomen Brothers ship their reindeer skins Outside to be tanned.

The reindeer industry was so much of a success that it aroused the interest of those who followed in the tracks of the whalers and others who had exploited the wild life of Alaska. In 1914 the Lomen Brothers—who contrary to fairly widespread belief Outside are not Eskimos!— Norwegians of several generations back plus an English grandmother, who came to Alaska in 1903, bought some Lapp herds, following this up the next year by buying mission herds, against the strong protest of the superintendent of the Northwest district. The Lomens bought

them when allegedly it was illegal to do so; but it certainly was no crime for white men to buy them, though
it may have been for the natives and missions to sell them,
since the Regulations ("a mere Department fiat not backed
by Congress, hence a big bluff for years") said they could
be sold only to other natives.

Then the 1929 Act made it all legal, allowing all over
one hundred females to be sold, while males could be sold
at any time. "The Lomens have a big government pull,
Carl especially is a great lobbyist," is the way the other
side of the controversy puts it. I had met Carl Outside
years before and had a long talk with him and his two
brothers in Nome; two more live in the States. He tells
me that they and the government made all sorts of experi-
ments. They crossed reindeer with caribou and sent bulls
to different herds, producing a larger animal than those
in Lapland. The Lomens formed a stock company and
had stockholders in all the northwestern states, and they
all bought reindeer meat. In the 1920s they started reindeer meat companies and did a lot of advertising, but
eventually found it not practical to ship reindeer meat to
the States. The government undersold them by 3½ cents
a pound; the high cost of transportation to Seattle became
prohibitive; the meat did not compare with beef; above all
the U. S. packers had all the publicity sources. In Lapland the meat is simply put into the holds of steamers,
covered with hides, and reaches the nearby markets at
small expense. To ship it from Alaska is another story.
During the past few years the only reindeer exported have
been approximately a thousand carcasses yearly, bought
from Eskimos and shipped on the *North Star* on its return
from its annual Arctic cruise, and this meat has been dis-
posed of almost entirely at the various stops in Alaska
on the way back to Seattle.

The natives accuse the Lomens of "jumping" ranges,
making raids on native herds, even of kidnaping a rein-

deer owner on Nunivak Island, whose land the Lomens wanted as a trading station, keeping him falsely imprisoned for a year. They claim that the Lomens appropriate the natives' animals and tried to make them join a cooperative that would make the native owners take care of Lomen debts. They say bad management killed the reindeer market in the States and that the Lomens used lobbying and similar tactics common to all big companies.

"The Lomens had invested (or promoted) about $1,500,000 of capital and were losing from $50,000 to $100,000 a year. So they tried to sell a minority interest in a $4,400,000 company, incorporated by putting the steamer lines, mining dredges, trading posts, their lucrative lighterage and other business into separate corporations, and sell enough reindeer stock to clear their $1,500,-000 investment that is practically a loss. The company failed through the slump in speculation and now they are trying to unload on Uncle Sam. Of course this raised a rumpus."

When there were 30,000 people in Nome reindeer got to be worth $150 each! Prices ran from $18 to $30 a head when the Lomens went into the business, but as they began to get a monopoly the price fell to below $3 a head. Now they are probably worth about $10, but it costs $5 to round them up and send them through the chute and butcher them. Today the Lomen (Baldwin) interests have a White Rover Dog Food and are hoping to gross 10 cents a pound for meat for which they are now getting 6 cents.

"Their herds and those of the natives have been all mixed up since the depression forced them to give up helpers. It is hard to keep track of young reindeer; there used to be the same problem among western cattlemen—except that here there are no six-shooters. In answer to the prayer of the natives for relief a ruler was sent up from a cattle ranch, but he tried to force them into a partnership with a corporation involved in debt. Besides, it is only a business for a Lapp or an Eskimo, who can follow his herds, live with them, live off them and sell a little surplus. It will not pay on overhead, speculation, borrowed capital."

In September, 1937, Congress passed a law which authorizes the Secretary of the Interior to buy back all the reindeer owned by white individuals, by Lapps and by missions, together with abattoirs and other equipment, and return them to the natives. The sum of $2,000,000 was authorized for this purpose, but at the time no appropriation was made. The government suggested to the Lomens that the government acquire their holdings, including $500,000 worth of equipment, and buy out all other non-native owners at $3 a head, though this specific sum was eliminated later, as Congress did not want its hands tied. Those who favor the natives say the time is not too late to turn back to the original idea—make it strictly a native industry. Either give the reindeer back to the natives, they say, or let the Department of the Interior hold the animals in trust for the natives, which, in the meaning of the Act, means any Indian, Aleut or Eskimo "and their descendants of whole or part blood who were living in or came to Alaska from Canada prior to this Act." After that, they should not be allowed to sell or even devise reindeer to other than natives without the written consent of the Secretary of the Interior, and those must be killed within thirty days or forever taken out of the Territory.

The Lomens asked payment for 250,000 animals, but Congress is still to be convinced. It wants an exact count, for instance; to have them actually counted in chutes or corrals. The case has been before the courts and the Department for years, but no decision has been reached. Committees have gone to Alaska time and again, but their reports have been pigeonholed and ignored. Today

Alaskans interested in reindeer are eagerly waiting for action on the report of three Congressmen who had a nice three-months' vacation in Alaska last summer, who attended a number of reindeer roundups, inspected slaughterhouses and took testimony from various interested persons, and were expected at least to ascertain the value of the property which Uncle Sam is planning to acquire from non-native owners and return to the natives.

The Lomens admit that a count is impossible, but they guess they have at least 250,000 reindeer; their opponents say "they have at no time counted as many as 50,000." It is now estimated that there are 600,000 or 700,000 reindeer in Alaska; some say only 300,000—they can't agree even on numbers—and that they feed, partly at least, 13,000 natives. The chief government "reindeer man" in Nome estimates that there are now 540,000 deer, two-thirds of them in the hands of natives, half the other third belonging to the Lomens—though he was "careful not to say so, as they might raise their estimates." The latest official count showed 78 reindeer herds, 59 of them owned by natives. Many of the non-native owners are Lapps. They brought their families with them but married natives when their own women gave out. They are good herders and fairly good citizens. Squaw men are counted as white if they hold title to the deer themselves. Most of them don't. The government estimates the holdings of almost all owners at less than they claim themselves.

The Lomens claim that "Squawman O'Connor" dominates the natives and that they fear him and do as he says. Duffy O'Connor is an Irishman, as you may have guessed, sincere but mentally erratic, an intelligent man with a completely undisciplined mind. He was born in Boston, 75 years ago, came in by way of Skagway in 1898, spent three years on Hershell Island around 1907,

is still physically hardy. He married two Eskimo women
(not simultaneously of course, the first one having died
in 1918), "partly at least because he wanted to hold reindeer, which you can do either by marrying or adopting
a native, thinking them a paying venture."

I met Duffy O'Connor on the streets of Nome and he
took me to his house to explain his grievance, but made
little clear in his chaotic torrent of words. "Buck big business and you are pushed out of a job and have to shovel
beach sand into a sluice to try to feed your family." He
was almost in tears. "The Eskimo will be satisfied with
nothing less," he said, "than complete separation of Lomen
and native grazing grounds and herd management."

A reindeer herd looks, even from the air, like a forest
of antlers. Both males and females have horns and both
drop them in the fall, so that until they are in velvet again
in the spring they look harmless and—oh, sort of unsophisticated. The male looks a bit more formidable than
the female, but they are not a big animal; 100 to 125
pounds dressed. Reindeer must scratch for a living. They
need little care but they do require herding. It takes
tundra moss fifteen to fifty years to come back if it is
cropped down to the roots, and deer starve because they
eat the moss down on a closed range. Yet it is a common
thing for natives to keep a reindeer herd corraled in one
small spot, instead of ranging far and wide, as it should,
and as caribou do. "The Eskimos loaf and keep their
deer in 'potlatch' so they can go sealing or fishing or
merely visiting." Caribou make a huge circle on the range
and the moss regrows. The natives, white Alaskans contend, need a "reindeer czar," a white ranger to see to it
that they keep their deer moving. They say there is danger of reindeer feed being exhausted on the western slope
of the Seward Peninsula, and they want the government
to do something about it.

It seems to be the general impression in northwestern

Alaska that many reindeer stray and join caribou, inter-
breed with them and may in time be absorbed, as the
Chinese absorb their conquerors. But Carl Lomen and
some others say that very rarely does a reindeer go caribou permanently; "about as often as a non-Gipsy goes
permanently Gipsy." It was long thought that reindeer
always mill clockwise, which caused them to be branded
on the left flank, until it was discovered that their skins
are too thin for branding. Now their ears are nicked.
Then to the Lomens' surprise it was found that other
herds in other places mill counter-clockwise. The same
herd always mills the same way, but no one knows why
others do it the other way around. Maybe they are Re-
publicans and Democrats.

Eskimos claim that wolves kill many of their reindeer.
The constant cry of the natives is "Wolves!" But white
men say this is mainly an alibi, to cover up their illegal
killing of reindeer for dog meat, because they are too lazy
to catch and dry fish for them. They kill the females because they are fatter, but tell the government that wolves
are killing them, and the government believes it. Many
deer carcasses which the natives say were killed by wolves
were really starved, an investigator reported. But the
natives are beginning to get it through their thick heads
that, the allotment of deer to each family having been
sharply reduced, there is some danger of deer extinction;
so maybe they will wake up and cooperate with the government.

Logan Varnell had spent the previous winter trying to
get the natives of Noatak and vicinity to trap wolves, if
it was really true that they were killing their deer. He
showed them the best methods of trapping; how to set
traps to the best advantage, what to use as bait—"wolf
scent," he called it. He came back two months later, in
January, and found neither the traps nor the wolf scent
distributed; asked the chief when they would take their

equipment out to the herders on the range, and the reply was, "Some day."

Varnell says the depletion of reindeer herds is due, in the order named, to ineffectual herding, overgrazing the ranges, deer joining caribou herds, killing deer for dog food—a thousand were killed for the dogs during the corraling a year ago—and wolves. When he was out looking for wolf dens last spring he found no herders, though it was fawning time, the most important time for careful herding. He went down to the coast and found the herders sealing, the chief herder gone to Point Lay on a visit. Since wolves come mainly from the caribou country north of that line, Varnell recommends a trap line from Kelly River to Point Hope, along the northern rim of the range, with small sod shelters every twenty miles, so that a man could move along it without breaking his back with the load he must otherwise carry. Such huts could be thrown up in two or three days by a crew of three men, and watchers could also keep an eye out for reindeer eloping with caribou herds.

Probably the most romantic episode in the story of reindeer in Alaska was what is still known as the Great Trek. The Lomens were to get $195,000 for delivering 3,000 reindeer to Canada (Yukon Territory). The trek started on Christmas Day, 1929, with 34,000 deer. They had eight reindeer dogs, half a hundred sleds drawn by one or two sled deer each (500 pounds was a load for two deer) and one dog sled to run errands. Reindeer, like salmon, always want to return to the place where they were born. Moreover, they want to go down to the sea in summer, for salt, and breezes that protect them from mosquitoes. Deer constantly wanted to run home, or go to sea, and many succeeded.

The Lomens had expected the trek to take not more than two years, but that was before they knew the delays involved. They did not know that reindeer can travel only in winter; the ground was too soft for them in summer. The herders had to stop for fawnings. In places clouds of mosquitoes hung about each deer, driving them mad; at low temperatures the trekkers could see only a great cloud of steam over the herds, and the deer were blinded by it. They had to knock ice off the animals' eyelids and nostrils in the morning before they could be driven onward. Female reindeer eloped with male caribou, but male caribou also joined the herd and were welcomed. Small caribou herds were encouraged to enlist and the trekkers shot the males for food; ate also deer killed by accidents or wolves.

Often the Lomens had no idea for months where the herds were. After they had been gone a year and contact with them long since lost, Joe Crosson flew over them on his way to Point Barrow with antitoxin, and stopped on his way back. The Lomens had offered him $250 for a note from chief herder Andrew Bahr. It was so cold that Crosson dared not turn off his plane motor, and Bahr was not much given to writing notes. Finally he produced barely 25 words, less than a night telegram, asking for food. Crosson flew a thousand pounds of food to them at a dollar a pound.

At the mouth of the Mackenzie they had to drive the deer out on the frozen Arctic Ocean, because willows were so thick along the banks of the river that the deer could not get through them. Many wise old animals had run home during the trek; 90 percent of the original herd were killed by wolves, men, accidents, starvation, died natural deaths, or had escaped. But there were five fawnings on the way. So of the 2,370 animals delivered to the Canadian government five years and three months after the trek started only 10 percent had ear nicks, the others having been born on the trek. But there were more than the contracted 3,000 a few weeks after delivery, as the spring fawns numbered between seven and eight hundred.

But in the delivery count the Canadians not only refused to include these but even fine female caribou, more valuable than female reindeer—or rather, they accepted them as they came through the chute into the corral but refused to count them in the contract. So after all their trouble the Lomens got no profit, Carl tells me, out of the transaction.

CHAPTER XVII

THE ALASKAN CAPITAL

Back to Fairbanks—on Second Try . . . On to Juneau . . . Tom Johnson . . . Alaska's "Panhandle" . . . An Outside Atmosphere . . . Juneau's Mine . . . Patsy Ann

WE tried twice to leave Nome before we succeeded. For two hours Al Munson flew us eastward in Electra comfort, the last half hour a devious search for a way through battalions, whole divisions, of clouds, then had to turn back. A four-hour flight for nothing—except the never-failing pleasure of riding the clouds.

We went back to the other hotel, the one with the un-washed barber in the front room and the museum-like bar behind it, rather than bounce and sweat and listen to the dredge all night. But financially that turned out to be no improvement. For Harry, finding his room hermetically sealed, with double windows, broke one of them in a vain attempt to get some air and up came an irate landlady built like a Finnish wrestler and took away most of his small monthly allowance. I doubt whether a pane of glass costs $2 even in Nome, but probably two thirds of it was a fine for flouting her European fear of fresh air. We were far from there before Harry confessed, so I was denied the privilege of asking whether even a bed-ridden husband is excuse enough for a Senator's wife to take it out on one of her most loyal guests.

About ten next morning Al Munson said, "Let's go," as casually as if to a restaurant across the street. Your experienced pilot doesn't pace the floor deep in thought but is casual and chatty between weather reports. Nome had been perfectly cloudless the afternoon before, but we couldn't get through. This morning Nome was buried in clouds, yet off we went . . . and got there.

There were plenty of clouds all that day, yet at 6,500 feet we could see for a hundred miles in any direction. Maybe some poet could give you a hint of the beauty of half Alaska a mile and a half below, while you sit warm and cozy in an easy-chair; but I can't. When we got a long clear space ahead Al turned the controls over to Walt Hall and came back and "unlaxed" with the passengers. Later on he took a nap while a young Department of Commerce inspector of aeronautics took his place, lovingly working the controls, like a boy with a coveted plaything in his hands at last. It was reassuring to know that government inspectors have more than a speaking acquaintance with airplanes.

Fairbanks was almost hot compared to Nome. On September 8 it was already noticeably dark by seven o'clock. The country was magnificent with autumn colors, growing more autumnal by leaps and bounds. It was rather like Vermont toward the end of October, with less variety but more intensity of colors: yellow and greens in beautiful shades—but one misses the reds of maples in Alaska. Yellow-green hillsides, getting more and more yellow almost visibly before your eyes; much more interesting than all-green July. The yellow cinquefoil was turning, the fireweed was now snow-white, like a very old man's hair. Out on Elam Harnish's street two men were cutting up a caribou they had brought in by truck. The hunting season had opened on September first and only a few miles out whole election-night processions of caribou were crossing the Steese Highway.

In money matters Alaska is rarely petty-minded. There was the makings of a fine dispute in that Richardson Highway disaster of ours, for instance. An Outside garageman

would probably have taken my last pennies away from me
for leaving a rented car 150 miles away on such a highway
—assuming that you can find one like it in the States.
Whereas, when we got back from Nome and I found time
to drop in on the man who buries 'em and insures 'em and
rents cars to 'em and all that sort of thing in Fairbanks,
he did mention that he had paid a fellow some fabulous
sum to go and get the car, and that for some reason one
of the rims had to be pounded back into shape; but . . .
well, yes, he realized that I had been put to some trouble
and expense, too, so if I was willing to call it square—and
he'd refund what I had paid for that windshield-wiper job,
too. No, in Alaska gentlemen, or he-men, don't quibble
over cents.

Our unscheduled return from Nome cost us our places
in that day's plane to Juneau and there was no room left
for Harry in the Electra leaving three days later. Moreover, he had missed the semi-weekly train that would catch
the next steamer at Seward. But Don Victor of the
Star Airlines came to the rescue by flying him down to
Anchorage, with a whole day to spare before the train he
had missed left there for the coast.

There was an hour or two of waiting next Sunday morning, until the fog roundabout Fairbanks lifted. Then Bill
Knox and Walt Hall gave her the gun and we were soon
out of the clouds; down the Richardson Highway as far
as the ferry crossing, then off across country. We flew
right over Harding Lake, still resentful at Dr. Schwartz
for just having killed its only, and his only, moose, tame
as a cow! Hillsides were gorgeous in their wealth of
color, at times almost bewildering in its variety and intensity. Fewer reds but more yellow than in the Adiron-
dacks or New England; beautifully clear creeks, even
rivers, obviously virgin country, with very rarely a sign
of man's trespassing, none of the unsightliness of civilization. We had a marvelous view of Alaska Range, though

it was too cloudy to see McKinley—I still don't like the name!

A word from the cockpit had not reached those of us farther back when the inbound Electra, held up by weather the day before, flashed past us, gleaming in the sunshine. "There she is . . . there she goes!" I have never seen anything made by man more instantaneous than that. As between us we were going some 380 miles an hour you can picture how brief the greeting was.

Nearing Whitehorse a kind of tiny chaparral gave the whole upland hillslopes a rusty-red color that under an overhead sun becomes a deep pink. But what now? Barely in the air again, we swung around in a complete circle over Whitehorse, beside the Yukon below, and sat down again on the airfield carved from the forest on the bluff about it.

"I don't like that right motor's smoking," said Bill. "Take twenty minutes to clean it up, if any of you want to stretch your legs again."

Just a bit of oil spilled in the servicing, as Bill had suspected; but wise pilots take no foolish chances.

We had with us a tottery old-timer named Tom Johnson, born in Norway, who had mushed in over Chilkoot Pass in '98—and never been out of the interior since. Lots of old-timers would probably never have come out again but for planes; or have found buyers for their holdings. Johnson had long had the trading post at Akiak on the Kuskokwim, and Bill Knox of Ridgewood Park, N. J., seems to have been the only pilot to make friends with the crotchety old fellow. Now, after four years of flying into the Kuskokwim, Bill had just been promoted to the Electra—looked well in his new uniform, too—and that gave Johnson his chance. Bill had flown him from Akiak, or Bethel, the day before, after waiting more than a week there for "weather," and now he was taking him to Juneau. "It's all right; Bill is going to fly her." Amusing, the confidence these old boys have in fellows whose parents had not met when they "went inside" back in '98.

So now for the first time in forty years Tom was "going Out . . . never coming back," retracing his steps—and how! Bill flew him right over the trail up which he had laboriously climbed four decades ago. He didn't seem to show great interest; later I found out why: "I enjoyed the flight to Whitehorse, but I didn't like it through that Chilkoot canyon. I thought the plane's wings would scrape those mountains." Flying through that narrow canyon is rather an experience; it did seem as if those silver wings were almost touching the mountain sides, though of course that was optical illusion; really lots of room, even to be buffeted by high winds. But isn't it funny that an old fellow with at most half a dozen years left to live should care much if life suddenly ended for him on the old trail?

Mountains, close on either side of us, rocky, high and fantastic in formation; clouds skudding through that great cleft in the shore range; glaciers like mighty rivers suddenly frozen solid as they were about to plunge into the ocean, their fronts higher than Niagara Falls. Crater lake on our level; intensely blue lakes and fjords, Skagway, right below us. . . .

High winds come down the Lynn Canal from Skagway and from a side estuary and sweep across the town and cantonment at Haines, three or four flying minutes farther on. Chilkoot Barracks, at Haines, now our only army post in Alaska, seemed to look enviously up at us; barracks around a hollow square as large as the town itself. About 350 soldiers, officers and men, spend the whole three-year hitch at Haines, according to half a dozen of them we met on the homeward steamer, going Outside to be discharged. Only two years are required there, but most of them don't bother to change for the last year. Yet life in Haines is pretty dull, they admitted, especially since the major now in command came along and made natives and "breeds" out of bounds. The "breeds" especially were hurt, because until then they had always considered themselves white, or at least had mingled freely with the soldiers.

Most old-timers go to the Gastineau Hotel in Juneau. But the Hotel Juneau is more quiet and homelike. It has the only elevator in Alaska, too, except in two or three Federal buildings, if that means anything to you. Right behind it is the six-story Federal building from which Alaska is governed; back of that, two big schools . . . but nothing bores me like describing buildings or just another American city.

Still, Juneau is not exactly that, American as it is. It is crowded thin along Gastineau Channel on a very narrow strip of land overawed by an almost sheer mountain wall, dark-green with trees below and rising to bare, jagged summits. Pushed close down to the sea by lofty aggressive mountains sheer as a rocket almost at its back door, it is still not much on the level in its narrow space. For this is broken up in high rocky knobs, on which stand many a fine residence, some of them far aloft and all of them, unless I missed one, frame buildings. The greenly wooded mountain above it rises to what I understood to be perpetual snow, and even in mid-September streaks of snow lie in the valleys and fissures well down its steep sides, down which milk-white streams come tumbling headlong.

Streets go upstairs in Juneau; wooden stairs posing as sidewalks climb quite a little way up the almost sheer skirts of the mountain, to soggy wooden houses—though not high of course compared with its full height. Sheer white ribbons of water; dense green against gray rock . . . you feel as if the whole mountain might come tumbling down upon you if you picked a weed.

Parts of it have, in fact, from time to time. Juneau's

most famous landslide took place on November 22, 1936, at 7:20 P.M. There had been a small slide the month before, day after day of incessant rain, and people had been warned; but you know how people are. The slide took a boarding-house and an apartment building, a dozen or more houses. It cost (Juneau disagrees on the exact number; prefers to forget) thirty-some lives, all white people. Some had left after the warning and many were at the movies, or a great many more would have been killed. The mark is still plain on the hillside, but time gradually covers over all sorts of depredations.

The Alaskan capital since 1912 is a little modern metropolis, probably with nearly 6,000 inhabitants by now. It seems a big city after a summer in the interior: cars rushing about, dock workers busy (except when they are on strike), much activity ashore. There is moss on some of its roofs and on the one pair of stone steps I saw, a church. Most "Southeastern" towns are paved in planks, but Juneau has some concrete streets and sidewalks, muddy streets and more wooden sidewalks; houses on piles down on the shore. There are 75 miles of roads; taxis will take you anywhere in town for two-bits. "Juneau is in the same latitude as London and never gets as cold as Washington, D. C., sometimes does"—I quote rather than check and verify, but it has been said so long and so often that it must be true. All this, "Southeastern" owes to the Japan current, about the only good thing the Japs have ever sent us. It rarely gets down to zero in Juneau, but "when it does it is terrible." Winds come down from the plains of Canada by way of Atlin and Taku Valley two or three times a year and blow it within doors. There is so much rain that all its better and newer stores have overhangings covering the sidewalks.

Alaska's capital is a mining town; its saloons are full of men, sawdust boxes and big spittoons, nickel-in-the-slot "music," even on Sundays and late into the night.

The Alaska-Juneau mine and the Alaska government, shipping, and commerce with the interior, support it, for it does very little fish-canning. You must look up telephone numbers in Juneau; it has the only U. S. mailboxes I saw in Alaska. There are cheap lodgings, hardly to be found in Fairbanks; bath houses; Finnish steam baths open only on Friday and Saturday nights and catering only to white trade. The capital is not as friendly as towns inside, yet it is so small that everybody knows your name and business before you get settled in your hotel room. Juneau takes on some of the surliness of Indians, some of the indifference of Outside. Don't misunderstand me; even Juneau is a pleasant town, with lots of very hospitable fellows, but it does not have the free and easy ways of the interior.

Juneau's fur and souvenir shops have an atmosphere redolent of Fifth Avenue, New York. Show any liking for a thing and, "Yes, that's a lovely one"—even if it is obviously not worth carrying home. Indian moccasins are made for tourists to the point of having "Alaska" in large letters embroidered upon them. The clerks, women clerks at least, do not know the difference between walrus-skin and moose-hide, though they would never think of admitting it. If trappers get one-tenth what tourists pay for skins in Juneau they are better paid than they admit. Just in case you may have in mind buying furs in Alaska, let me drop a hint: You can buy them as cheaply in New York or Seattle as in Juneau, though you can save your plane fare to Nome by buying there. If you want anything of that kind don't make the mistake I did—believe the Nomites who tell you that you can get just as large a choice of Alaskan native products, and at "perhaps a little less," down in Juneau on your way out. In all Juneau I saw exactly one pair of those genuine Eskimo-woman-chewed sealskin, fur-lined, walrus-skin-soled moccasins that fill whole store windows in Nome, a pair so poorly made that Nome would hesitate to offer them for sale. and the price was three times what a better pair costs in Nome.

In a way Juneau is not in Alaska at all, certainly not in Alaska proper, though for heaven's sake don't tell Juneau I said so! What Alaska calls the "Southeastern" or the "Panhandle" is 600 miles long and 700 miles from the United States, or at least from Seattle. But if it were possible to pick up Alaska and shake it, this panhandle, the "tail," would probably drop off, since it is attached to the whole only by a glacier. Yet here is one case where the tail wags the dog. Juneau, with more help from Washington than it likes, governs Alaska. Don't conclude that you can see Alaska by coming to Juneau; "Southeastern" has as much in common with Nome and the Seward Peninsula as Maine has with Texas.

A great many small boats ride at anchor in Juneau harbor. They are going to build them a new berth, so that steamers cannot crash into them. Surly-looking Indians and "breeds" live on the boats or go to their homes in them. They smell of fish; are far from spotless inside. Indian girls in pants and sweaters, lip-rouged, with curled hair, roam the dock streets like street-walkers. Farther out, half a dozen cribs house frowsy-looking women of several races and their mixtures, who tap and wave an invitation to all passing males above fourteen. Yet over Juneau has crept a film of respectability and its consequences that makes it very different, I suspect, from pioneer days.

Down at the docks there is a labor union atmosphere and many foreign accents and rather dull people. Alaska's coast towns are all unionized; inside, unions are hated. "A man of independence has to go farther and farther inland to get away from the restrictions and exactions of this sort of gangsterism," one of them complained. Agitation for labor unions all comes from Outside; the typical Alaskan considers it a form of tyranny and will move north to get away from it. The unions of course want to organize all workers in the Territory, but they have made little progress inside. Alaska is still the land of rampant individual initiative.

Tom Johnson, after forty years of unbroken isolation in Alaska and the Klondyke, twenty-four of them at lonely Akiak on the Kuskokwim, was already longing for "some place that isn't so dawgone crowded. Juneau? Too damn many people; I wouldn't stay here for all the dawgone money in the world. Alaska is still a good country for the young man, but I haven't got the strength to go on doing business these days, when a fellow has to fight his own government along with regular business competitors."

I saw him outside the Gastineau Hotel the morning after we arrived: heavy new woolen pants, red-and-black lumber-jacket, a battered green felt hat, sneakers with a slit in one of them for his favorite corn, no recent haircut, but even in Juneau an old-timer's queer rig gets no attention. He was talking with an old friend he had just met, an old-timer who had been inside for 52 years—came to Juneau in 1886, only a year after Joe Juneau and Dick Harris—who was urging him not to go Outside for good. Both of them had a trace of Scandinavian accent left.

"Why, I went Outside a couple of years ago," the old friend was saying: "went to San Francisco and had a swell time—for a month. Then I wore out several pairs of shoes just walking around. It's so different, Outside. No one even looked at me. I couldn't say, 'Hello, Bill,' 'How are you, Jim,' 'Go to Hell!' to anybody. I never was so glad of anything as to get back, and I'm never going Out again. My children were born, brought up and married here, though of course they went to school Outside. No, you'll be back."

"Not even any cuspidors [no, he didn't say spittoons] any more," Johnson grumbled, back in the hotel. I pointed out several of the high things that serve nowadays

as cuspidors. "But can a man spit in those?" Tom wanted
to know. I offered to drive him south, mentioning our
car in Seattle and an engagement I had in San Francisco
on the way home. But he immediately turned suspicious;
he didn't carry more than $10 in cash on him even in
Juneau.

The Alaska-Juneau Gold Mining Company, whose big
gray mare—I mean mill—you see piled up the hillside just
before you dock in Juneau takes out a surprising amount
of gold, a little lead and a trifle of silver a year. Lode
mining here, contrasted to placer mining at Fairbanks and
Nome. They tear down a rock mountain from the inside
and dump whole trainloads of ore, grind it up to sand and
mud and pan out gold on huge shaking tables, riffled tables,
with water constantly running over them. Filipinos stand
along a traveling belt and pick out rocks with any white in
them; or rather, let those go past and throw the others
down chutes into chasms below, to be added to the great
windrows of waste rock that have formed a peninsula just
below the mine out into the Gastineau Channel. The
rocks with white in them are smashed up by big steel balls
in immense drums, finer and finer; are reground and re-
washed until they are reduced to mud. They use tons of
starch and other chemicals and reagents, sparingly, because if they used them plentifully it would cost them more
than the gold recovered is worth. For this is low-grade
ore; hardly $1.25 a ton. The biggest piece of gold ever
taken out of these rocks was by no means as large as a
quarter; most of it you can barely see with the naked eye.
Like kids picking over a dump heap.

Finally a man in a locked room puts what is left into
bowls and flushes it with water. He uses a big magnet to
pick out iron shavings and knocks them off into another
bowl. Mercury recovers the rest, which goes to a safe in
the office each night. Once a month they put this stuff into
the furnace and the mercury is recovered, and used again

and again. Even with all this immense machinery to get tiny particles of gold, some escape; it would cost more to recover it all than these would be worth.

There is a concrete road out to the Alaska-Juneau office, past those cribs with the perpetually beckoning women. The manager said he rarely received visitors, then let me look at some of his statistics. Alaska-Juneau miners get an average of $6.60 for eight hours' work. About a thousand men work six days a week, half of them underground. Two-thirds of them are American born. The others were of more than a dozen nationalities. None of the 46 Filipinos, and only one native, work underground. There used to be lots of natives when it was an open cut, but now, "I like to go fishing." The tunnel goes three miles into the mountain; then shafts and "raises" go up or down, some as much as 2,000 feet. There are sixty-five miles of drifts and shafts and "raises."

It is interesting how the mine piles up the mountainside. Miners climb slowly up the trail or the covered stairway at 2 P.M. "How d'ye like to climb this 365 days a year?" As a matter of fact they get one day off every eight days, in rotation, and when that day falls on a Saturday they get Sunday off also. It took a woman in the office a long time to work out that complicated system.

The Alaska-Juneau miners had only recently been unionized and there has been little union trouble. Now they were unable to prove a majority for either of the big unions and two NLRB men had come all the way from Washington to look into the matter. They would be at the office at ten—so the early-rising manager got in a day's work before they arrived. Snippy young fellows, who patronize the old-timer and real producer. One of the last bunch sent up turned out to be a fellow who had been fired as a bank clerk in Seattle as incompetent. No doubt they recommended an election, so that several more bright young men can have a free trip from Washington to Alaska and back.

When we left Alaska the Wages and Hours Act was worrying Alaskans, workers as well as companies. They did not know whether Uncle Sam would be intelligent enough to realize that mining in Alaska is distinctly seasonal work and that to subject it to rules fair enough, perhaps, in year-round factories would be seriously to hamstring Alaska's second industry. Fishing is exempted, because it is seasonal; but how about mining? Mine employees to a man signed a protest against being subjected to the Act, saying a 44-hour week is too short in such a seasonal occupation. But the latest reports are that Uncle Sam is determined to stick to the letter of the law.

It seems the sun *can* shine in Juneau, and then climbing her stairway streets is warm work even in mid-September. On my last afternoon there I took a walk across the big modern steel bridge over the Gastineau Channel to Douglas Island and on to the town of Douglas. It is hardly an island at low tide, and they are going to fill in what makes it so then, I understand. You can drive out the Glacier Highway, past the airport, eighteen miles of good road for Alaska, to the face of Mendenhall Glacier. They will tell you it is the only glacier in the world to which you can drive, but Norway might protest. Nor can you touch ice without getting out of the car. But it takes little walking to reach it, and it is a beautiful sight without even that exertion.

Mendenhall is a "dead" glacier, which means that it is receding instead of advancing. A marker shows that it has shrunk back a quarter of a mile or more since 1916. It looks three miles wide and the front face must be several hundred feet high. The top is very old and very dirty, slants upward and seems to grow narrower, like a cone. But this is only a glacier tentacle; you must fly to see it in its immense entirety. The glacier ice is good and Juneau used to use it; but it is cheaper to make ice now.

Old cars with heaps of big salmon, bleeding, beside them stood along a branch road that bordered a stream. Fox farmers are allowed to gaff salmon, so if one gets through all the nets set for him he still has a gauntlet to run before reaching the spawning grounds. There is much forest about Juneau, but they tell me not much of it would make good lumber. The trees rot on their feet and what look like excellent timber are dead at the top and found to be hollow, like some pompous men. Since they will die and fall down, Alaskans would like to see a paper pulp industry established—one was started here in 1929 but did not prosper. Firs are unknown in Alaska; its hemlock is no good except for flooring; spruce was at one time used for airplane propellers, but metal has taken its place. "Southeastern's" red cedar has some value, but bull pine growing on muskegg is considered worthless. "We can get better lumber for less from Outside," say the Alaskans.

By the time you read this Juneau's new hotel, 100 rooms with bath, will be open and Pacific Alaska Airways will probably have a regular twice-weekly air service between Juneau-Ketchikan and Seattle. I see the Civil Aeronautics Authority has at last installed two radio beams. Juneau is famous for, and proud of, its old white dog, Patsy Ann, who meets all steamers. Patsy Ann is not only old but lame, like many an old-timer; has the same look and manner, and is deaf into the bargain. Originally from Portland, she was a prize winner, a pure English bull bitch, but lost her hearing when she was spayed. The man who brought her up gave her to a minister. But Patsy Ann evidently didn't take to the religious life and became a tramp, or rather, a wharf loafer. The city has bought her two or three collars, but they were all stolen as souvenirs and now she is as naked as the day she was born. Now and then the longshoremen chip in to reduce her nudity.

One Fourth of July Coast Guard sailors painted her red, white and blue; the Coast Guard and several others have taken her Outside, but she always comes back, like a true old-timer.

Patsy Ann is good for a handout at any restaurant in town, but the minute a steamer whistle blows (or even if it doesn't; and anyway, she can't hear it) she gets out from under a boiler somewhere, dusts herself off, and ambles down to the dock, day or night. There she walks the length of the steamer—and she knows the right portholes—scorning a bun but accepting roast beef. I told you she is English. I'm sorry it isn't a lost owner she comes down to meet; that would be much more romantic. But even as a dock loafer Patsy Ann is one of the characters of Juneau. The last time I saw her she was making her way down to a steamer as unerringly as if the captain had sent her a radiogram.

CHAPTER XVIII

EVEN ALASKA INDULGES IN POLITICS

*A Biennial Election . . . Alaskan Longings—
and Complaints . . . Official Visitors . . . That
Gross Gold Tax . . . Relief, Amid Plenty*

I REACHED Juneau on the way Out just in time for the
Alaska elections, on September 13. Alaskans vote every
two years, and vote early, because it used to be quite a
long job to get in all the returns. If and when Alaska
becomes a state, assuming it continues its present election
date, it will join Maine in showing how the wind is
blowing.

Alaska's governors, of course, are appointed by the
President, for four-year terms. But like Hawaii, it sends
a Delegate to Congress, where he has every perquisite of
a Congressman—$10,000 salary, a $5,000 secretary, 20
cents a mile for real or imaginary traveling expenses, free
printing and postage to keep his fences in order and all the
rest of it—except the insignificant right to vote. If I
am any judge of men at a glance, Alaska's present Delegate is at least as worthy of the office as either of the two
men who tried to take it away from him last September,
though I don't like his politics. But then, if he didn't play
ball with the present administration he could of course get
nothing done in Washington for Alaska. In fact, as the
nation goes, so goes Alaska. One lone Republican was
elected that September—Senator Sullivan of Nome, with
a lead of 24 votes.

Though they are both glad and proud to be a part of
the United States, Alaskans generally are not entirely

pleased with the present Federal administrative set-up in
the Territory. In 1912 the "Organic Act" gave Alaska
what virtually amounts to a Territorial constitution. But
it does not have as much autonomy as our States had as
territories. Congress may disapprove laws passed by the
Territorial Legislature or make Alaskan laws of its own.
There are no local governments except in the seventeen
incorporated towns. Yet . . .

"We don't want statehood, but we do want more lee-
way," runs the consensus of Alaskan opinion. "We lack
lots of rights Nevada had as a territory. We can't levy a
property tax, except in municipalities; we can't form coun-
ties; we have no control over lands and forests, not even
school lands. We probably can't even legislate liquor
away from the natives, though the next Legislature will
try it again. We are perpetually fighting labor unions,
Bridges, Dave Beck and the rest of them, and Federal
officials, especially the Secretary of the Interior. Yet it's
all politics to want statehood. Besides, we can't afford to
become a state."

The only Alaskan I heard talk in favor of statehood was
a former mayor of Fairbanks, born in Norway, later in the
Legislature, whose son, born in Dawson, is now mayor of
Fairbanks. He thinks statehood will be a good thing; believes a majority of Alaskans want it, which is probably
wishful thinking, for I did not find a baker's dozen Alaskans who agreed with him.

Undoubtedly it will be quite some years before Alaska
reaches a statehood status, or is even granted a full territorial form of government. It has a Legislature but is
directly under the Department of the Interior and indi-
rectly controlled by nearly all the other Federal departments, "all scrambling for Federal funds, until it's a
wonder anything at all is accomplished up here." The
Department of Commerce runs its fisheries, including
Pribiloff Island sealing; the Department of Agriculture

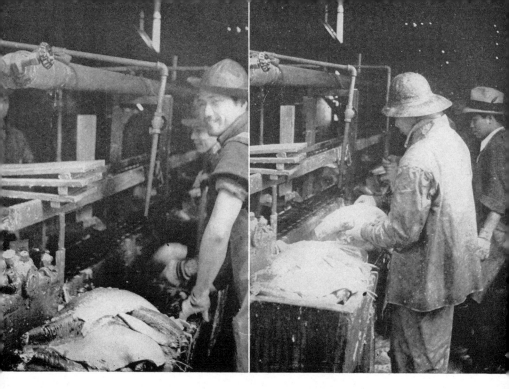

A glimpse of life in a salmon cannery

A typical waterfront in southeastern Alaska

Alaska's totem poles are mere relics now

Sitka has one of the most entrancing sites in Alaska

governs its trapping; the State, War, Navy, Justice, Labor and Post Office Departments all have their share in its government. The Game Commission has to do only with land animals—yet has no jurisdiction over them in national parks. The National Park Service has nothing to do with the national forests. The Bureau of Fisheries has charge of sea animals; the black bear is under one department; the brown bear enjoys the protection of another . . . in short, it is estimated that 57 Federal departments or agencies have a finger in Alaska, and very few of them have any Alaskan representation. No wonder there is constant complaint in Alaska against rule by Washington bureaucrats.

Two Cabinet members and two assistant secretaries of Federal departments made an excursion to Alaska on official duty last summer. Our northwestern Territory is a favorite summer mecca among high Federal officials, perhaps because it is cool and far away—for it may not be news to you that official travelers seldom have to spend as much as they are allowed per mile for traveling expenses. One argument in Alaska for—in Washington against—making it a state is that then many people in Washington would no longer be able to make these annual taxpayers' summer cruises to Alaska.

The Postmaster General refuses to ride in airplanes, but "Alaska's Dictator," in other words our Secretary of the Interior, made fewer friends, though he outdid his fellow Cabinet member by actually coming to Alaska and not merely skimming its edges. That is, he took the railroad all the way to Fairbanks—and publicly called it hard names for the shaking it gave him; yet its roadbed is under his jurisdiction. Then, instead of coming into town to enjoy the hospitality Fairbanks had prepared for him, he slept at the University, three or five miles out, in a private car. Alaska was not amused by other tactless remarks, such as the statement that there are no hotels in Alaska fit for him and his bride; and he capped the climax by refusing to ride down the Richardson Highway for which his Department is responsible. But, assuming that it was original with him, he did get off one good line: "Alaska needs more substantial visitors than postcard shoppers."

Alaska dislikes Federal employees telling the Territory what to do, as a boy hates a bossy father. "We resent Jim Farley, Harold Ickes and a lot of junketing Congressmen and their wives coming up here on government money and telling us to reelect Tony (Anthony J.) Dimond. We resent Uncle Sam, under the present management, urging the cities of Alaska to borrow money, to increase our bonded indebtedness, which means perpetual debt. But I suppose he doesn't feel good with a part of the United States out of debt; is unhappy if any one is solvent.

"Alaska needs a thorough survey as to its agricultural possibilities, oil, tin, pulp, not to mention tourist trade and aviation. It needs more roads and commercial airports that can be used also by the army and the navy, more Federal navigational aids to aviation, government cooperative trading-posts to keep traders from skinning the natives. It needs more Federal money for schools and hospitals. It needs expert study to help the Alaskan farmer to find cheaper methods of production and transportation, so he can compete with Outside crops. It needs the development of an Alaskan consciousness Outside, as many are now Hawaii-minded, stressing the constant consideration of Alaska as a defense outpost. Above all Alaska needs population.

"It needs a change in its court system. As it is now, Federal judges are appointed for four-year terms, subject to change with each administration. Judges should be appointed for life, so they won't play politics; and Alaskans should be appointed to such jobs instead of Outsiders unfamiliar with the requirements of Alaska, in payment for political debts. . . . Alaska wants more home rule; we

want to run our own fishing, mining, trapping, hunting,
pass our own laws, levy our own taxes. Now we have a
virtually powerless Legislature, whose acts must be con-
firmed by a Congress four thousand miles away. Alaska
is tired of being a political football." Aren't we all!

The Washington program for Alaska seems to be confined to defense: $100,000,000 for naval bases at Sitka
and Kodiak, perhaps Unalaska also; army bases, particularly a large army aviation field at Fairbanks, and possibly
an Alaskan National Guard. Alaska also wants the International Highway, and above all elimination of fish
traps and the toll on the Richardson Highway.

Seems as if every one, except the big Outside packers,
is against fish traps; "but it will take four or five years to
abolish them." The Alaskan Delegate, on the spot in this
controversy between the big fish canneries and the majority,
now has bills before Congress which would gradually
eliminate all fish traps in Alaska within five years and abolish the highway toll at once. But of course his job is to
a considerable extent a poker game, in which, unlike a Congressman, he does not hold even a log-rolling ace, in the
form of a vote with which to swap favors.

Alaska, its loyal sons and daughters protest, produces
more Federal revenue than the figures indicate. Income
taxes paid by large mining and fishing companies and
others, to States where they have their home offices, far
exceed the annual Federal grants to the Territory. Alaskans want among other things an expert revision of this
question and an increase in the so-called Alaska Fund, so
that Alaska will get a greater share of the wealth she
produces.

The Legislature, dating from 1913, meets on the second
Monday in January every odd year, following those biennial September elections. There are sixteen Representa-
tives and eight Senators. Thus there must be five Senators
in favor of any bill before it can become a law. Four

Senators can tie up legislation—or even three, as happened when Senator Devine of Nome became ill last session.

At the last election Alaska snowed under a proposal, sponsored from Washington and favored by the Alaskan Delegate, to give the Territory a one-house Legislature. The uni-cameral system was not favored in Alaska for several reasons: first, two houses are best, because bills hurried through one can be quashed in the other; second, only Nebraska has so far tried the plan and has done nothing to prove that it is an improvement; lastly (to skip a few other arguments), the matter of expense does not register with Alaskan voters, because the cost of the Territorial Legislature is borne by Uncle Sam, and anyway it is not high. Members get $15 a day only during the session, which is limited by law to sixty days every other year. True, they get the familiar old 15 cents a mile for traveling expenses, but transportation costs more nearly that up there than it does Outside. They have no allowance for secretaries, no senatorial lunchrooms or barbershops, and cannot vote themselves 20 cents a mile for trips home which they do not make. The Governor can call a special session, but so far only one has been called; and that was tacked right on the end of the regular one.

Ninety-nine and a half percent of Alaskan real estate is owned by the Federal government. Except in municipalities there is no property tax, but there is a tax on production. Fishing has been paying a production tax for some time; gold miners claim they are willing to pay their share but they object to the present ungraduated tax, a 3 percent gross tax on gold, with a $20,000 exemption to help the small miner. Uncle Sam let mining alone until the industry could get going, but is now showing signs of wanting his cut increased.

"Alaska's Dictator" wants the 3 percent gross gold tax, which brought in more than $6,000,000 last year, raised to 10—well, at least to 8 percent on gross production, "on

all products extracted from the earth." Also he wants
every miner or prospector, "any man hauling gravel or
marketable earth," required to post a minimum bond of
$2,500. He is afraid they will run away without paying
the gold tax; but experience shows that they do so far less
often than politicians fail to keep their promises.

That is the usual politician's idea of business, say the
miners of Alaska, who claim they hardly make a reasonable
profit under the present tax; say that should be lowered,
and seem to have the figures to prove it. They cite as
an example a mining company that grossed $61,000 but
had a net profit of only $5,126 *before* the present gross
tax was paid, which made it amount to a 35 percent tax
on profits! Companies have to pay a gross tax even when
their operations net them a deficit. The average profits
of companies is 5.6 percent; the average lone panner probably totals not much more than the fun of digging. Seems
to me it was Marshall who said, "The power to tax is
the power to destroy"—or was it something about a 5-cent
cigar?

Alaskans say that an 8 percent tax would promptly kill
mining in Alaska; that the bond for $2,500 would prob-
ably cost at least $300 and would be hard for most and
impossible for some miners and prospectors to get. The
dictator retorts that Uncle Sam spends a million dollars
a year on roads in Alaska, many of them for the almost
exclusive benefit of a few mining companies. He may
have something there, but . . . Alaska's Legislature introduced at this year's session a bill based on the dictator's
demands, "merely to show respect to the Secretary of the
Interior," but turned it down in twelve minutes flat. But
that perennial raiding of producers by politicians calls for
eternal vigilance even in Alaska.

"The government does everything for the natives, even
the part-breeds, but nothing for the white man doing his
darndest to raise good citizens; no free airplane rides to

school for white kids, no free boarding-schools for them, but everything for the natives." The speaker was an old-timer in the Kotzebue district, seeing his son off by plane to Juneau for his last two years of high school. Kotzebue, even Nome, he said, does not have the grade of teaching he wants his children to have; and while the son would be only two days away by air, the cost of transportation made his destination seem as far away as if he were going to the other side of the world.

"It's all politics to give the natives relief and all the rest," some one else avowed. "The young natives are being ruined because the government feeds and woods and schools and doctors them, instead of letting them learn the crafts and initiative and endurance of their forefathers. The government pays the Eskimo to go out and cut his own wood—but not the white man. Bringing in reindeer made the natives lazy; they used to have to get out and kill caribou."

"We'll soon have more than a million dollars for unemployment pensions," said another man, this time in the "Panhandle." "It's silly to give unemployment relief to an able-bodied man in Alaska. Any man in Alaska should say to himself, 'Here, as far as I can see, this is all mine, and if I can't make a living on it I don't deserve to live. It's no use sending up CCC boys or proved failures. But any young man with pep and guts, who has not been deadened by the dole, can make good in Alaska."

Others in a position to know deny this vehemently, saying that all Alaska is marginal land and that all worthwhile claims are now owned, mostly by loafers or people who can't be found, hence can neither be rented nor bought. Donald MacDonald tells me that he spent months exploring with some CCC boys, "just as hardy and enterprising as the old '98ers," and that they could not find a place free to prospect. There should be no ownership without use, he concludes, especially in a place like Alaska.

Yet Alaska communities, especially on the coast, have considerable difficulty in caring for their own unemployed. There are people on relief and a growing CCC contingent, and the hardy old-timers are wroth about it. It would have been bad enough if government charity had been confined to residents of the Territory, they protest, but to ship in reliefers from Outside, send up CCC boys from the west coast. . . . Nor does Alaskan air seem to improve the working speed of Uncle Sam's—that is, the taxpayers' —beneficiaries. "It took ten CCC boys months to do a job one white boss and two good natives could do in a week. The waste of money—we have it; the Federal government has sent it up here and it has to be spent, so—is less serious than the ruination of the pioneer spirit in the younger generation." In short, nothing is more natural than that the Hyde Park philosophy of life should be especially abhorred in Alaska, where rugged individualism still operates.

"There were 275 out-of-works in Juneau the first year of the depression, 1,700 the first year of free government money, 2,700 the next year. The first year the merchants collected $7,000 and had the Salvation Army see to it that any one who needed a sack of flour or a slab of bacon sawed wood for it. Then the government sent up tramps who had been six months in transient camps in Seattle, gave them $20 a month and found. Naturally, they were no good and had all the social diseases. Why, bums came up here from Outside, a blanket bundle on their backs, and immediately asked the way to the relief station, without even asking if there was any work in town. There never was any trouble before, until Outside bums came up here for CCC or relief; agitation, labor trouble and all that stuff has come since. Sure, we could do with a few more roads. But most of the natives are on CCC in winter, when roads can't be built—which just suits 'em.

"In intelligent times a fisherman who made good money

in summer laid aside enough to rent a cabin, say $10 a month for six months, and to buy enough grub to see him through the winter, and went on a big spree with the rest. Now they spend all their earnings on a big spree and go to the CCC or on relief—that is, ask you and me to carry them over the winter."

It would be interesting, don't you think, to know how many good sprees relief has made possible. But I suppose the New Deal answer would be that the poor fellow on relief has the same right to life, liberty and the pursuit of alcoholic happiness as the rest of us, and that anyhow sprees put money back into circulation.

CHAPTER XIX

ALASKA'S CHIEF INDUSTRY

The Mysterious Salmon . . . Fishing Rules . . .
Rival Unions . . . Cannery Life . . . Watching
Them Can . . . Pumping a Returning Fisherman

MOST of us, when we think of Alaska at all, think first
of mining. There is a lot of gold in Alaska, but her
greatest material contribution to the world is fish. It is
a very shopworn statement that Alaska has returned many
fold that mere $7,200,000 which Congress howled so much
about when presented with the bill. Since 1867 Alaskan
waters have yielded up a billion dollars' worth of fish;
fisheries products have far exceeded all others combined.
The fishing industry gives work each summer to 30,000
men, most of them from Seattle, or at least from Outside.
Eighty percent of Alaskan workers are engaged in its
fisheries; fifteen percent in mining. Alaska shipped out
$50,000,000 worth of fish products in 1937, of which
$44,547,769 was for 6,669,665 cases of salmon of 48 cans
each. In 1938 Alaska shipped $44,000,000 worth of
fishery products to the States—and imported $8,000
worth of canned salmon! Its chief import last year was
$7,764,019 worth of tin cans.

In other words, Alaska, or at least those who take it
upon themselves to speak for Alaska, is typically American
in boiling everything down to dollars and cents. But before we get ourselves hopelessly lost in a morass of figures
may I mention in passing that Alaska has fully justified
its purchase even if it had never repaid that measly
$7,200,000 plus cable tolls, if only as a place where he-men

stay he-men, and women . . . but let's not go too deeply into that, either.

There is a fascination in the life story of the mysterious salmon, the world's champion high jumper. No doubt it is too old and well-known a story to need repeating. Yet it is the mystery fish, sure enough. How long do salmon stay at sea before coming in to spawn, for instance? Some of them get to weigh fifty—yes, even a hundred—pounds before they give up the ghost in a cannery or on the banks of the stream where life began for them.

For, like boys who run away to sea, or to see, salmon come home to die . . . unless they get canned before they get there. When his time comes, the salmon goes exploring along the seashore, looking for the mouth of a stream up which he can go and spawn; and the consensus is that he always finds the stream up which he was born. No one can exactly prove it, but it is one of those things every one is sure of, such as immortality, the crookedness of politicians, the superiority of contract over ordinary bridge, even though Einstein himself has never been able to prove any of them.

The moment it reaches fresh water the salmon begins to die. But for a dying thing it is pretty lively as long as there are falls or swift streams up which it must struggle. At the mouth of the stream it turns red, except in the face; by the time it reaches the spawning grounds it is all covered with a kind of fungus and is no longer edible. But chivalry does not completely abandon the male even during his last hours. For he digs a bed in the gravel bottom of the stream for the female's eggs. Then, she having laid them, he swims over them and squirts his milt upon them, nearly always making a direct hit the first time. Then, their duty to life over, they cease all exertion and float away down the stream, tails first, to fetch up on the first low gravel bar and become shriveled corpses.

During the spawning season every one eats salmon eggs: trout, birds, bears, people. . . . Seagulls, for instance, eat whole masses of eggs, swallow chunks of them half as big as themselves—if they get hold of the end. If a gull grabs a bunch of eggs in the middle, other gulls snip off the ends while he is struggling to make away with it. But as each mama salmon lays an average of 3,000 eggs . . . why worry?

The little salmons, known as fingerlings, stay where they were born clear through the first winter, then go to sea for several years. No one knows exactly where they go or what they live on, though in hatcheries they seem to thrive on a kind of meal, much the same kind that makes corn-pone down south. They return (except some mavericks) to their birthplace when they are between two and eight years old depending on the species—though one tagged "1928" was caught last summer, which knocks out a lot of theories.

– Since they would all soon die anyway, and death at the cannery saves them a mighty struggle, during which they do not even eat and when no one has any proof that life is any fun for them, though it probably is, the soft-hearted, who cannot bear to be reminded before a sirloin steak or a succulent drumstick that animals, even fowls, must be killed before we can eat them, need not shudder at sight of a can of salmon.

There are five kinds of salmon, at least as far as Alaska is concerned. First and foremost is the king salmon, a royal fish indeed, which fights its way up to the spawning grounds from late in April to the end of July. King, also known as chinook or spring, salmon are veritable goliaths in size and strength, compared with other species. Then comes the red or sockeye, five to eight pounds, which begins to run about May 15 and is on the whole the most valuable. These are followed by the coho, known also as the silver or medium red, which averages somewhat

heavier than the sockeye and is believed to have a life
span of only about three years. Next comes the hump-
back or pink, which evidently does not take time to grow
up, for it lives only two years and does not average five
pounds in weight. It is the poorest and most numerous,
like grades of human beings, and is used almost exclusively
for canning; runs from July 12 to around the end of
August. Finally there is the chum or dog salmon, which
loses much of its color in canning and therefore is the
lowest priced. Kings and reds are best, most canners
contend, but the others are almost as good—if they were
not so often taken when too near spawning. The closer
any salmon is to the spawning grounds the poorer it is;
not merely is it worn out with travel but, like many an
English lord and most sailors, it turns senile with incredible
rapidity when it comes in contact with fresh water. In
other words, the farther up toward home they are caught
the less they are worth, just like tourists.

The first cannery in Alaska was established at Sitka in
1878; put up 7,000 cases. In 1929 there were 156 canneries, though now there are barely 120. The working
or at any rate the commercial fishing season varies in each
district of Alaska. The Secretary of Commerce, or at
least his Fish Commissioner (a political job paying $9,000
a year) sets the time, occasionally advancing or extending
it a few days, even a week or so, if conditions seem to
warrant. Get caught fishing out of season and they will
confiscate your boat, gear, even the cannery, for all I know.
Canneries could run another ten days, but Uncle Sam wants
to be sure enough salmon get up the streams to spawn—
so there will be salmon to can next year.

It is illegal to fish from 6 P.M. on Saturdays until 6 A.M.
on Mondays. So the big canneries have fish traps in which
they impound enough fish to be able to keep running those
two days. These are so huge that an entire large boatload
can be "brailed" out in one operation, with an immense

net worked by winches. Fish traps make it possible, too, to can for several days after the season closes, and there are now nearly 500 of them in Alaskan waters.

Fishermen are about half natives and all fishermen must be American citizens. Forty men who overlooked that little detail of citizenship paid $20,000 in fines last summer. Except for the natives the fishermen are mainly Scandinavians—who soon become citizens, so they can go fishing. A non-citizen can do anything except take fish out of the water. On seiners even the cook has to be a citizen, since he must help pull in the fish. The trap-eliminating bill now before Congress would also gradually confine commercial fishing to residents of Alaska only.

San Francisco canners bring their own ships. Big packers ship their entire crews up and have lots of overhead, so they want to get the job over as quickly as possible. The union now requires that white salmon workers travel first class (the operator of course paying the fare), which leaves the Alaska Steamship Company with a problem on its hands. For fishermen used to travel steerage, and now steerage is never filled.

Large canneries have from sixty to eighty boats fishing for them. Length and depth of nets are prescribed by law, varying for different species and localities; so are mesh sizes, because yearlings often come up with Mother and Dad, not to spawn but just for the trip, and they must pass through unharmed. Fishermen used to destroy great numbers of them and it was a big bother, as they are no good for canning. Salmon could easily get out of the nets set for them if they would only turn back, as we could out of some of our troubles. But their instinct is to fight their way on, no matter what the obstacle, like bull-headed human beings.

Thirty thousand fish in one haul is nothing unusual when salmon are running at their best. Fishermen get paid per fish. That is, fish are all bought at the same price, irrespective of size. The cannery we visited was paying $90 per 2,000 salmon. Union rules require fishermen to deliver to a specified cannery. The company furnishes boat and gear to some, and of course pays less per fish. The best fishnets, by the way come from Norway; the best wire rope from a small town in Scotland—they tell me U. S. Steel even imported its (the small town's) water, but couldn't make as good ropes.

Indian girls work in the canneries, but cannery workers are largely Spanish-speaking: Mexicans, Puerto Ricans, especially Filipinos. Today the "ladies known as Lou" follow the salmon run instead of the gold rush. The Filipinos belong to the C.I.O., fishermen to the A.F. of L. White men complain that Filipinos get better wages than they do, because they have a union behind them that forces good contracts. "If there is no trouble they send up a union delegate to create a fuss. Now you have to slap your Filipinos on the back," instead of using a more natural stroke. They earn from $58 to $80 a month and found. In the winter they go back to California and Arizona and, being rated "smooth" lovers, enjoy the favors of American girls.

"The Indians don't want to belong to a union, but they are afraid only of God and the union. The Scandinavians are very radical; unionism is a religion with them. The Swedes and Danes are worst; Norwegians and Finns are not so radical-minded."

Each cannery has a store in which fishermen and cannery workers can buy anything within reason—some canneries say at no profit to themselves. "It is still a feast or a famine with the Indians. A man is either in jail or canning." That is, they get drunk as soon as payday comes and are let out only in time to go back to work. Alaskan law does not allow the working of prisoners. So natives, especially Indians, contaminated by too much contact with "civilization," like to go to jail, to sit and read and smoke.

It has been nice of Uncle Sam to add the ability to read to the other amusements of his voluntary shut-ins.

The government pays Indians on the CCC $60 to $70 a month and they were told they could work for the CCC all summer if the strike stopped the fishing; in fact, they can stay with the CCC or go fishing, as they prefer. So they don't care whether they work or not—except that "I like to fish." They do not go trapping in the winter any more; CCC is better. Asked where he thought the CCC money came from, an Indian replied: "Why, the government makes it!"

The only cannery we actually visited, since we were "inside" most of the summer, until fishing was over, was rather a small one across the bay from Valdez. The owner was a southerner and had a "nigger" cooking for the workmen. "The C.I.O. slipped him in; all canneries have a few extras foisted upon them, because the union wants all the dues it can get." This cannery, now called Dayville, stands where once stood Fort Liscomb, an army post abandoned about 1924. Bought by the Days in 1929, the army hospital became the cannery; they use all the other buildings. When it was an army post there were about 600 men there.

The law requires that salmon must be canned within twenty-four hours after they are taken (from the sea or from traps); often they are canned within twelve hours. The eight-hour day prevails, with 50 cents an hour for overtime. As the eight hours not counted as overtime must be between 8 A.M. and 6 P.M., canneries try to get the boats to come in the morning. The fish are washed into the cannery by water pressure, sorted by species and sent to the "iron chink," so named because Chinese used to do the same work by hand. This deheader and degutter is so nearly automatic that, with two men tending it, it does the work of forty men. Heads, eggs and other waste are thrown into the bay, hence clouds of seagulls constantly circle over canneries. "Yet the best eating is the head, made into head chowder." A "slimer" cleans out the rest of the blood along the backbone. Once they had to scrape out more than that but now the "iron chink" almost com- pletes the job. Automatic knives cut the salmon into strips just the length of the can. The fish are packed raw, salt is sprinkled automatically into each can, and they are cooked by the case of 48 cans, for an hour and a half at 240 degrees. Retort trucks carrying a dozen cases are pushed into the cookers. All cans are "exhausted" by machine now before cooking, and the old method of punc- turing the cans so that gases and steam can escape, then soldering over, is no longer used.

All machinery except the "iron chink" is rented from the American Can Company. The cans come soldered but flattened; cost about 2 cents each. A machine makes them round, then puts on the bottom; another puts on the top after they are filled. A can of salmon must weigh sixteen ounces; often weighs seventeen. An Indian woman cuts up fish by hand and fills the cans rejected by the machine as underweight. You can't run a soft salmon through the "iron chink," as it would tear it to pieces. Also there is a close inspection; so no more "high" salmon gets on the market. The inspectors condemn by smell. That is, if there is no smell it is bad! Machines must be thoroughly cleaned every night; otherwise there will be "high" salmon in the morning. Labels have nothing to do with the cannery. I mean, while the label does specify the grade, to the sharp-eyed, you have no way of knowing which can- nery put up the can of salmon you buy.

One king salmon may fill several cases; eight chums to twelve reds fill one case. Last year the best red salmon brought $10 a case, $2.50 a dozen cans, set down in Seattle. But prices were now down to $1.75, chums 95 cents, a dozen. Check that with your grocery bill. Yet salmon is almost a luxury, as the depression proved. Even the salmon business is a gamble, thanks to labor-union restric-

Gordon Bettles

Father Kashavaroff

A gallery of old-timers

Elam Harnish

Martin Ravenkilde

Tom Berryman of Kotzebue   Mrs. Tom Berryman

A gallery of old-timers

Why, here's Paul Davidovics again!   Patsy Ann of Juneau

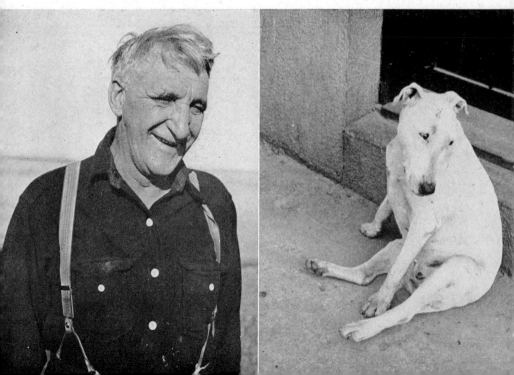

tions, government restrictions, canneries operating on borrowed money, capital graft tied up with the whole American economic system.

An agreement between traders at Bristol Bay for the past few years not to sell liquor between June 15 and August 15 was made official this year, with their consent, by Judge Si Hellenthal. But to the average American, Bristol Bay of course means Japanese poaching. The Japs use nets three miles long and sweep the ocean floor; whereas U. S. regulations allow nets, if I understood my informant, only 500 feet long and 10 wide. The Japs can drop such a net far out in Bristol Bay over the school channels and leave us none—and sell their take to us!

The Japs came to Bristol Bay, famous for its red salmon, again in 1937, as they had for years. But the Japanese government promised they wouldn't in 1938, and apparently they had actually pulled out by the time we got to Alaska. The explanation there is that they already had more salmon than they could sell for several years, and that they would be back again when they need more, State Department notes notwithstanding. They obey no rules, so they have cut down the sizes as far as regulations had built them up. They send huge floating canneries, mother ships and a training ship to back up their fishermen, who fish right up on our doorstep, so to speak. The saucy fellows ask our help if one of their men is hurt, but if we send an injured man on board a Japanese vessel the doctor may come up on deck to look at him but under no circumstances will they let him down below.

On September 22 the streams about Ketchikan were still fairly full of salmon, constantly fighting to get upstream; and trout, especially the dolly varden, hung about in quiet pools alongside, like Soapy Smith's men, waiting to eat eggs. In April, 1937, the Alaska Legislature appropriated $25,000 (which the canners matched) to pay a bounty of 2½ cents on dolly vardens in Bristol Bay, because they destroy the salmon spawn—as what doesn't? You can turn their dried tails in for groceries at trading posts and the traders turn them over to the Bureau of Fisheries, which destroys them. Well over a million had already been turned in when we left Alaska. Salmon feed on herring, so they were thinking of prohibiting for two years the taking of herring—used mainly as meal for fertilizer. Next to salmon and herring the halibut is Alaska's most valuable fish, especially since it has been found that the livers fishermen formerly threw away are worth more than all the rest of the fish.

A lot of bright university men, and some girls, work at jobs ranging from fishing to freight clerking on Alaskan boats in the summer. I am glad we waited to see the exodus of these and the like from Alaska—and to meet lots of Alaskans "going inside" for the winter. On the *Denali* on which we returned to Seattle was a man, his hands calloused with a summer's fishing, who lives in the San Juan Islands, just off the coast of Washington. He had left there in March and was now (September 22) on his way home, first reporting in Bellingham, when his wages would stop. "You can't find work Outside [though he was obviously a good workman] so I just sit on my tail until fishing starts again in the spring."

About 8 P.M. that night the whole horizon was a row of lights, like a city, of fishermen. Big steamers can't help running through nets now and then, said the man on his way Out, then proceeded to tell us a lot about salmon fishing. The nets here, I understood him to say, are 20 feet deep and 300 fathoms long. They have a white light on the tail of the net and a red light, with a white one above it, on the boat. It is against the law to tie a net to the shore—though fish traps can do so. They do not knock fish on the head, as Alaskan stories have it, he said; the better they are treated the more valuable they are. They shake out most of the fish, but some are so well "gilled" that they must be taken out by hand. Skates and other "scrap fish" are caught in the nets, and provoke profanity.

"This summer I caught a 750-pound sturgeon in my net and it took me the whole day to clear it; he had wound it all up in a ball. I got $35 for the sturgeon, but I was sure sore at losing a whole day's fishing. The biggest salmon I ever saw weighed 120 pounds; kings average about 25 pounds. I have seen kings so big their tails drag on the ground when you carry them over your shoulder. Here they pay by the fish; on Columbia River by weight. The best salmon comes from the Columbia River; second best from Puget Sound; the poorest from Alaska. Red salmon is the most expensive, but the idea that it is best is not always true. It looks rather than tastes better, like a red apple. They all have about the same nourishment. Formerly you couldn't sell red salmon in the East; they thought it had not been properly bled. Now they use staining to make the other kinds look red. Down south, on the other hand, they like their salmon meat nearly white, because years ago a smart canner put up chums and printed on the cans, 'Guaranteed not to be artificially colored.' Sockeyes and 'whites' or chums and especially humpies are good eating, but the East wants 'em red."

Fish traps ought to be abolished, according to this fisherman. Neither fish traps nor fish wheels are allowed on the Washington side of the Columbia River, but both are on the Oregon side; and Washington, I gathered, is just as well off. "Yes, the Coulee Dam will kill off the salmon in time, as they can't make their way up those fancy fish ladders the government has built for them; and the small fish are ground up in the turbines when they come down in the spring. Then, too, acids from the pulp mills are killing salmon and the salmon industry wherever they are located.

"There ought to be a law," he went on, "to compel canneries to make fertilizer out of the waste—heads, tails, innards—and the eggs could be made popular as caviar.

[I wonder.] And they should allow only so much pack to each cannery; Atlantic salmon, you know, were extincted by bad fishing laws, though they do not die when they spawn. Then there will always be salmon in Alaskan waters . . . and especially the Japs should be kept out."

I mentioned an Indian, who looked like a "natural" as a fisherman, whom I had seen in the streets of Juneau, looking very disconsolate. He had told me he had fished for canneries all his life but that now "they" wouldn't let him fish any more. He was going over to Metlakatla and join the cooperative village there, so he could fish again.

"They," according to the man from the San Juan Islands, meant the union, the C.I.O. "Union members have to grease the palms of union officials to 'pass' and get a fisheries job. This is how it works: A man comes out of the union's place with a glum face and says, 'I didn't pass. I don't know why.' A man outside the door asks, 'What's the matter, mate?' 'I didn't pass,' says the fisherman. 'Oh, I'll fix that,' says the man at the door, 'but it will cost you ten dollars.' The fisherman slips him ten dollars and he goes inside and swears the other man has fished in Alaska before: 'I saw him up there myself.' 'Oh, in that case,' says the official, 'I only wanted somebody to vouch for him. Let him go.'"

Good workers are sore, too, because "punks" are allowed to join the union and get the same wages as experienced men. "I think the union would have more prestige if it had an apprentice class; let young fellows help at fishing for a year or two before they are allowed to join the union. But then of course the fellows who get the big money, the labor leaders, the fellows who wear the white collars and do the least work and get the most money, wouldn't get so much, for the young fellows wouldn't pay dues. Two years of unions now and there are good men who won't knuckle down to them—and they can't fish any more."

CHAPTER XX

ON THE HOMEWARD TRAIL

Mary Joyce's . . . Flying to Sitka . . . Memories of Russian Days . . . Pioneers' Home . . . Petersburg . . . Ketchikan, Vancouver, Seattle

ALEC HOLDEN, flying a Marine Airways Fairchild pontoon plane, flew me to Mary Joyce's Taku Lodge—except that fog closing in over the Gastineau Channel before we were halfway there forced him to sit down on the water and transfer us to Mary's motorboat. Mary, with one lone Indian as a companion, once drove a dog team all the way from Juneau to Fairbanks, where she took part in two annual Dog Derbys. She met us in Alaskan garb and introduced us to a cow that eats dried fish and drinks crankcase oil—no, I wouldn't believe it myself if I hadn't seen it. Her hide-out near Taku Glacier would be just the place on a sunny day, but we spent an evening of rain, rain, rain before a welcome open fire.

A young customs officer and his wife lived in a tent down at the end of Mary's clearing, checking the supplies that fly in and the gold that is flown out of a mine high in the mountains beyond, for the Canadian boundary is never far away in southeastern Alaska. One winter L. H. Barr, an American free-lance pilot, landed at Mary Joyce's on a fine day, but found it so comfortable that he stayed . . . and that night it snowed. So he spent all the month of November there, but finally, since most of us eventually tire of the best of everything, Barr made a pair of airplane skis out of lumber from an old abandoned barn, so fastened that he could drop them when he took off, and landed on wheels in Juneau. Just another example of the ingenuity of Alaskan aviators. I heard of another one who made his skis out of two spruce trees.

By ten next morning it was clear and bright, so Alec dropped in on his way back from the Canadian mine and flew us over Taku River and Twin Glacier Lake, with a grand view of Taku Glacier, before hopping back to Juneau. Harry turned up at last that night, his steamer having wandered all over the map loading fish, and next morning Lon Cope flew me in the same Marine Airways seaplane to Sitka, which is off the beaten track. Rain and fog, or clouds scraping their bottoms on Gastineau Channel, soon gave way to a higher ceiling, but winds buffeted us like gulls. Swanson's Harbor, with little fishing vessels snoozing in it, two others speeding across the sea as if Sunday meant nothing to them, sped past beneath us, but we landed a passenger at Hoonah. With nothing else to do in an Indian village like many others I went to church. The white pastor had a native elder beside him, as if to keep him posted on the native point of view. A young white man sat at the organ, but a pucker-lipped old lady (the pastor's wife surely) was the only member of our race in the congregation. The rest of it consisted of two small Indian girls, a little Indian boy, seven Indian women (each weighing 200 or better, dressed) and one young Indian woman in very modern dress, even to one glove on and one off, who looked as if she dieted for her figure, and obviously knew all the modern tricks of cosmetics and hairdress. Otherwise it was exactly what that particular Protestant sect's service is in Iowa or Maine.

It was not easy to land at Angoon, a strong east wind being one of its almost perpetual bad habits. We circled over it four times before Lon got his passenger ashore on a reed-grown, jagged-rock-strewn beach with the surf dashing over it. A sprinkle of wooded islands of all sizes and many fantastic shapes, heavily wooded mountains, even the lowlands evergreen with vegetation, marked the rest of the flight to Sitka. But I don't care particularly for flying over wooded mountains in a pontoon plane, even for only a few minutes. Lon Cope and four passengers lost their lives in this region a few months later.

I was on Chichikoff, Admiralty and Baranof islands on that Sunday morning flight. One of the richest mines in Alaska, they tell me, is the quartz gold mine on Chichikoff. Pulp mills once planned to make Admiralty Island their domain, but a goodly portion of it is now a sanctuary for bears.

Sitka has one of the most entrancing situations in Alaska, if not in the United States. Its bay is full of those heavily wooded islands of fantastic shapes; when the weather is at all clear nearby Mt. Edgecombe, though only 3,467 feet high, rivals Fujiyama in beauty. Yet Sitka is crowded down almost into the water in pile-held shacks, and what is known as Sitka village or the Ranch, inhabited by natives, is a long vista of ugly, unpainted commonplace frame houses. Sitka is one of the most Indian towns in Alaska, and only Kodiak, they say, is more Russian.

Sitka was founded in 1799, six miles from its present site, to which it was removed in 1804. Some two hundred lives were lost when the Indians massacred the Russians in 1802 and wiped out the settlement at old Sitka, then known as New Archangel. Sitka was a thriving city before San Francisco was founded. The first steamboat to ply California waters was built there; bronze bells were cast at its foundry for the missions in southern California— though, the makers being Russian Orthodox instead of faithful Catholics, the pious padres said little about the origin of the bells at the time. It was the capital of Russian America from the time the seat of government was moved from Kodiak, and of Alaska until Juneau was chosen in 1912 as more convenient.

When the American flag was first raised at Sitka there were only a few hundred whites in what is now the Territory of Alaska. In the early days Alaska was officially dry, but Sitka, with less than 2,000 inhabitants, imported hundreds of barrels of molasses a month! Both whites and Indians drank freely of the "hootch" made of molasses and almost any other ingredients handy. There were no marshals, judges, commissioners, virtually no government in Alaska for nearly two decades after we took it over. Detachments of U. S. soldiers were stationed at Sitka and four other places soon after we took possession, and they had nominal jurisdiction, but their specialty seemed to be abusing the native inhabitants. They were tough babies left over by the Civil War, who drank and got the Indians to drink, and worse, during the ten years they were there. The report of the then Secretary of the Interior said that within six months after the arrival of the soldiers the whole Sitka tribe of 1,200 had venereal disease. Being apparently of no use except to provoke war with the Indians, the soldiers were withdrawn from the rest of the Territory in 1870 and from Sitka in 1877, no doubt so they could do their Indian fighting in our Wild West.

For the next two years there was no government of any kind in Alaska. Even after Congress ruled that Alaskan cases were to be tried in the Washington or Oregon courts there was no one to arrest bad men and no transportation provided to get them to court. The Indians clung to their tribal customs, even had slaves; there was no such thing as valid title to property, until Alaska was made a "district" in 1884 and officials were appointed.

Baranof Castle, where the official transfer of Alaska took place on October 18, 1867, has since been burned down, but in its place stands rather a distinguished looking old semi-colonial frame building on a hill close to the harbor. Today Sitka has the distinction of having no telephones and no bank. But PWA Project No. AAA 102F is now providing it with a sewer system. Strikes in which Alaskans were not really interested had shut down all canneries in Sitka and vicinity for the year and most of the natives were working for Uncle Sam or not at all.

Across the harbor, on Japonski(!) Island officers and men were training at a Navy airplane base that has now been made permanent. Each morning the six big seaplanes slid one after another down the paved way and bumbled over the vicinity. The officers at least seem to have very comfortable homes there, but they say that most of the men stay here for only three months of training. I see our government has decided to spend $2,240,000 of our hard-earned money at Sitka and $8,471,000 at Kodiak. Dutch Harbor, Unalaska, has long been an auxiliary Naval base and now there is talk of building defenses on Attu Island, our closest point to Japan. The prevalence of Japanese fishing craft along the Alaskan coast has led some cautious persons to wonder if they are preparing submarine bases for future reference.

The Russian aspect of Sitka is still distinct. Its collector of customs is a part-Aleut whose grandfather was a Russian political exile to Saghalien—though you'd never suspect it except for his features, so completely American is he in every word, gesture, thought and point of view. I never cease to marvel how completely we absorb the alien in one, or at most two, generations. Other countries of the New World do not; almost anywhere in South America the grandson of a German is still "un alemán."

Sitka's Russian Orthodox church, begun in 1816 and dedicated in 1848, might have been brought intact from Russia. It contains what are said to be valuable ikons, ceremonial robes and jeweled chalices from St. Petersburg, and a very good Madonna and Child—for which J. P. Morgan once offered $25,000 but was turned down. Services are held in a nearby chapel in summer, because tourists got into the habit of crashing the gate into the famous old church when they should pay admission. There are some three hundred members of the Orthodox congregation, mostly natives; hence this church, unlike the one at St. Michael, is kept up in spite of the drying up of funds after the Bolshevik revolution.

There is a younger Russian priest, who seemed to speak no English, but I take it that Father Kashavaroff is still his Orthodox superior. Father Andrew P. Kashavaroff, born at Kodiak but a resident of Sitka for 58 years—except that he now spends more time running the museum in Juneau and only just happened to be over here on his vacation—is a sturdy little fellow, physically, with hints of that histrionic love of being noticed and the naïveté mixed with hard-boiled knowledge of the world common to Russians. Yet he, too, is intensely American and a fascinating authority on Alaskan history.

Out along the shore where Sitka begins to disappear is the Sheldon Jackson mission boarding-school for natives and part natives, in buildings more imposing than those of the University of Alaska. Beyond, high trees so thick that it is a gloomy walk through them on a rainy day, frequent in Sitka, cover one of the smallest of our national parks, a mere 57 acres. Sitka National Monument, I believe they call it, and its historic associations are legion. Sixteen totem poles, donated by the Indians of southeastern Alaska, line the way to a restored Russian blockhouse. The totem pole, as you know, is the Alaskan Indian's family tree. But contrary to common belief it is confined to southeastern or coastal Alaska and is as unknown in most of the Territory as in the United States. Some of those in Sitka's park are nearly as lofty as its trees. Expertly, not to say fantastically, carved, they are almost always topped by the wooden replica of a diplomat's high hat. Some say the Indians got this idea from a picture of President Lincoln; others, that it was original with the Indians, or at least in vogue long before Lincoln was born.

But totem poles become mere tourist exhibits when they are removed from their settings and no longer serve their original purpose. The native name for totem is "ko-te-a," meaning image or likeness, and while they were hardly objects of worship they did have much the same significance as the spirit tablets of their ancestors have to the Chinese and Japanese. When they adopted Christianity the Indians destroyed or gave away their totem poles, at the instigation of the missionaries. Broader-minded people urge them to keep them, to keep up the old arts by carving new ones. But the chiefs say, "No, my belong Jesus now."

The national cemetery on a knoll behind Sitka is a well tended array of white marble stones in memory of bygone government employees, including a former Governor of Alaska. Mere civilians, many of them no doubt natives, lie beneath row upon row of mainly wooden markers, most of them fallen and all rotting away, on a lowland overgrown with weeds beyond. But does it matter much whether your remains are given perpetual attention? The CCC had recently uncovered a hundred or more flat stones still farther on and within a disintegrating chain fence are a dozen large monuments, also lost in the weeds now, to people no doubt of importance in their day. Sitka must have been a populous place when it was Alaska's capital.

Back of quite another part of town is the grass and weed-obliterated Russian cemetery, with hundreds of those queer double wooden crosses, the crosspieces always slanting, peering above the vegetation. Farther back still, in the edge of the woods, is the once rather elaborately stone-marked grave of a Russian princess, whose life as the wife of a high Russian official is said to have been glamorous. Across the bay, twelve miles from Sitka, is Sitka Hot Springs, reputed just the place to recover from what ails you. But the bay is often rough and Sitka is unanimous only in demanding a road to it, not as to whether it would be a simple or a costly job.

The most imposing building in Sitka, the one you will wonder at as you land, is Alaska's Pioneer Home. It sits on a prominent knoll just above the small-boat and seaplane harbor. The old-timers were farmed out in Sitka and vicinity, even at Sitka Hot Springs across the bay, for a year and a half while their new building was being constructed at a cost of $350,000. You may mistake it for a stone building, but it is of fireproof reinforced concrete. Few government retreats for the aged, however, or for that matter not many Elks' or Masons' Homes, Outside give their inmates better housing than Alaska does its pioneers.

We first became aware of Alaska's Pioneer Home at the Hotel Seward in Seward, where a delightful old-timer (Taylor was the name, I believe) had been waiting for weeks to be admitted to it. There is nearly always a long waiting list and already they are talking of adding a new wing or even duplicating the present structure. Taylor had come to Alaska from Nova Scotia in 1903; has never been Outside since. A lone wolf, like most Alaska prospectors, he had packed heavy loads in over the hills around Seward until now his heart was ailing; he was seventy-four, he said, though he hardly looked sixty. So he had found two honest (we hope) men to take over his claim and was waiting for word from Sitka, meanwhile gazing across Resurrection Bay at the range he will never climb again. Oh, well, most of us come to the same end, painfully soon, no matter what we do with our little lives.

"I don't feel exactly as if it were charity, going to the Home," he said, "or I'd go down to the dock and jump in. Without fellows like us Alaska would never have developed"—which is Alaska's attitude also toward her old-timers.

I was glad to find Taylor installed in the Home when I got to Sitka, and already chummy with his bed-ridden roommate. He was insisting on paying his own keep—

well, at least on giving his income and pension ($35 a
month) to the Home; hoped maybe there would be more,
from those honest partners.

The Territory maintains the Pioneer Home and in theory at least a man assigns to the Territory all he owns
when he is admitted. If they can pay it the charge is $2 a
day, but "between you 'n' me," said the superintendent,
"none of them is paying now." It costs Alaska about
$1.20 a day ($1.02 is the record low per diem rate so far),
besides the investment and the overhead, to keep the old-
timers. A hundred and eighty-seven of them, not so
young as they were years ago, were tottering about, riding
in wheel-chairs or lying permanently abed when I was in
Sitka. The prospector's life certainly takes its toll. The
main trouble among the pioneers seems to be "heart
trouble," though paralytic strokes are common. Probably the youngest inmate in the place is a man barely forty,
who sits in a wheel-chair because he was caught in a blizzard and froze his legs off. Seems to me I was told that
the fellow who lost both his feet and his fingers by lying
drunk at the roadside all night had died the year before.

The average age is seventy-three; Matthew Bruce, not
from Scotland but from Kentucky, is "somewhere around
ninety-five," but is one of the liveliest of the inmates. He
takes two-mile walks, makes canes and sells them to the
tourist trade. Last year he wrote the authorities on
Japonski Island across the harbor offering to fight if the
United States went to war again. The Navy station commander wrote him a "very grateful" letter telling him his
patriotism would be duly made use of if the occasion arose.
Hardy individualists, Alaska's pioneers. That never-failing optimism of the true prospector stays with most of
them to the end. Many of them are planning to go back
to their claims as soon as they can get another grubstake.

There are only 176 beds in the Home, but "we crowd
in 187." Only half of them are American born and at

least half the others came originally from Scandinavia. There is no more room for them in Sitka's three cemeteries, but space around them that can be cleared will do for another twenty years. "But we want a mausoleum, and a crematory for those who do not object to cremation." Seems to me after forty Alaskan winters I'd look forward to that.

You can enter the Pioneer Home now if you have lived five years in Alaska. There are roommates who never speak; some prefer two in a room, some even a ward. Not that they are gregarious by nature; a prospector is hardly that, but in many cases they have been living alone so long that "I got to talking to myself." Being largely Scandinavians, however, and nearly all northerners, they tend to prefer single rooms. Eiler Hansen, the superintendent, puts "the seamen in front so they can look at the sea and the miners at the back so they can look at the hills"— though you can see mountains on every side in Sitka. So far 150 varieties of Alaskan flowers and shrubs have been planted in the grounds of the Pioneer Home to make the old-timers feel at home. The latest improvement was a ring of benches around the flagpole, where a collection of them sat like aging birds on a limb whenever the sun was shining.

Pretty girls wait on them in the dining-room, though I believe only male orderlies go any farther than that. In addition to food, shelter and medical care inmates get smoking tobacco—several brands, "but not always my brand"—chewing tobacco and snuff, even their pipes. No cigars or cigarettes. (It's a wonder our cigarette companies haven't complained!) However, few of them are cigarette smokers; old-timers consider it a sissy habit. The Home spends about $1,500 a year for pipes and tobacco. On Mondays the local movie house gives the Pioneers free admission. At Christmas they get from $11 to $15 each from donations, "and we sit around hoping other fellows will die during the year, so our Christmas cut will be larger."

There is no Pioneer Home for women. Alaska pays them a pension, ranging from $25 to $45 a month and something in addition if they have a family to support. I heard complaints that it gives larger pensions to those who have gone Outside than to those who remain in Alaska, but found no time to investigate this grievance.

The *Denali,* with Harry on board, picked me up on her last call at Sitka that season. A roundabout route through many narrow waterways brought us to Ketchikan, stretching long and thin at the foot of mountains not quite so imposing as those behind Juneau. It is an old saying that to those going inside, Ketchikan doesn't look like much of a town, but on the way out it seems an important city, stocked with most of the things that stores Outside offer, though prices are high even there. If you comment on them, the retort is, "Well, what do you expect? This is Alaska."

Not far from Ketchikan is Metlakatla, an experiment in communism which antedates that in Russia. The Reverend William Duncan moved Metlakatla to Annette Island from British territory in 1887, when the Canadian authorities refused to play ball with him. Later the island was made an Indian reservation and today Metlakatla has some 500 inhabitants. The land belongs to the community but individuals can acquire enough of it on which to build homes. Indians hold stock in the communal enterprises and get dividends as well as wages. The cannery is leased to outsiders; Metlakatla's own electric light and power system supplies electricity to every house in the village free of charge. It has a 60-piece band said to be worth hearing and its new $50,000 town hall is the largest in Alaska. Taxes, assessed only on adult male residents, are $3 a year. Most of those who live in Metlakatla say they would not live anywhere else on earth. It is considered the most successful of all Indian settlements in Alaska.

It seemed queer to see the *Denali* loading spruce lumber for Seattle, when so much of our lumber comes from our northwestern States. Petersburg, which we reached by another series of devious channels with some striking scenery, and much fog, is another of those towns on stilts, out on a wooded nose of land surrounded across narrow waterways by high mountains. It was dark and, of course, raining when we got there early in the evening, Alaska's short winter days already beginning. Not merely the board sidewalks common all over Alaska but whole streets made of planks stretch as far as I climbed up the slope in several directions. Some of the frame houses were almost luxurious residences. The main street and all the business section of the town sit on piles; there is a big Sons of Norway Hall and saloons were as numerous and wide open and orderly as you expect in a Scandinavian-American community.

Wrangell was a total loss as far as we were concerned; we never even woke up there. They say it is picturesquely situated down on the fringe of a much indented shore with a wooded mountain background, so that, like man, it has barely a toe-hold in Alaska. It is proud of its collection of totem poles, some of them bush-grown at the top, and has all the comforts of home—which is merely to describe any of the white man's towns in Alaska's "Panhandle."

Clouds of seagulls escorted us back to Seattle, by way of the unexpected pleasure of a day in Vancouver, where the *Denali* unloaded many cases of fish. But Vancouver today is just another big American city, with all that implies, though it happens to be in Canada. A customs officer at the gangway saved us the trouble of going through any formalities when we landed next morning where our car was patiently waiting for us.

THE END

Arctic

Siberia

Barrow

Wainwright

Kivalina
Noatak
Kotzebue

Brooks

Bering Strait

East Cape

Cape Wales

Seward Peninsula

Deering

Teller

Nome

Golofnin

Nulato

Tana

St Lawrence I.

Norton Sound

Ruby

St Michael

Yukon River

Hughes

Iditarod Flat

McGrath

Mt McKinl

Bering Sea

Bethel

Akiak

Pribilof Islands

Kuskokwim Bay

Bristol Bay

Aleutian Range

Kodi
I

Unimak

Alaska Peninsula

Unalaska

Pacific Ocean

Charles 2 Pont